Pat Williams's new book points the way to a life filled with meaning and purpose. I'll be recommending *What Are You Living For?* to many people for years to come.

GARY L. BAUER
Chairman, Campaign for Working Families
President, American Values

What a great book! In a time when someone has "changed the price tags" on what's valuable and what isn't, it is so refreshing to get back to the basics of what life is really about and what really matters. That would be enough, but to say it in such a refreshing manner is a gift. Read this book, and you will owe me for having recommended it to you.

STEVE BROWN
President, Key Life Network

When Pat Williams writes, trust me, you want to listen. *What Are You Living For?* is a very powerful book, and I found Pat's counsel extremely applicable in my personal battle against the common temptations of this fallen world. It won't be long before I reread it.

PAUL BYRD
Pitcher, Cleveland Indians

Few men in America are learners and leaders like Pat Williams. Pat is committed to helping people invest their lives in what really matters. His family life and career model what really matter. If you are ready to grow, be stretched and pursue the true priorities of life, read this book. The world needs what Pat Williams has lived and written about.

DR. RONNIE W. FLOYD
Senior Pastor, First Baptist Church of Springdale, Arkansas

If your life lacks meaning, significance and direction, you have picked up the right book. Pat Williams has been where you are and knows how you feel. In these pages, he points the way to a life filled with purpose and hope.

BILL GAITHER
Gospel singer and songwriter

When Pat Williams writes it, I read it! Once again, this splendid communicator describes life at its best and gives us vivid illustrations as to how we can live abundantly and effectively for Christ.

JACK GRAHAM
Senior Pastor, Prestonwood Baptist Church, Plano, Texas

Pat Williams has done it again! He's written a remarkable book that makes one stop and remember what is really important in life—and what isn't!

GOVERNOR MIKE HUCKABEE
2008 Republican presidential candidate

What Are You Living For? reminds me so much of the apostle Paul's exhortation to young Timothy when he told him what to pursue—and what not to pursue. Pat Williams has done us a favor in talking about the things we chase after that are equivalent to grasping the wind in our hands, while showing us the things we should pursue that would not only be worth living for but also worth dying for. Read and be blessed!

JOHNNY HUNT
Senior Pastor, First Baptist Church of Woodstock, Georgia

After a lifetime of leadership in business and sports, Pat Williams has written a book about character and faith in Jesus Christ that is suffused with wisdom and wit. *What Are You Living For?* provides powerful lessons, drawn from real life, about real heroes and stunning failures. Throughout it all, Pat leads the reader toward life's greatest laurel and deepest magic: a profound relationship with the God who made us.

TONY PERKINS
President, Family Research Council

What Are You Living For? will cause you to think deeply about every facet of your life. Do not rush through this important book. Read it, reflect on it, and then apply the results.

JIM RYUN
United States Congressman and three-time Olympian

The great thing about this book is that it teaches you what matters most about living. Pat Williams asks the right questions about life so that you can live the right answers before it's too late.

DR. DAVID UTH
Senior Pastor, First Baptist Church of Orlando, Florida

As a successful leader in the powerful world of professional basketball, Pat Williams has unique insight to address the question, *What Are You Living For?* He knows the game of fortune, fame and pleasure and how it leaves its players empty-handed when they lack deeper reasons for living. Pat's winsome influence has been a great encouragement to many, and I know his book will offer you lasting direction and hope.

RAVI ZACHARIAS
Author and speaker

WHAT ARE YOU LIVING FOR?

PAT WILLIAMS

WITH JIM DENNEY

WHAT ARE YOU LIVING FOR?

INVESTING YOUR LIFE IN WHAT MATTERS MOST

Regal

From Gospel Light
Ventura, California, U.S.A.

Published by Regal
From Gospel Light
Ventura, California, U.S.A.
www.regalbooks.com
Printed in the U.S.A.

Williams, Pat, 1940-
What are you living for? : investing your life in what matters most / Pat Williams with Jim Denney.
p. cm.
Includes bibliographical references (p.   ).
ISBN 978-0-8307-4664-4 (hard cover)
1.   Christian life.   I. Denney, James D. II. Title.
BV4501.3.W5528 2009
248.4—dc22
2008025827

1 2 3 4 5 6 7 8 9 10 / 15 14 13 12 11 10 09 08

Rights for publishing this book outside the U.S.A. or in non-English languages are administered by Gospel Light Worldwide, an international not-for-profit ministry. For additional information, please visit www.glww.org, email info@glww.org, or write to Gospel Light Worldwide, 1957 Eastman Avenue, Ventura, CA 93003, U.S.A.

In memory of Dr. Wendell Kempton,
friend and mentor,
and a true role model of character,
influence, parenting and faith

CONTENTS

FOREWORD

By Tom Osborne

What are you living for?

Great question.

You've got to admire someone who asks the tough questions. And that's what Pat Williams does in this book.

What are you living for?

Can you think of a more important question than that? Whether you are young or old and no matter where you live or what you do in life, you need to deal head-on with this question. Your answer will determine whether you are living a life of meaning and significance, or just marking time until you die.

You might say, "Well, I'm young, I'm building my career, and I'm enjoying life. I'm doing fine. Don't bother me with philosophical questions."

Life is short. It passes in the blink of an eye. You think you've got all the time in the world, and then suddenly you turn around and wonder where your life went. If you think your goals of a good career and a lot of shiny possessions will give your life meaning, you're destined for disappointment.

If you're only living to make a reputation for yourself, or to acquire wealth and status, or to enjoy all of life's pleasures—then you are wasting the gift of your one and only irreplaceable life.

Life is uncertain. You could be eating all the right foods, getting plenty of exercise, staying trim and fit, and tomorrow you might be diagnosed with a terminal illness or be killed on the freeway. Or the economy could go south, taking your brilliant career, your nice house and your expensive car along with it.

If everything you're living for turns to dust and ashes, what then?

You can't wait until "someday" to find your purpose in life. You can't wait until tragedy strikes before you get serious about living a life of significance. It's time for you to pause, turn these pages, and consider the question, *What are you living for?*

Pat Williams, the man who asks you that question, has been where you are. In this book, he lays his life open and tells you about his ambitions as a young man—how he was chasing money, fame, power and pleasure. And he not only *pursued* them all, but he *had* them all! In his mid-twenties, he was an up-and-coming professional sports executive, making good money, driving a big car and attracting attention in the national sports media. He was a big success at an early age, and he was heading for even bigger things.

But he was empty inside. He knew something was wrong with his life, but he couldn't say what it was or even give it a name.

Maybe this story sounds familiar. Maybe this is *your* story.

The good news is that something happened to Pat Williams. The eyes of that ambitious young sports executive were opened to a deeper and wider reality. I won't give away the story here; I want you to read it for yourself. But for now, just take my word for it: You need to read this book. Pat Williams not only asks the question "What are you living for?" but also shares with you the answer he has found.

This book is filled with stories that will grip you at a deep level. It's also packed with life-changing principles and insights you can put into practice right now. I believe you'll find your life and your thinking being changed long before you reach the final chapter.

So I commend this book—and this question—to you: *What are you living for?*

Tom Osborne
Athletic Director, University of Nebraska
Head Football Coach, Nebraska Cornhuskers (1973 to 1997)
Member of the U.S. House of Representatives,
Nebraska, 3rd Congressional District (2000 to 2006)

WHAT ARE YOU LIVING FOR?

As this book was nearing completion, I went to Boston to run in the Boston Marathon. While there, I visited my son Thomas, who is a senior accountant with the Red Sox organization. He got tickets for his brother and me for a Sunday afternoon game, the day before the Marathon. So there we were, Thomas, his twin brother, Stephen, and old Dad at Fenway Park, watching the Red Sox take on the visiting Texas Rangers.

I was shaking a handful of sunflower seeds into my palm when I heard the stadium announcer say, "Now batting for the Rangers—Josh Hamilton!"

Well, *that* name made me sit up straight!

My thoughts went back almost nine years, to the 1999 Major League Baseball draft, when 18-year-old Josh Hamilton was the number-one draft pick overall. He was a pitcher and outfielder straight out of Athens Drive High School in Raleigh, North Carolina. Scouting reports said he had the makings of another Mickey Mantle. He threw a consistent 95-mile-per-hour fastball and was called a "five-tool player," meaning he was one of those rare players who excelled at hitting for average, hitting for power, base-running, throwing and fielding.

The Tampa Bay Devil Rays paid Josh Hamilton a $4 million signing bonus, making him a multimillionaire at the tender age of 18. Few players ever came into pro baseball with a brighter future awaiting them—yet Josh Hamilton kissed it all away.

The Devil Rays started him in the minors so that he could acquire some seasoning in pro ball. That's when his life began spinning out of control. Maybe all that money was too much for him to handle. He quickly developed serious addictions to alcohol, cocaine and assorted street drugs. In 2003, he walked away from spring training camp and no one knew where he went. When he returned six weeks later, the team manager turned him away, saying, "Come back when you get your life straight." Josh missed the rest of that season.

After that, he checked himself into drug rehab several times, but he couldn't shake the addiction. He attempted suicide multiple times, usually by overdosing on drugs. He told reporter Bob Nightengale of *USA Today*, "There was even a night I thought about jumping off a building. I had nothing to live for. So I tried to give up. There were a lot of days like that. I let down so many people. . . . I really didn't think I deserved to live."

His addiction reached the point where he chain-smoked crack cocaine. "I remember one time I woke up in a trailer with about five or six total strangers," he said. "It must have been 98 degrees inside. There was no air conditioning. Nothing. My truck was gone. I had no money. But I didn't care. I was just looking for that next high."

For a while, in 2004, he seemed to get his act together. In November 2004, Josh married a lovely young woman named Katie. Two months later, he relapsed into his full-blown addiction. He got back on track for a while, but in May 2005, he decided to celebrate his birthday with a drinking binge. He fought with Katie, did several hundred dollars worth of damage to a friend's pickup and was arrested.

By this time, Josh and Katie had two girls, Julia and Sierra, and Katie feared for their safety. Josh's behavior was simply too scary and unpredictable when he got drunk. She told him to move out, and then she filed a restraining order against him.

Josh Hamilton was out of baseball and had lost his family and home. "I had nowhere else to go," he later recalled, "but something clicked in my head. My grandmother had always told me I could come to her for any reason, at any time." So in the middle of the night, he knocked on his grandmother's front door. When she opened the door, she saw a young man so thin and wasted from drug abuse that she hardly recognized him—but she took him in.

A few months later, Katie called Josh and told him she needed him to come home. The baby had come down with a serious case of the flu—and now Katie was sick with it as well. So Josh went home and helped care for his wife and daughter. Then, when he came down with the flu himself, Katie cared for him. "Taking care of each other that whole week," Katie later recalled, "we thought, well, maybe we still care about each other—maybe there's still something here."

Around that time, Josh received a phone call from a man he hadn't seen in years—Roy Silver, who had been a minor league manager in the Devil Rays' farm system. Silver owned Winning Inning, a baseball camp in Clearwater, Florida. He'd seen Josh's story in the news. Silver promised that if Josh wanted to pull his life together, the camp was just what he needed.

So Josh went down to Clearwater. The baseball camp was located at the old Jack Russell Memorial Stadium, the longtime spring training home of the Philadelphia Phillies. Winning Inning had taken it over after the Phillies moved to nearby Bright House Field in 2004. Josh lived in a little apartment above the locker room, sleeping on an air mattress. The work he did was far from glamorous: cleaning toilets, mowing the grass, trimming shrubs, sweeping the dugouts, taking out the trash. But the hard work and the Tuesday night Bible study were good for his soul.

Trading his labor for use of the batting cage and other baseball amenities at the camp, Josh focused on rebuilding himself physically, mentally and spiritually. He also worked hard at rebuilding his marriage. Katie recalled, "I'd visit him down there and we had time to just get reconnected with each other. It really gave him a chance to show me he was serious about staying clean and sober."

Without the chaos of drug abuse in his life, Josh worked his way back into organized baseball, starting with a Devil Rays' farm team. He was drafted by the Cincinnati Reds before the beginning of the 2007 season—his long-delayed rookie year in the majors. And what a season it was! With 19 home runs, he came in second to the Milwaukee Brewers' rookie left fielder Ryan Braun for the honor of National League Rookie of the Year. In December 2007, the Reds traded Josh to the Texas Rangers. In 2008, he settled in as the Rangers' starting center fielder and the third slot in the Rangers' batting order.[1]

So there I was at Fenway Park, with my son Thomas, on a Sunday afternoon in late April 2008, watching Josh Hamilton step up to the plate and face the fastballs—not just in a baseball game, but in the only game that matters, the game of life. Knowing his story as I did made it much more exciting to watch him on the field.

And as I sat there in the stands, I reflected on the fact that the theme of this book is really the theme of Josh Hamilton's life. Here's a guy who had it all—a mountain of money, incredible fame, the power to achieve any kind of future his heart desired. Yet he squandered it all on pleasure, the intense but soul-destroying thrill that comes from a hit of crack cocaine.

Most of Josh Hamilton's $4 million signing bonus went to either drug dealers or drug rehab clinics. His fame turned to shame when the story of his downfall made national headlines. He traded the power to become a Hall of Famer for a humbling but healing experience of cleaning toilets and emptying trash at a baseball camp. The first seven years of his playing career literally went up in smoke—the smoke from a crack pipe.

But Josh is coming back strong. The experts say that his Mickey Mantle-type talent is still there. At 6' 4" and 250 pounds, now entering his late twenties, he's still got the physical prowess to make a lasting impact on the game. Josh can hit a ball out of sight; he's got great running speed and he's one of the most naturally gifted players ever to come along. Given another decade or so to play, he could still have a Hall of Fame career.

Most important of all, Josh Hamilton has finally discovered what he is living for—and it's not money, fame, power or pleasure. The Josh Hamilton story isn't over, not by a long shot. He may still have a few rough innings ahead of him. I pray that he stays strong and never stumbles. One thing's for sure: The Josh Hamilton I saw at Fenway Park looks like he's got his whole life ahead of him—and it looks like a very good life.

"What am I living for?" I don't know if Josh ever asked himself that question in those exact words. But I do know this: We can't truly live whole, purposeful, effective lives until we ask ourselves that question. "What am I living for?" was the question that motivated him to rebuild his marriage and his career. It was the question that led him out of the darkness of addiction and into the sunshine of the life he now leads.

What about you? Are you investing your life in the things that matter most? Or are you living for money, fame, power and pleasure? Maybe it's time you ask yourself: "What am I living for?"

PISTOL PETE

Josh Hamilton's story reminds me of a basketball star I knew a number of years ago. His name: Pete Maravich.

I became personally acquainted with Pete during my brief stint as general manager of the Atlanta Hawks in 1973. "Pistol Pete" Maravich was the team's crowd-pleasing guard—and the first NBA player to earn over $1 million a year. From our first handshake, I knew that Pete would be a handful. He was brash and cocky. While other NBA players had their last name on their jerseys, Pete's jersey read "Pistol." He loved that nickname.

The '73 Atlanta Hawks roster was loaded with talent, and we should have easily made it to the playoffs that year. Instead, we racked up a dismal 35-47 record. Head coach Cotton Fitzsimmons hated losing. He tried every trick in the book to motivate his players. Nothing worked.

Before one game, he told his players, "We need to change the way we think about ourselves. So tonight, I want you to *pretend* you're the greatest basketball team in the world. I want you to *pretend* you're playing for the NBA championship. I want you to *pretend* that you're out to extend a three-game winning streak. Now go play like winners!"

So Pete Maravich and the Hawks went out on the court—and got massacred by the Boston Celtics. At the end of the game, Coach Fitzsimmons stared up at the scoreboard, unable to comprehend the lopsided score. Maravich sauntered up, clapped the coach on the back and said, "Cheer up, Coach! Just *pretend* we won!"

Maravich was one of the greatest showmen in the NBA. He dazzled crowds with his behind-the-back dribble, through-the-legs pass and pinpoint shooting from way downtown. Pete put on a brilliant show, but he refused to play within Cotton's system. We were a talent-laden team that couldn't win games. One of my last official acts as general manager of the Hawks was to trade Pete Maravich to the expansion New Orleans Jazz. Years later, the Jazz moved to Utah and released Pete. He signed with the Boston Celtics, where he played alongside Larry Bird.

Pete retired in 1980, having never won a championship. He later admitted that he quit the game because of immaturity and ego. "I didn't need to quit," he said regretfully. "My last game with the Celtics, I

scored 38 points, and that night I quit." After Pete retired, the Celtics
went on to win the NBA championship without him.

Pete became so bitter that he destroyed all of his career memorabilia
and shut the game completely out of his life. He couldn't even look at a
basketball for the next two years. His personal life went to pieces. After
his mother's suicide, Pete tortured himself, wondering if he was somehow to blame. He turned for consolation to alcohol, drugs, astrology
and Eastern religion. He drove his sports car down country roads at 140
miles an hour, hoping to kill himself.

What went wrong with his life? Money was certainly no problem.
He had plenty of money stashed away from his playing days. And fame?
He'd had all the fame and adulation anyone could want. It ultimately
meant so little to him that he tossed it all away. Power? He'd been one
of the most powerful and intimidating sports figures on the planet.
And pleasure? With his wealth and fame, he could have had any wish
granted with a snap of his fingers.

Yet here he was, miserable, bitter and wanting to die.

One night in November 1982, at about 5:40 in the morning, Pete
cried out in the predawn darkness, "Oh God, can You forgive me? If You
don't save me, nothing will save me. Come take over my life."

He later recalled that he didn't *feel* changed after praying that prayer,
but somehow he knew he *was* changed. Everyone who knew him was
amazed at the difference in Pete's life. All the anger, bitterness and arro-
gance were instantly replaced by a quiet humility. Moreover, it became obvious to everyone that Pete was living his life for a whole different reason.

In 1987, Pete was inducted into the Hall of Fame. Around that same
time, Pete's father, retired college and pro basketball coach Press Maravich, was diagnosed with terminal cancer. Pete was present during his
father's final hours. He leaned over and whispered in his father's ear,
"Dad, I'll be with you soon." Though Pete himself couldn't explain why,
he had a strange sense that his own time was short.

A few weeks later, Pete was in southern California to be interviewed
by Dr. James Dobson on the *Focus on the Family* radio program. Dr. Dobson, a longtime fan, asked the former NBA star to play a pickup game
with him at a church gym near the studio. They played for a little less
than an hour, and Dr. Dobson was dazzled by Pete's skills.

"Pete," he said, "you should come out of retirement! You're too good to quit this game!"

"Actually," Pete said, "this is the first time I've played in a long time. I've been having chest pains for the past year or so."

"Oh? How are you feeling today?"

"Today? I feel great!"

Those were Pete's last words. In the next instant, he collapsed to the floor. Dr. Dobson rushed to his side and applied CPR while someone called 911—but Pete was already gone. An autopsy later disclosed a previously undetected heart defect—an unconnected left coronary artery. The coroner was astonished that Pete had survived a strenuous 10-year NBA career. He died on January 5, 1988, at age 40.

He had spent the first 35 years of his life chasing money, fame, power and pleasure. His chase had left him empty and bitter. One question haunted him: "What am I living for?" He had no answer for that question until the night he called out to God. After that night, Pete Maravich was a changed man. During the last five years of his life, Pete knew exactly what he was living for.

Life is uncertain and all too short. We have no way of knowing how many years—or seconds—are left to us. So it's important that we invest our lives in the things that matter most. It's important that we ask ourselves, *What am I living for?*

A LIFE THAT TRULY MATTERS

In August 2006, I was invited to speak in Lamesa, a West Texas cow-and-cotton town of about 10,000 people, located out on the wide-open spaces of the Llano Estacado. I was there to speak to a student gathering at Lamesa High School, and everyone I met was warm and gracious.

After my talk, a man pulled me aside and introduced himself. "I'm Ray McCall," he said, "and I coach here at the high school." We talked for a while about how young people desperately need parents, teachers and coaches to be mentors and role models in their lives. I signed a copy of my book *Coaching Your Kids to Be Leaders* for him.

A day or two later, after I returned home to Orlando, I was pleasantly surprised to receive an email from Coach McCall. He reflected on our conversation and closed with these profound words:

> Some of the kids I coach tell me I can't relate to what they're going through in their lives because I'm an adult. It's as if they don't realize that I was actually their age once! I have vivid memories of my life in those days, and I can identify with their experiences more than they realize.
>
> The other day, a thought hit me: Every kid who's growing up is dying to live his life. When kids are little, they're dying for Christmas morning to come so they can open their presents. As teenagers, they're dying to turn 16 so they can start driving a car. Next they're dying to be 18 so they can get out of the house and be "free" and "independent." What are they really dying for? They're dying to live!
>
> But as people get older, things change. Instead of dying to live, they start living to die. They plan for their retirement age so they can stop working and go fishing or cruise the Caribbean and generally mark time until death catches up to them. They write wills and leave instructions about who gets what when they're gone. Some even prepare themselves spiritually for the judgment day.
>
> So here's the question that's always on my mind as I teach and coach and influence kids: "What are you dying for?" The writer of Ecclesiastes wrote, "A good name is better than fine perfume, and the day of death better than the day of birth" (Eccles. 7:1). In other words, what do you have at the end of your life? Nothing but the merit of your name.
>
> In closing, Mr. Williams, I have a thought for you: What are you dying for?
>
> After hearing you speak to our students, and after having the chance to talk to you, I think I know.

Wow! Those words from Coach McCall grabbed my mind and wouldn't let go! What a powerful and crucial question he posed! It's a question we all need to answer for ourselves: What am I living for—and what am I dying for? How can I live a life that truly matters? How can I leave a legacy that will live on after I'm gone?

FOUR *FALSE* REASONS FOR LIVING

As I rolled that question around in my mind, it occurred to me that most people on this planet really only have four reasons for living their lives. The life of almost every person in the world today is ruled by at least one of those four driving obsessions.

Reason 1: Fortune. For many people, money equals meaning in life. They see their lives as a competitive game, and their bank account is the scoreboard. The more their net worth grows, the farther ahead they are in the game of life. But what good does their money do them on the day they draw their final breath?

Reason 2: Fame. For many people, fame equals meaning in life. They derive their status and self-worth from being recognized and applauded. "Fame" doesn't have to mean being on the cover of *People* magazine. For most of us, fame can simply mean recognition, having the people around us think, *He's a big wheel in the company,* or, *She's a key leader in her church.* A lot of people think their lives will be meaningful if everybody knows their name and envies their position in life. Some even feel that being *infamous* is just as good as being famous; they would just as soon be hated and despised as loved and admired.

Reason 3: Power. For some, power equals meaning in life. Some people are driven to attain power to control others, to control circumstances, to have total mastery over their own lives. This is often called the drive to be the "alpha male," though there are many women today with an equal drive to be the "alpha female." Many think that wielding power will give them meaning and satisfaction in life. But power is fleeting and never truly satisfies.

Reason 4: Pleasure. Many people think they can substitute pleasure for meaning in life. Pleasure is a lure that takes many forms: the lust for sex or fine food or luxury or entertainment. If it feels good, do it! If it tastes good, eat up! If you want it, buy it! You only go around once, so grab for the gusto! Pleasure can make us forget our problems and anxieties for a while, but pleasure can't satisfy and fulfill us. In fact, those who are driven to seek pleasure often have the emptiest lives of all.

For each of these four driving obsessions, there is a corresponding philosophy of life. Many people around you, and perhaps you yourself, have been seduced by one or more of these four philosophical mindsets:

1. *Materialism.* This philosophy is used to rationalize the obsession with fortune—with the acquisition of money and possessions. According to the materialist philosophy, we live in a material world, and only material wealth can satisfy. To the materialist, our sense of worth is measured by the quality and quantity of our possessions. Piling up money and "stuff" is all that matters.

2. *Humanism.* This philosophy is often used to rationalize an obsession with fame, the exaltation of the self. Humanism, in a general sense, enshrines human reason and rationalism while denying belief in God and rejecting religion-based morality. In its extreme form, humanism says, "Humanity is glorious! Be your own God!" It teaches that we human beings are the captains of our own souls and suggests that the greater our fame and reputation, the more meaning and fulfillment we will experience.

3. *Fatalism.* People often adopt this philosophy to rationalize their obsession with power. Every human aspiration and all human events are destined to end in death and corruption. Ultimately, there is no meaning in life except the meaning you choose for yourself. So take charge of your life while you can. Seize as much power as you are able. This grim philosophy is the reason so many power-driven people often seem obsessed with dividing the world into winners and losers. Fatalists are determined to win at all costs, because they know that death, the ultimate defeat, will get them sooner or later.

4. *Epicureanism.* This philosophy, based on the teachings of Epicurus (340 B.C.–270 B.C.), is often used to rationalize living for sensual pleasure and luxury. Epicureans delight themselves in fine foods, drink, books, art, and sexual experiences. Epicurus taught that the greatest happiness in life comes from seeking pleasure and eliminating pain, so Epicureanism sometimes takes the form of a hedonistic, pleasure-obsessed lifestyle.

People often say, "If I just had more money, fame, power and pleasure, I'd be happy. My life would be complete. There would be no more gaps or holes in my life." But then you look at the lives of the people who have it all, and they seem to be the most miserable people on Earth.

While this book was being written, former *Playboy* model Anna Nicole Smith killed herself with a toxic cocktail of prescription drugs. Actor Owen Wilson, riding the crest of Hollywood fame, power and wealth, narrowly survived a suicide attempt involving drugs and slashed wrists. Heiress Paris Hilton and actress Lindsay Lohan got in trouble multiple times for driving under the influence of alcohol, and with suspended licenses. Kiefer Sutherland, star of the hit Fox TV series *24*, racked up his fifth DUI. Actor Heath Ledger, Oscar-nominated for his role in *Brokeback Mountain*, was found dead of a drug overdose in his New York apartment. And pop princess Britney Spears is melting down in full view of the entire world—losing custody of her two small boys, a hit-and-run incident caught on tape, shuttling in and out of rehab clinics and psych wards, and on and on.

These are the "beautiful people," living the "lifestyles of the rich and famous." They have it all—money, fame, power and pleasure—yet they feel an obsessive need to drown themselves in alcohol, numb themselves with drugs and seek oblivion through suicide. If the rich and famous can't be happy with all of their money, fame, power and pleasure, then who *can* be happy?

In a segment on the cable news show *The O'Reilly Factor*, host Bill O'Reilly asked comedian Dennis Miller why people who had reached the pinnacle of success were killing themselves or numbing themselves with drugs and alcohol. Shouldn't they be happy? Miller replied:

> Bill, when you say, "They have everything," at the end of the day "having everything" just means you can look at all of your problems through a jeweler's loupe. If you *don't* have everything, you think, "If I ever have everything, I'll be happy." Guess what? When you get everything, the areas where you're messed up become more clearly delineated. You find out that the gaps in your life don't go away because you've got a hit TV show and you're making a good buck. You find out that your gaps are your gaps,

and your problems go a lot deeper than show biz. I think that's
what happens with a lot of these kids. They have their list of all
the things they think will make them happy—and then they fill
up that list. They get it all! And they're *still* not happy! That's
when they get the drugs or hit the bottle.[2]

Dennis Miller is right. Those four false reasons for living—money,
fame, power and pleasure—can't satisfy. They can't fill the real gaps in
our life. When we live for those four false reasons, and we achieve them,
we find that our lives are still empty—and that's when disillusionment
and boredom set in. That's when we reach the terrifying realization that
time is catching up to us, death is closing in on us and all the money,
fame, power and pleasure in the world are mere diversions from the in-
escapable fact of our own mortality. If these four false reasons are all we
are living for, then we inevitably reach the realization that Peggy Lee
once sang about: "Is that all there is?"

In another *O'Reilly Factor* segment, guest host Laura Ingraham interviewed psychotherapist and TV personality Robi Ludwig, Psy.D. "What
about those celebrities," Laura Ingraham asked, "people who have looks,
talent and a lot of money? I think of Owen Wilson, who attempted suicide. I think of the sad saga of Britney Spears. Now Heath Ledger's dead.
They are constantly hungry, and they're filling themselves up with things
that take them away from their own conscience. And I believe, the further
you get away from God—ultimately you're going to be really unhappy."

"That's right," said Robi Ludwig. "There is this feeling that once a
person achieves fame, it's an ideal state, and that somehow they're not
affected by the normal conditions that affect every human being. Very
often, for the celebrities who pursue fame, they do it because internally
they want to prove their lovability. And the problem is they get out
there and they feel loved for their ideal state, their celebrity image, and
not for who they really are. And that can create a lot of conflict."

"The focus on the self and the narcissism doesn't work."

"Exactly," the psychotherapist concluded. "It doesn't work, and it
leaves them very depressed."[3]

Please understand, I'm not pointing a finger of blame at anyone in
Hollywood. I like to think I'm living for God, not for money, fame,

power and pleasure. But, my friend, I have to be honest with you. I, too, easily succumb to those four false reasons for living. I have to continually re-examine my life and my motives. I have to repeatedly ask myself, "What is the focus of my life? How am I investing my time and my money? What am I living for? And what am I dying for?"

FOUR *TRUE* REASONS FOR LIVING

What, then, should we live for—and die for? Coach McCall of Lamesa, Texas, really forced me to think deeply and carefully about this question.

It came to me that, just as there are four false and meaningless reasons for living our lives, there are also four true and satisfying reasons for living and for dying. Those four reasons give purpose and value to our life so that we can know that our life has eternal significance. The good we have done continues on, even after our dying breath. Most important, our existence doesn't end; the life God intended for us to experience from the beginning of time is just beginning.

The four *true* reasons for living are:

1. *Character.* God wants to shape us and make us like Him. He wants our character to be like His character. The more we seek to pattern our lives after God, and after His Son, Jesus, the more we achieve His goal and purpose for our lives.

2. *Influence.* Our influence is the impact we have on the lives of others. Instead of living only for ourselves, God wants us to live for others and to pass on to the next generation our best traits, values, beliefs and dreams for the future. Through our influence, the very best part of us lives on even after we physically die.

3. *Parenting.* Parenting is the process of raising another generation to carry on our faith, values and meaningful traditions. I am a "dad" to 4 birth kids, 14 adopted kids, and a daughter by remarriage. I've also done quite a bit of coaching and mentoring over the years. So my definition of "par-

enting" includes any form of guiding, discipling, training, leading, encouraging and affirming of young people, whether we are biologically related to them or not.

4. *Faith*. What do we believe in? How are we investing in our lives? Are we using our time in ways that count for all eternity—or are we merely marking time until time runs out? Our faith is our most important reason of all for living.

In the coming pages, you and I will explore together how to move from the four *false* reasons to the four *true* and *satisfying* reasons for living—and for dying. As Dr. Martin Luther King, Jr., once said, "If a man hasn't discovered something that he will die for, he isn't fit to live."

In these pages, I believe you will discover something worth dying for—and by making that discovery you will truly begin to live. Once you have something to die for, you know that your life has a purpose and eternal significance. Your life will count today, and it will continue to count after you've left this planet because you have left behind a legacy that will never die.

I'd like you to think of this book as a conversation between just the two of us. You and I are sitting down over coffee, talking together about the things that are most important to us. So let's get started. Turn the page with me, my friend.

Let's talk about life.

CHASING FORTUNE

Money does strange things to people.

In early 1965, after two years as a catcher with the Philadelphia Phillies farm club in Miami, I accepted a position as general manager of a minor league baseball team in Spartanburg, South Carolina. Just a few weeks after settling into the job, I received an urgent call from one of my former associates with the Miami team. He said he was in serious financial straits and needed a thousand dollars right away. Could I lend it to him?

I was 24 years old and just starting my new career in sports management, so a thousand bucks was really serious money. I gulped hard. "You need a thousand—"

"Pat, old buddy, if you could rush a check to me," he said, "I promise I'll pay you back in three or four days, tops. You don't have a thing to worry about. I'm in a short-term pinch, but I'm expecting my money any day now. You know I'm good for it."

So I rushed the money to him. He and I had gone through a lot together during our time in Miami. I knew he'd pay me back.

A week went by. I didn't hear from my good friend in Miami—not a peep. Another week went by. And another.

Finally, when a month had gone by, I phoned Miami and left several messages for him. He didn't return my calls. After a week of phoning, I finally tracked him down and got him on the phone. Feeling awkward and embarrassed, I asked him about the money.

My old buddy was apologetic—and he was still tapped out. "I'll get a check to you soon," he said. "I won't let you down."

"No worries," I said. "I know you'll pay me back when you've got it."

Weeks went by. My buddy called, and when I heard his voice, I thought, *I knew he'd come through!*

But as he started talking, my heart sank. He wasn't calling to tell me my check was in the mail. He actually wanted *another* loan! I couldn't believe my ears.

After hearing him out, I said, "Give me some time to think about it."

I hung up and went straight to the office of my employer, Mr. R. E. Littlejohn, owner of the Spartanburg Phillies. Mr. Littlejohn was not only my boss, he was also my friend, mentor and advisor. He listened quietly as I poured out my tale of woe.

"Pat," he said when I had finished, "here's what you need to do. Call your friend back. Tell him firmly that you are not in a position to lend him any more money, and you want to be paid back. But don't be surprised if you never see that money again. You've probably lost a friend—and your money. But this is a good lesson to remember the rest of your life: If you want to give money to someone as a gift, then do so. But the minute you start lending money, it will cause you nothing but grief."

And Mr. Littlejohn was right. I never saw my money again—and I never saw my friend again. I took Mr. Littlejohn's advice and decided to simply let it go. I had a couple of phone conversations with my friend over the next few years, and though I didn't bring up the debt, I could feel a tenseness in his voice. Our friendship was never the same.

A few years later, I moved to Philadelphia to work with the 76ers organization. One morning, I picked up the newspaper and was shocked to read that my friend had died of a heart attack. I thought, *What a tragedy that a loan of a thousand dollars came between us. Yes sir, money does strange things to people. And to friendships.*

As I mentioned in the previous chapter, the lives of people today are ruled and motivated by at least one of four driving obsessions. All of us, without exception, are affected by at least one or two of these obsessions, and most of us have been at least partially seduced by all four. To recap, they are fortune, fame, power and pleasure. In this chapter, we will look at the obsession with wealth.

DROWNING IN AFFLUENCE

Rose O'Neal Greenhow was killed by her money.

Mrs. Greenhow was a beautiful and famous society woman in Washington, DC, during the American Civil War. Her husband, Dr. Robert Greenhow, was an official in the State Department. She was a friend to politicians, Union generals and Northern industrialists. But she secretly used her friendships in the North to obtain military information, and then passed those secrets to the Confederates. Simply put, Mrs. Greenhow was a spy.

One of her most important assignments involved obtaining the battle plans drawn up by Union Brigadier General Irvin McDowell and passing them along to Confederate General P. G. T. Beauregard. Jefferson Davis, president of the Confederacy, later declared that Mrs. Greenhow's spy work gave the South an important victory at the First Battle of Bull Run.

A month after the battle, the Secret Service arrested her, searched her home and found top-secret maps and documents that proved her to be a spy. She was tried and convicted, and she served her sentence in the Old Capitol Prison in Washington. She was permitted to keep her eight-year-old daughter, Little Rose, and care for her in the prison.

In May 1862, after only four-and-a-half months in prison, Rose Greenhow was released and deported to Virginia. Southerners gave her a hero's welcome and President Davis appointed her as the Confederacy's ambassador to Europe. She traveled throughout the Continent and was received by Napoleon III in France and Queen Victoria in England. She published her memoirs, which became a bestseller on both sides of the Atlantic.

In September 1864, Mrs. Greenhow boarded the British blockade runner *Condor*, bound for the Confederate states. She took with her several thousands of dollars worth of gold coins, the royalties she had been paid on sales of her memoirs. On October 1, 1864, while being pursued by a Union gunboat, the *Condor* ran aground on a sand bar near Wilmington, North Carolina.

Mrs. Greenhow realized that Union sailors would soon board the ship, arrest her and seize her gold. She hid the gold under her clothes and got into a lifeboat. Two men, both Confederate agents, went with her to row the boat. They didn't get very far from the *Condor* before a wave capsized the boat. Weighed down with bags of gold, Rose Greenhow was dragged beneath the water and drowned—*killed by her wealth*. Rose Greenhow epitomizes many of us today. We are wealthy, but we are not secure. Our wealth is killing us, destroying our sense of security, robbing us of peace and joy. We are drowning in our affluence.

According to statistics reported in the *Wall Street Journal*, in *Parenting* magazine and a 2003 MetLife Study of Employee Benefits Trends, 70 percent of all Americans—the richest people on Earth—live from paycheck to paycheck. Nearly half of all Americans would not be able to cover one month's living expenses if their paycheck stopped coming. They have little or nothing set aside in savings or liquid assets. It's not surprising that this is true of 87 percent of low-income wage earners (people who earn $30,000 or less annually). But it is nothing short of astonishing that 37 percent of high-income earners (those who earn at least $75,000) are in the same boat.

As a nation, we appear to be wealthy. We have big homes, multiple cars and pleasure boats parked in our driveways. We spend boatloads of money on entertainment and dining out. Yet, a 2002 survey by the Consumer Federation of America shows that fully a quarter of U.S. households—including many households of high earners—have net assets of $10,000 or less. We owe more than we own. We live seemingly prosperous lifestyles, but on paper we are bankrupt. It would take no more than a bit of bad luck or a hiccup in the economy to put us in the poorhouse.

Why do Americans seem so wealthy when they are actually living life without a financial net? The answer: debt. We insist on lining our lives with tons of stuff we don't need, can't afford and hope to pay for later. According to CardTrak LLC (May 2004), the average household with at least one credit card owes about $8,000. Many American households are servicing high-interest credit card debt in the tens of thousands of dollars. No wonder banks are earning more than $30 billion in annual profits from credit card interest alone.[1]

Like Rose Greenhow, we are weighed down with our glittering treasures, and all it would take is one wave of adversity to swamp our boat and send us to the bottom. We think we need our "stuff," but our "stuff" is drowning us, weighing down our minds and our souls with financial worry and robbing us of our joy and peace of mind.

THOSE WHO TRUST IN RICHES

I have long been fascinated with the paradoxes in the life of Omaha-based billionaire Warren Buffett, the largest shareholder and CEO of

Berkshire Hathaway. According to *Forbes* magazine in 2008, his $62 billion fortune makes him the richest person in the world. But unlike many of the rich and famous of our society, he lives quietly and modestly, and would rather give money away than spend it on himself. In 2006, for example, he announced his plans to deal out his vast fortune to an assortment of charities, with the bulk of it going to the Bill and Melinda Gates Foundation.

While this book was being written, I went to Omaha for a speaking engagement. My limo driver while I was in that city was a genial man named Walter. He told me all about the city, the interesting places to visit and some of the notable people he had chauffeured around town. Without question, his most interesting guests of all were Warren Buffett and Bill Gates.

"Mr. Gates comes to town a lot," Walter said. "He and Mr. Buffett are fanatical about playing bridge. They're both great kidders. One time, while I was driving them both someplace, Mr. Gates said, 'Please drive carefully, Walter. You don't want to have a wreck with the two of us in this limo. It would adversely affect the global economy.'"

I asked Walter if he would drive me past the Buffett home, and he agreed. So we went to the Dundee-Happy Hollow section in the center of Omaha, a beautiful and stately residential area with many historic homes. Walter stopped the limo in front of a two-story gray stucco home surrounded by mature landscaping. It's a nice, comfortable, well-kept home—but driving by, you'd never suspect it was the home of the richest person in the world.

"Mr. Buffett bought this place in the 1950s," Walter said. "It was priced in the low thirties then. Even after he became a billionaire, he would always mow his own lawn and cut his own hedges."

I've never met Warren Buffett, but judging from his modest lifestyle, I'd say he's a man who understands the limitations of wealth. He doesn't use money in an attempt to buy happiness or security. He has an extraordinary ability to make mountains of money, yet he lives modestly and uses his wealth to help others.

What about you and me? Do we have a wise understanding of wealth? Do we see money as a tool we can use to do some good in the world? Or do we see money as the means to amass more "stuff"? Even though our affluence has not made us happy or secure, we continue to place our trust in money. We are as foolish as the wealthy and powerful Middle Eastern man who, in early 2003, said, "If anything goes wrong, I'll have my money. I will buy an island, be king on my island."[2]

This was no idle boast. The man owned numerous mansions; maintained a personal zoo filled with tigers, cheetahs and lions; owned over a thousand luxury cars (including Porsches, Lamborghinis, and Rolls-Royces); and stockpiled millions of dollars worth of fine wines, expensive liquor, hand-rolled Cuban cigars, heroin and cocaine. He was the son of a dictator, and first in line to succeed his father as ruler of a powerful, oil-rich nation.

Who was this wealthy Middle Eastern man? Uday Hussein al-Tikriti, the eldest son of Iraqi dictator Saddam Hussein. He made that boast a few days after U.S.-led coalition forces invaded his country on March 20, 2003.

Just four months later, on July 22, 2003, members of America's elite Task Force 20 and the Army's 101st Airborne Division raided Uday Hussein's hideout in Mosul. When the smoke cleared, both Uday and his brother Qusay lay dead in the rubble. There was no security in money for Uday Hussein.

Wealth can never make anyone secure. It doesn't matter how much you have to live *on* if you have nothing to live *for*. As Jesus once said, "How hard it is for those who trust in riches to enter the kingdom of God" (Mark 10:24, *NKJV*). This is as true for you and me as it was for the son of the Iraqi dictator.

In his book *Lies That Go Unchallenged in Popular Culture*, Charles W. Colson, founder of Prison Fellowship, wrote about former General Electric CEO Jack Welch. Colson described Welch's myopic view of life this way:

> Even after Welch retired, General Electric provided him with a luxury apartment on Central Park West, free travel on company jets, and good things of life such as flowers, furniture, opera tickets, and even stamps.
>
> These disclosures about sticking GE with the tab for his lifestyle embarrassed Welch, who agreed to reimburse the company.

But there's no evidence that Welch is rethinking his idea of the good life.

Quite to the contrary, during an appearance at a public forum, Welch was asked what he had learned from a brush with death seven years earlier. Had he had an epiphany during his heart surgery? His answer was, "I learned I didn't spend enough money." When pressed—they thought he was joking—he added that, after his bypass surgery, he vowed never again to drink wine that cost less than a hundred dollars a bottle—and he was completely serious.

What a sad answer! What's even sadder is that Welch is hardly unique in this regard. . . . Materialistic worldviews have deprived people of any sense of purpose in life. . . . Whether it's drinking the best wine, eating the best food, or flying in a private jet, it makes no sense not to spend more money if this life is all there is.[3]

I'm not saying there is anything intrinsically wrong with money, nor with working hard and investing wisely to provide for your family. When we place wealth in a proper perspective with everything else that is important in life, it's an important force for good in the world. Our society, our businesses, our churches, and our families should all be run on sound economic principles. We should use our wealth to improve our own life and the lives of the people around us.

Money becomes a trap, however, when it becomes an obsession—the thing that drives us and rules our life. One of the wisest men I've ever met is Dr. Billy Graham. I first met him decades ago when I was a college student at Wake Forest University and I interviewed him on my campus radio program. Years later, I was privileged to stand on the same platform with him on two occasions and share my faith in God with his audience. Dr. Graham is one of my heroes, and I admire his wisdom—especially his wisdom regarding money.

"There is nothing wrong with possessing riches," Billy Graham once said. "The harm comes when riches possess us." On another occasion, he said, "A checkbook is a spiritual document. It tells you who and what you worship." And on still another occasion, he said, "If a person gets his attitude toward money straight, it will help straighten out almost any other area of his life."

Those who know Dr. Graham well will tell you that he practices what he preaches. His younger brother, Melvin Graham, once said, "I've never seen a man in my life who cares as little about money as Billy Graham."

God never intended for human beings to order their lives around the acquisition of wealth. Yes, we live in a material world, but we are not just material beings. We are spiritual beings, and we can never be satisfied by the accumulation of piles and piles of material "stuff." We can never find lasting meaning in things that do not last. We can never find satisfaction in material wealth, because the essential nature of wealth is that "enough" is never enough. We will always want just a little bit more—and that is why material wealth never satisfies the soul or brings peace to the human spirit.

As humorist Will Rogers sagely observed, "Too many people spend money they haven't earned to buy things they don't want to impress people they don't like." Isn't that an uncomfortably accurate diagnosis of your life and mine?

Look at any coin or dollar bill, and it will tell you, "In God We Trust." Our money tries to tell us where we should place our trust—*but we don't listen*. We look to money to provide our needs, to bring us joy, to give us peace of mind, to provide a sense of security—*all the things that we should look to God for*. If we were honest with ourselves, the tragic motto of our lives would probably read, "In Money We Trust."

The first step in getting our priorities straight is to admit that our values are out of whack.

WHAT IS MONEY?

There is a story told about a Mexican fisherman and an American investment banker. I've tried without success to learn where this story originated (if you know the author of this story, please let me know).

On a vacation trip to a coastal village in Mexico, an American investment banker saw a fisherman tying his boat at the dock. There were several large yellow-fin tuna in the bottom of the boat.

"Hey," the American said, "that's a nice catch. Did it take you long to catch that many fish?"

"Only a little while," the fisherman replied.

"Well," the American said, "why don't you stay out longer and catch more fish?"

"I caught enough fish to feed my family," the fisherman said with a shrug.

"But what do you do with the rest of your day?"

"I sleep late, I fish a little, I play with my children and take a siesta with my wife. At night, I take my guitar into the village and I sip wine and make music with my amigos. It is a good life."

"Mister," the American said, "you should let me help you. I have an MBA from Harvard and I can show you how to make good money fishing. Follow my advice, and you'll be able to buy a bigger fishing boat and, eventually, a whole fleet of fishing boats. You'll be able to open your own cannery and set up a processing and distribution chain. With my help, you'd be able to leave this little fishing village and move to the big city, and maybe even to New York, where you could run a global seafood enterprise."

The fisherman looked troubled. "How long will this take?"

"Ten, maybe twenty years."

"But what then?"

"Eventually you'll take your company public and become a very rich man."

"Then what do I do?"

"Then you retire. You can move to a little fishing village right here in Mexico. Then you can sleep late, fish a little, take siestas, sip wine, and make music with your amigos."

We success-oriented, goal-oriented *norteamericanos* think we have all the answers when it comes to making money. But sometimes, in our headlong drive for success, we fail to take stock of what life is truly all about. What is the point of setting career goals and making money if we never pause to experience those quiet, meaningful, reflective moments that truly make life worth living?

Colonel Harlan Sanders, the founder of the Kentucky Fried Chicken fast-food empire, put it this way: "Make sure you don't end up the richest person in the cemetery. You can't do business from there." Or, as columnist Dave Barry put it, "You should never confuse your career with your life." And psychoanalyst Charles Spezzano, in *What to Do Between Birth and Death*, observed, "You don't really pay for things with money. You pay for them with time. . . . The phrase 'spending your time' is not a metaphor. It's how life works."[4]

What is money, anyway?

"Money is a singular thing," observed economist John Kenneth Galbraith. "It ranks with love as man's greatest source of joy, and with death as his greatest source of anxiety." And former baseball pitcher and manager Larry Dierker said, "Money is like a legal drug. You can become addicted, enslaved, and all the while people will think how lucky you are."

Dorothy Parker, the New York writer who had such a keen eye for human foibles, once said, "If you want to know what God thinks of money, just look at the people He gave it to." And humorist Vic Oliver offered this perspective on money and the people who have it—or want to have it: "If a man runs after money, he's money-mad. If he keeps it, he's a capitalist. If he spends it, he's a playboy. If he doesn't get it, he's a ne'er-do-well. If he doesn't try to get it, he lacks ambition. If he gets it without working for it, he's a parasite. And if he accumulated it after a lifetime of hard work, people call him a fool who never got anything out of life."

Some of the most perceptive assessments of the human condition are found on the rear bumpers of our cars. Here's a sampling of bumper-sticker insight I've seen: "I have no desire for money. I just want *STUFF*." And, "The one who dies with the most toys wins." And, "All I want is a little more than I'll ever get."

It's all true—and tragically sad.

WHO IS TRULY RICH?

There is so much wealth sloshing around in our society today that people sometimes lose all sense of perspective. Jerry West enjoyed a legendary 14-year career in the NBA, playing his entire professional career with the Los Angeles Lakers. He once observed, "Players have every amenity that you can possibly have today. The life of a basketball player is a life of luxury. The problem comes when you give someone so much money at such an early age. All of a sudden, a million dollars doesn't mean anything. You can make an offer to a player for an incredible sum, like wads of Monopoly money, and the response you get from the agent and player is, 'I am insulted with that offer.' That's hard for me to understand."

Actor Paul Newman once made a similar observation about Hollywood values. "Here's what happens," he said. "You start making more money than you ever thought existed. First, you buy a mansion so big that even the rooms have rooms. Your children have to have individual governesses. Comes April 15 and the income tax people want $200,000. You call your agent, but the only scripts available are real dogs. You have to take them anyhow. Either that, or fire a couple of governesses."

There is probably no one whose life better typifies the emptiness of Hollywood values than Paris Hilton's. In May 2005, she announced her engagement to Greek shipping heir Paris Latsis. Sigmund Freud probably would have had a lot to say about such a match: The playgirl heiress engaged to the playboy heir, both named Paris—why, it was probably the closest that two narcissistic people could come to marrying themselves!

To make their engagement official, Paris Latsis bought Paris Hilton an engagement ring worth more than $1 million. Ms. Hilton wasn't happy with the ring. So Paris Latsis took the first ring back and bought her a second ring made of white gold, with a 24-carat emerald-cut diamond, valued at more than $2 million. In an interview with *Vanity Fair*, she explained why she rejected the first ring. "I like it," she said, "but it's yellow, and I'm like, I didn't want yellow for my engagement ring." Even though it seemed like a match made in La-La Land, the engagement lasted about five months.

You may not believe this, but it's true: I feel sorry for Paris Hilton. Most people think she was very fortunate to be born a spoiled heiress. I think she's had a deprived life. Because she's always had anything and everything she ever wanted, she has never known what it means to be truly rich. A person who knows how to live a rich and satisfying life can do so on $5 a day. A person who doesn't know how to live a rich and satisfying life will turn up her nose at diamonds and gold, saying, "Eww! The gold is, like, yellow!"

Minnesota businessman Harvey Mackay, author of *Dig Your Well Before You're Thirsty*, tells a story from his boyhood that shows that being "rich" is a state of mind. As a boy, Harvey's favorite summertime delicacy was watermelon. His father had a friend, Bernie, a successful produce wholesaler in St. Paul.

At the beginning of every summer, Bernie would call and invite father and son to the warehouse. Harvey and his dad would go to the warehouse and sit on the loading dock while Bernie took a knife and cracked open the first ripe watermelon off the truck. Then Bernie would pass out huge slices to his two guests and the three of them would have a cold, juicy feast. They would eat only the sweetest, juiciest heart of the melon and throw the rest away.

"Bernie was my father's idea of a rich man," Harvey Mackay recalled. "I always thought it was because he was such a successful businessman. Years later, I realized that what my father admired about Bernie's wealth was less its substance than its application. Bernie knew how to stop working, get together with friends and eat only the heart of the watermelon." From Bernie, Harvey Mackay learned an important lesson: "Being rich is a state of mind." Those who are truly rich are the ones who dangle their feet over the dock and "chomp into life's small pleasures."[5]

How about you? Are you rich? If you answer no, then consider this: If the entire world population were condensed to a community of a thousand people, 180 would live on the mountaintop known as "the developed world," while 820 would live in squalor in land below. We privileged few on that mountaintop would own 80 percent of all the wealth—more than half of all the homes, 93 percent of all phones, 85 percent of all the cars, and 80 percent of all television sets. The 820 less-fortunate people in the lowlands would subsist on an income of $700 per year or less. As we look around at the world from our mountaintop in the developed world, how can you and I say that we are not "rich" in material things?

It has been said that there are two ways to be rich. One is to have all you want. The other is to be satisfied with what you have. A bulging bank account and a fat stock portfolio are not reliable measures of whether or not you are truly rich. In fact, you are not genuinely rich until you possess the things that money can't buy and time can't steal.

UNIMPORTANT—AND ALL-IMPORTANT

Many people think that artists and musicians are only in it for the art. This image of art-for-art's-sake musicians was especially prevalent during the counterculture era of the 1960s. Youthful rock musicians seemed to reject the materialistic values of their parents and the surrounding culture—but is that really true?

Ex-Beatle Paul McCartney has recently revealed a very different reality behind the anti-materialistic and counterculture image. He told one interviewer, "Somebody once said to me, 'But the Beatles were anti-materialistic.' That's a huge myth. John and I literally used to sit down and say, 'Now let's write a swimming pool.' We said it out of innocence, out of . . . working-class glee that we were *able* to write a swimming pool. For the first time in our lives, we can actually do something and earn money."[6]

One of McCartney's fellow Beatles, George Harrison, died on November 29, 2001, at age 58, after a long battle with cancer. His wife, Olivia, and son, Dhani, were with him when he died. Those who knew him well memorialized him as an accomplished artist and musician, a committed family man and a spiritual seeker. Early in his life, after losing several musician friends to drug abuse and suicide, Harrison became intensely devoted to discovering his place in the universe and finding the meaning of his life.

Before his death, Harrison said, "For every human there is the quest to find the answer to why am I here, who am I, where did I come from, where I am going. For me that became the most important thing in my life. Everything else is secondary."[7]

I pray that George Harrison found what he was looking for. But whether his search was successful or not, one thing is certain: The quest for meaning is a noble quest. We are not put on this earth to amass piles of money and material stuff, only to die and lose it all. We have been put here for a much deeper reason. We need to find out why we are here, who we are, where we came from, and where we are ultimately going. That truly is the most important issue of our life.

The eighteenth-century preacher John Wesley, who cofounded the Methodist movement, once accepted an invitation to the home of a Christian plantation owner. The two men rode horses around the plantation, and the owner showed Wesley all of his vast holdings. Near sunset, as the two men rode back toward the mansion, the man said, "Well, what do you think of my estate?"

"You have a very beautiful plantation here," Wesley thoughtfully replied, "and when the time comes, I think you are going to have a hard time leaving it."

It's true, isn't it? The more possessions we have, the more attached we become to this world. And the more attached we are to this world, the harder it will be to leave it. And sooner or later, we all must leave this world behind. As John Wesley said on another occasion, "When I have any money, I get rid of it as quickly as possible, lest it find a way into my heart."

Financier and industrialist John Pierpont Morgan (1837-1913) was one of the wealthiest men of his era. He helped form General Electric in 1892, and the United States Steel Corporation in 1901. He was also one of the leading art collectors in the nation. When he died at age 75, in 1913, a newspaper reporter asked one of his associates how much money J. P. Morgan left behind. The associate's reply: "All of it."

The Bible tells us, "Now listen, you rich people, weep and wail because of the misery that is coming upon you. Your wealth has rotted, and moths have eaten your clothes. Your gold and silver are corroded. Their corrosion will testify against you and eat your flesh like fire" (Jas. 5:1-3). It doesn't matter how fat our bank account may be, there isn't enough money in the world for any of us to buy our way out of the inevitability of death. What good will our wealth be when we have left it all behind?

Tertullian, a Christian philosopher of the third century A.D., observed, "Nothing that is God's is obtainable by money." What a powerful truth! There is nothing that meets our deep spiritual need for meaning that can be purchased with money—not one thing. Can money buy a sense of peace and purpose? No. As Rick Warren wrote in

The Purpose-Driven Life, "Self-worth and net worth are not the same. Your value is not determined by your valuables, and God says the most valuable things in life are not things."[8]

If we seek our security by stockpiling money, Money (with a capital M) will ultimately become our master. Jesus said, "No one can serve two masters. Either he will hate the one and love the other, or he will be devoted to the one and despise the other. You cannot serve both God and Money" (Matt. 6:24). Whatever we worship as the source of our security will become the master we serve. If you spend your life serving Money, you will enter eternity knowing that you have handed your life over to a master that is powerless to save you.

The New Testament also tells us, "For the love of money is a root of all kinds of evil. Some people, eager for money, have wandered from the faith and pierced themselves with many griefs" (1 Tim. 6:10). Those words are often misquoted as, "Money is the root of all evil." But there's nothing intrinsically evil about money. It is the *love* of money that is a root of all kinds of evil. Money itself is a fine servant but a cruel master. When we keep it in perspective and use it well, money is the source of all kinds of good in our lives and the lives of people around us.

The way we think about and use our money says everything about the kind of people we are, both morally and spiritually. As author-speaker Ken Blanchard once observed, "Jesus talked more about money than He did about anything else in the Bible. He wasn't against making money, but He knew the worship of money was the root of all evil."

The four Gospels—Matthew, Mark, Luke and John—record the life and teachings of Jesus. These four books preserve for us 38 parables of Jesus—stories that He told to illustrate profound spiritual truths—and 16 of them, almost half of all of His parables, deal with how we should use our money. In fact, of the nearly 2,800 verses in the four Gospels, 288 verses, more than one-tenth, deal with money. In the entire New Testament, there are more than 500 references to prayer, fewer than 500 references to faith, but more than 1,000 references to money and material possessions.

The genuineness of our spirituality will be revealed in the way we handle our material possessions. The most important outward indicator of inward spirituality is a lifestyle of generosity. As someone once said, "Generosity is not measured by how much you *give*. It is measured by *how much you have left*."

THOSE WHO HAVE THE MOST WANT THE MOST

Can money buy happiness? As entertainment executive David Geffen said in a 2002 interview on ABC's *20/20*, "Anybody who thinks money will make you happy hasn't got money." Other wealthy businesspeople have made the same discovery.

John Jacob Astor was the first millionaire in America, having made his fortune in real estate, fur trading and medical opiates. Reflecting on his wealth and the state of his life, Astor said, "I am the most miserable man on Earth."

William H. Vanderbilt, the heir of Commodore Cornelius Vanderbilt, was the richest man in the world during the nineteenth century. He once said, "The care of $200 million is enough to kill anyone. There is no pleasure in it."

Andrew Carnegie was a Scottish-born American industrialist in the late nineteenth and early twentieth centuries. He built railroads and founded the Carnegie Steel Company, and was not known as a happy man. "Millionaires seldom smile," Carnegie once said.

Henry Ford founded the Ford Motor Company and invented the modern assembly line. As sole owner of the then privately held Ford Motor Company, he was one of the richest men in the world. Yet, at the height of his wealth and power, he once reflected, "I was happier when doing a mechanic's job."

In their book *Compassionate Leadership*, Ted Engstrom and Paul Cedar tell the story of John D. Rockefeller. Beginning his business career as a clerk, Rockefeller earned $3.75 a week. Out of these meager earnings, he gave 50 percent to his church, set aside 20 percent in a savings account, and lived off the remaining 30 percent. He got involved in the brand-new oil industry and turned his fledgling company, Standard Oil, into the biggest petroleum supplier in the country. He made his first million when he was just 33 years old.

As his success increased, he gave less and less of his income to the church. By the time he was 53 years old, Rockefeller was a billionaire and the world's richest man—but he had stopped giving to God and others. Though he had been strong and vigorous in his youth, by this time he was approaching a complete physical and mental breakdown. He couldn't sleep. His digestive system was in such poor shape that all his meals consisted of milk and crackers. His doctors told him he had, at most, a year to live.

Rockefeller realized that all his financial holdings would do him no good in the grave. Like Scrooge in Dickens's *A Christmas Carol*, he underwent a radical transformation. He remembered the young John D. Rockefeller who had once given half of his meager clerk's income to his church. He hoped that it wasn't too late to rediscover the generosity of his youth.

He established the Rockefeller Foundation as a means of using some of his financial blessings to improve the world. Through his foundation, Rockefeller showered millions of dollars on churches, hospitals, universities, and organizations that helped the underprivileged.

Soon after his transformation, Rockefeller's sleep patterns and digestion returned to normal. He felt stronger and more energetic. His mental outlook improved. His doctors told him that he seemed to have discovered a miraculous cure. As a result, John D. Rockefeller—who had been scheduled by his doctors to die before he turned 55—went on to live to the ripe old age of 98. Late in life, he reflected, "A man who dies rich, dies disgraced. . . . Do everything you can for the betterment of your fellow man, and in doing this, you will better enjoy life.' "[9]

It has been said that there are things that money can and cannot buy. Money can buy a house, but not a home; a bed, but not rest; food, but not an appetite; medicine, but not health; information, but not wisdom; thrills, but not joy; associates, but not friends; servants, but not loyalty; flattery, but not respect. As motivational speaker Michael Pritchard once observed, "No matter how rich you become, how famous or powerful, when you die, the size of your funeral will pretty much depend on the weather."

From God's perspective, money is nothing but wads of paper and numbers on a computer screen—*unless* it is unleashed to do good in human lives. Money helps no one while it sits in a vault, collecting dust or losing value due to inflation. Money does no good if one man lavishes it on luxuries for himself while allowing his neighbor to go unclothed and unfed. Money provides no security, because calamity and death strike both rich and poor. We can have all the money in the world, but if we do not have meaning, purpose and contentment, then our lives are nothing but dust in the wind.

Many people say, "When I have enough money in the bank, *then* I'll be able to afford more charitable giving." The problem is, when we set such vague goals for our generosity, it's easy to keep moving the goal-posts. The fact is, few people ever really feel they have "enough" money. The more we have, the more we want. As journalist Ray Stannard Baker observed (in *The Friendly Road*, writing under the pseudonym David Grayson), "Believe me, of all the people in the world, those who want the most are those who have the most."

We see this principle in the life of an internationally known pop singer. In the course of her 2007 divorce proceedings, her attorneys filed financial disclosure documents as part of the child custody case. Those documents revealed that the pop star received average monthly earnings of $737,000. Out of that income, she managed to spend $49,267 per month on mortgage payments, $16,000 on wardrobe, $4,758 on restaurants, $102,000 on gifts and entertaining—and a mere $500 in charitable contributions.[10]

In her case, a huge income did not translate into generous giving. And let's be honest with ourselves: When you and I compare how much we earn with how much we give away, are we really in a position to judge her?

"GIVE, AND IT WILL BE GIVEN TO YOU"

Stephen King is the author of more than 50 bestselling novels. On the afternoon of June 19, 1999, he was walking on the shoulder of Route 5 in Center Lovell, Maine, when he was struck by a 1985 Dodge Caravan (the driver was distracted by a dog in the vehicle). King was thrown 15 feet by the impact and landed in a patch of grass. His injuries included a collapsed right lung, a broken hip, multiple fractures of the right leg, and a scalp laceration. After five operations, weeks in the hospital and extensive physical therapy, King was able to return home. He resumed writing on a reduced basis because he was only able to sit at his keyboard for a half hour before the pain became unbearable.

On May 20, 2001, King gave a speech at Vassar College, in which he reflected on the lessons of his ordeal. Here's an excerpt from his message:

> A couple of years ago, I found out what "you can't take it with you" means. I found out while I was lying in the ditch at the side of a country road, covered with mud and blood and with the tibia of my right leg poking out the side of my jeans like the branch of a tree taken down in a thunderstorm. I had a MasterCard in my wallet, but when you're lying in the ditch with broken glass in your hair, no one accepts MasterCard. . . .
>
> We all know that life is ephemeral, but on that particular day and in the months that followed, I got a painful but extremely valuable look at life's simple backstage truths. We come in naked and broke. . . . All you have is on loan, anyway. . . . All that lasts is what you pass on. . . .
>
> So I ask you to begin the next great phase of your life by giving, and to continue as you begin. I think you'll find in the end that you got far more than you ever had, and did more good than you ever dreamed.[11]

Jesus repeatedly encouraged His followers to adopt a lifestyle of generosity—for their own blessing as well as for the sake of others. He said, "Give, and it will be given to you. A good measure, pressed down, shaken together and running over, will be poured into your lap" (Luke 6:39). In other words, if you bless others through your material generosity, God will bless you in ways that may be tangible or intangible, material or spiritual, but always bountiful and overflowing.

Dr. Bruce Larson is a prolific author, the founder of Faith at Work, a parachurch organization, and the former senior pastor of University Presbyterian Church in Seattle. He once observed, "Money is really another pair of feet to walk where Christ would walk. . . . Money can go where I do not have time to go, where I do not have a passport to go. My money can go in my place and heal and bless and feed and help." And, as former British prime minister Margaret Thatcher put it, "No one would remember the Good Samaritan if he'd only had good intentions. He had money too." So money is a good thing when used generously to meet needs and bless others.

Jesus said, "Sell your possessions and give to the poor. Provide purses for yourselves that will not wear out, a treasure in heaven that will not be exhausted, where no thief comes near and no moth destroys. For where your treasure is, there your heart will be also" (Luke 12:33-34). We desperately need to learn to see life from God's perspective. From a human perspective, money is the treasure we pile up in vaults so that we can be secure. But Jesus warns us not to put our trust in treasures that can be stolen or corrupted. As the epitaph on an old tombstone reads, "What I gave, I have. What I spent, I had. What I kept, I lost."

Steven Spielberg's motion picture *Schindler's List* is the fact-based story of Oskar Schindler, a businessman in Poland during the Holocaust. Schindler is portrayed as a flawed man with a compassionate heart for the Jewish slave laborers in his factory. He takes great risks to save many Jews from extermination in the Nazi death camps.

Near the end of the film, we see Schindler (portrayed by Liam Neeson) surrounded by a crowd of Jews he has saved. One of them, Itzhak Stern (portrayed by Ben Kingsley), steps forward as spokesman and hands Schindler a letter of thanks. The letter has been signed by all the people he has redeemed. Then Stern places a gold ring in Schindler's hand, and Schindler reads the inscription, a quotation from the Talmud: "Whoever saves one life saves the world entire."

Schindler is speechless—and at first you think he is moved by the gratitude of the Jews. But then he speaks and we see that he is actually tormented by guilt and regret that *he didn't do more*. "I could have gotten more out," he says. "I could have gotten more—"

"Oskar," Stern says, "there are eleven hundred people alive because of you!"

But Schindler in inconsolable. "I threw away so much money! You have no idea! I didn't do enough!" He places his hands on his long black limousine. "Why did I keep this car? I could have sold it and bought ten more people." He takes a gold pin from his lapel. "This pin! It would have bought two more people!" He begins to sob. "I could have gotten more people, and I didn't! I didn't!"

As he is driven away in his limousine, he sees an endless line of faces beyond the window. They are the faces of the people he saved—yet they seem like the ghostly faces of those he could have saved, but didn't.

At the end of our lives, when we look back on the way we used our money and our material possessions, what will we think of? Will we remember all the people we helped, all the lives we saved?

Or will we wish we had spent less and given more?

CHASING FAME

In 1983, I served as general manager of the Philadelphia 76ers, a team whose roster included such legendary names as Julius Erving, Moses Malone, Bobby Jones and Maurice Cheeks. We capped that magical season by roaring through the playoffs and sweeping the Lakers in four straight games in the Finals. As NBA champions, the victorious 76ers were feted by a ticker-tape parade and a ceremony before 50,000 ecstatic fans at Veterans Stadium.

On opening night of the following season, NBA Commissioner Larry O'Brien presented us with our championship rings at a pre-game ceremony. As we put our rings on our fingers, the fans cheered and the new season was underway.

But in the days that followed, I noticed something strange happening to me. Wherever I was, no matter what I was doing, I'd find my eyes being drawn to that big, sparkling ring on my finger. I would gaze at it as if hypnotized. I'd think about what it represented—not just the accomplishment of a championship season, but the fame and acclaim of millions of fans. Suddenly, a realization hit me: I was so dazzled by that ring that I had not truly focused on the new season. I was so lost in thoughts of *last* season's glory that I didn't have my head in *this* season.

So I took the ring off my finger, put it in a box and placed it in a drawer. That was more than 25 years ago, and I've never taken the ring out, unless a friend or family member asked to see it. I've moved on from past glories and past dreams of fame. I've learned that chasing fame is a fool's game—and even more foolish is the game of dwelling in the glories of the past.

THE EMPTINESS OF FAME

By the time he was 28 years old, Tom Brady had acquired immense fame and fortune. As quarterback of the New England Patriots, with a 10-year contract worth $60 million, Brady had won three Super Bowls. He also collected millions of dollars for product-endorsement deals that took advantage of his enormous fame.

In 2005, Brady was interviewed on TV's *60 Minutes* by CBS news correspondent Steve Kroft. As Kroft asked Brady how it felt to be so successful, the quarterback turned pensive and seemed a little lost within himself. "A lot of people would say, 'Hey, man, this is what is. I reached my goal, my dream, my life.' But me, I think, 'It's got to be more than this.' I mean this can't be what it's all cracked up to be."

Kroft seemed startled. "Well, what's the answer?" the newsman asked.

"I wish I knew," Brady said. "I wish I knew."[1]

My heart goes out to Tom Brady. He was finding out what I had learned 25 years earlier—the emptiness of fame. Many other famous sports figures have made that same discovery.

American Olympic runner Evelyn Ashford competed in an unprecedented five Olympic Games and was possibly the greatest female sprinter of all time. She was asked how it felt to win two gold medals in the 1984 Summer Olympics in Los Angeles. "When the gold came," she replied, "it was anticlimactic. I thought, 'Is that all there is?' You work so hard, and it's over so fast."

That same year, Czechoslovakian tennis star Hana Mandlíková defeated the legendary Martina Navrátilová in three sets in the finals at Oakland, California. Her upset victory ended Navrátilová's 54-game winning streak. Asked how she felt about the victory, Hana Mandlíková replied, "Any big win means that all the suffering, practicing and traveling are worth it. I feel like I own the world." The reporter then asked her how long that feeling lasts. Mandlíková's reply: "About two minutes."

Martina Navrátilová had a similar comment on the emptiness of fame. In 1984, she compiled a 74-match winning streak that has never been equaled. By mid-1985, Navrátilová had lost only 8 of her last 290 tennis matches and had amassed more than $2 million in prize money in a single year. Yet an article in the *New York Post* (May 22, 1985) quoted her as saying that she felt "alone all of a sudden. After winning at Wimbledon, I had it—the letdown."

One athlete who has a good perspective on fame is retired baseball catcher Dave Valle, who played from 1984 to 1996. Dave, who, with his wife, Victoria, cofounded the Christian Third World development organization Esperanza, said, "We spend the first half of our lives looking for success. The second half, we look for significance. At the end of the race, you want to be able to look in the mirror and say, 'This was a life well lived.'"

NO SUBSTITUTE FOR LOVE

In the summer of 1973, I moved to Atlanta to assume my duties as general manager of the Atlanta Hawks. Upon my arrival, several people told me I needed to meet the owner of the TV station that carried the Hawks' games. I called the station and made an appointment for lunch at a club downtown.

That luncheon meeting was my first encounter with Ted Turner.

This was before he became an international celebrity. He had not yet launched the Cable News Network (CNN), nor had he yet become owner of the Braves and the Hawks. But he was definitely the king of Atlanta media and a force to be reckoned with.

I had no idea what to expect when I sat down with Ted Turner—but what a luncheon that was! He had a boundless supply of emotional and physical energy. As he talked, he would become loud and boisterous, to the point of yelling. He was passionate about everything he said, and to emphasize his words, he would actually jump up from the table, wave his arms, dance and gesticulate wildly. It was quite a show.

During a recent trip to Atlanta, I encountered a woman who had worked closely with Ted Turner for nearly a decade. I asked for her impression of Mr. Turner. She said, "Ted Turner is the most unusual man I've ever met. In spite of all of his success, his accomplishments and his flamboyant personal style, no one really knows him. He has built up walls around himself and won't let anyone in. To tell you the truth, I don't think Ted himself knows who he is. I'm convinced that he's deeply insecure. Out on his sailboat, Ted is fearless and in control. Yet he's such an insecure and frightened man that he can't sleep alone at night by himself."

Time magazine called Ted Turner "perhaps the most openly ambitious man in America . . . a prototypical modern celebrity, famous above all for being famous." Turner himself admitted, "My desire to excel borders on the unhealthy." Where does Ted Turner's compulsive drive for fame come from? Perhaps he is driven by a tragic lack of feeling loved, approved and affirmed in his early life.

He was born Robert Edward Turner III, the son of Ohio billboard entrepreneur Ed Turner. When Ted was nine years old, his father moved the family from Cincinnati to Savannah, Georgia. Young Ted was sent off to military academy, and like many kids who spend their formative years in boarding school, he may have interpreted this move (whether consciously or unconsciously) as a demonstration of his parents' rejection. Also, the Ohio-to-Georgia transplantation muddled his identity: Was he a transplanted Northerner or an adopted Southerner?

"There is a haunted side to Turner," said *Time* magazine. "He is as acutely aware of childhood traumas. . . . His memories are shot through with a ceaseless struggle to prove himself worthy, with a sense of rejection as a Yankee in the South and a Southerner in the North." His boyhood pain and identity struggles bred in him a hunger for attention, demonstrated in grandiose actions and frenetic activity. To this day, he is known for doing and saying outrageous things, and for driving his subordinates crazy with his moodiness, restlessness and frantic hyperactivity. He also appears to be continually compensating for the devastating tragedies of his past, including the tragic illness and death of his only sibling, Mary Jane.

During his teens, his younger sister, Mary Jane, was diagnosed with severe lupus, a chronic and degenerative autoimmune disease. Though there are many effective treatments for lupus today, there was little that could be done for Mary Jane in those days. Turner still has a difficult time talking about his sister's five-year ordeal of nightmarish pain, ending in her death.

Though Ted recalls that his relationship with his father was "close," Ed Turner was a strict disciplinarian who often inflicted corporal punishment with a wire coat hanger. During Ted's teen years, his father hired him in the summer to work for his billboard business. Ted worked 40 hours a week, maintaining billboards. His father took back half his salary for room and board at home.

When Ted wanted to attend the Naval Academy at Annapolis, his father put his foot down and insisted that Ted apply to Harvard. After

Harvard turned him down, Ted enrolled at Brown and majored in the classics. Ed Turner wrote Ted a scathing letter, which read in part: "I am appalled, even horrified, that you have adopted classics as a major. As a matter of fact, I almost puked on the way home today . . . I think you are rapidly becoming a jackass, and the sooner you get out of that filthy atmosphere, the better it will suit me."

Stung, enraged and insulted, Ted lashed back at his father by publishing the letter in the Brown University student newspaper. But Ed Turner kept the pressure up on his son, and Ted gave in, changing his major to economics. Losing interest in his studies, Ted was suspended twice and finally dropped out of Brown. He eventually returned to Georgia and went into his father's business.

As a boss, Ted's father was a teacher, a mentor and an intimidating taskmaster. He taught Ted everything he knew about running a business, including the lessons he had learned from past business failures and successes. Ed Turner was a millionaire and a risk-taker who was constantly buying up companies and piling up assets on one side of the ledger while running up debts on the other side. While in the middle of a major expansion effort, Ted's father became convinced he had made a major mistake that would collapse his business empire. On March 5, 1963, Ed Turner went alone to a plantation he owned in South Carolina. There, at age 53, he turned a gun on himself and committed suicide.

"My father died when I was 24," Ted Turner recalled in a 1982 speech at Georgetown University. "That left me alone, because I had counted on him to make the judgment of whether or not I was a success." In another speech the previous year, Turner surprised and unsettled his audience by stopping in mid-sentence, picking up a copy of the *Success* magazine with his picture on the cover, and raising it over his head. Turning his eyes toward the ceiling, Ted whispered, "Is this enough for you, Dad?"

After his father's death, Ted Turner took over the business his father had founded, Turner Outdoor Advertising. In 1970, he purchased a failing Atlanta television station and turned it into the world's first cable TV "superstation." A decade later, he created CNN, the world's first 24-hour cable news network. He cultivated the image of a bold, brash swashbuckler of the business world.

Turner made a failed bid to acquire CBS, then succeeded in purchasing the Hollywood film studio MGM/UA Entertainment for $1.5 billion. This acquisition gave him a film library with which to launch new cable networks such as Turner Network Television, Turner Classic Movies, and The Cartoon Network. In 1996, his Turner Broadcasting System merged with Time Warner, Inc., with Turner himself serving as vice chairman of one of the largest media empires in the world. He portrayed himself in several television series and films, and acted in two Civil War TV-movies he produced (appearing as Confederate Colonel Waller Tazewell Patton).

Clearly, Ted Turner seems to be driven to pursue fame. Why? Perhaps it's because, at some deep level of his wounded psyche, he equates fame with love. We all need to be loved in order to live. Those of us who failed to receive the affirmation and approval of those who matter most to us tend to have a hole in our lives that we desperately try to fill with other things. Some try to fill it with fame.

In 1977, after successfully defending the America's Cup as skipper of the yacht *Courageous*, he told a press conference, "Fame is like love. You can never have too much of it." In that statement, Ted Turner may have said more than he realized about the inner forces that drive him.[2]

You may say, "Well, I'm not looking for fame. I don't have any ambition to get my picture on the cover of *Forbes* or *Time* or *People* magazine. I couldn't care less about being famous." Maybe not. But—

Wouldn't you like to be popular? Don't you enjoy being noticed? Doesn't it feel good when people pat you on the back and acknowledge your accomplishments? Haven't you caught yourself inserting a sly "brag" into a conversation so that people will be impressed with something you've done or someone you know? You may not think of it as an ambition for "fame," but you felt that tug, that desire to be recognized, that need to be admired, acknowledged and possibly even envied.

We all feel it from time to time. Some of us feel it all the time. And for some of us, that need to be recognized is like a hole in the soul that consumes us from within. It's a hole that is supposed to be filled with a warm sense of being affirmed, accepted and loved. It's a hole that Ted Turner himself was unable to fill after his father committed suicide, because as he himself observed, "I had counted on him to make the judgment of whether or not I was a success"—that is, of whether or not he was worthy and approved and loved by his father.

Where is the hole in your soul? And to what lengths have you been going in a desperate attempt to fill that hole with other things?

FAME IS NOT THE ANSWER TO OUR SEARCH

At the beginning of his book *Into Thin Air: A Personal Account of the Mt. Everest Disaster*, Jon Krakauer recalled how he felt when he reached the summit of Mount Everest on May 10, 1996:

> Straddling the top of the world, one foot in China and the other in Nepal, I cleared the ice from my oxygen mask, hunched a shoulder against the wind, and stared absently down at the vastness of Tibet. I understood on some dim, detached level that the sweep of earth beneath my feet was a spectacular sight. I had been fantasizing about this moment, and the release of emotion that would accompany it, for many months. But now that I was finally here, actually standing on the summit of Mount Everest, I just couldn't summon the energy to care.[3]

Isn't that amazing? Krakauer had literally reached the lofty summit of his life goals. He stood upon the roof of the world and looked down upon a site of indescribable beauty—yet the moment seemed empty. He was emotionally numb and vacant. His victory was hollow.

Award-winning actor Dennis Weaver (1924-2006) had a long-running role as Marshall Dillon's sidekick Chester on TVs *Gunsmoke* before starring for seven seasons on the NBC police drama *McCloud*. He once said, "So many people in Hollywood are desperate for inner fulfillment. They chase false ideas of happiness and still feel discontented. They feel hollow and empty inside despite their fame, their big paychecks, their limos and their jewels. That's why they turn to drugs and alcohol and keep having affairs and getting married over and over again."

One Hollywood fame-chaser was Margot Kidder, the Canadian-born actress who played a quirky and assertive Lois Lane opposite Christopher Reeve in the *Superman* movies of the 1970s and 1980s. Coming to Hollywood from a childhood in remote Yellowknife in the Canadian

Northwest Territories, Kidder sought fame and found it. She dated former Canadian prime minister Pierre Trudeau and was married to (and later divorced from) playwright Thomas McGuane, actor John Heard and director Philippe de Broca.

In 1996, Margot Kidder made headlines when she was found hiding in the backyard of a stranger in Glendale, California. She was dirty and disheveled, her hair was crudely hacked off and her appearance and behavior were so wild and erratic that she was said to be unrecognizable. She had been reported missing three days earlier. When police talked to her, she claimed to have been stalked and assaulted; but though she was scratched from hiding in the bushes, she did not appear to have been the victim of a crime. Tests showed that she had not been taking drugs or drinking alcohol.

After being hospitalized and diagnosed with a bipolar disorder, Kidder issued a statement. "I think the truth is that I'd been insane for many years," she said, "probably from age 16, when I decided Hollywood and stardom was what life was all about and I turned my back on my parents. I was wrong. Fame gave me a totally empty life in which I turned to drugs and disastrous relationships. Now I've discovered what really counts. The tragedy is that it has taken me to the age of 47 to work out what really matters."

The emptiness of fame, coupled with a serious but treatable mental disorder, could have easily destroyed Margot Kidder's life. Fortunately, just in time, she discovered the pointlessness of chasing fame. Today, Margot Kidder is a strong advocate for mental health. She has devoted her life to helping others instead of seeking fame.[4]

It can be a deadly mistake to confuse fame with love, fulfillment, significance or happiness. Fame may get you the best table in the restaurant, but those who are famous will tell you that fame has not made them happy. Some of the unhappiest people I know are also some of the most famous people I know. That's especially true in the fame-rich environment of professional sports.

While riding high as the superstar shooting guard for the Los Angeles Lakers, Kobe Bryant was asked by a reporter if he was happy. Kobe shrugged and said, "I guess. Maybe. Not really. I really don't believe in happiness."

Dennis Rodman of the Jordan-era Chicago Bulls appreciated fame and notoriety as well as anyone in the NBA. His ever-changing hair color was nearly as legendary as his amazing rebounding ability. "The pro ball business is nothing but a fantasy," he once said. "It's like going to Fantasy Island and fulfilling all your dreams. But once you get out of the game, it's like you're still living a dream, but you don't have the applause and you don't have the cheers. All that is gone and everything is suddenly silent. Nobody knows who you are. You're a has-been. All people can do is say, 'Remember, he made a great move 15 years ago.'"

As Mark Twain once said, "Fame is a vapor." There is no lasting sense of security in fame. Pop singer Celine Dion expressed the insecurity of fame when she said, "In show business, you never know when it's going to end. I'm afraid I'll wake up and find it's all over."

When famous people fade into obscurity, they often find it easier to dwell in the applause of the past than to face the silent future. Playwright Lillian Hellman (*The Little Foxes*, 1939) put it this way: "It is a mark of many famous people that they cannot part with their brightest hour."

THE SOUND OF A GREAT NAME

While I was working on this book, I had a conversation with my two Korean sons, Stephen and Thomas. I told them I was writing a book called *What Are You Living For?* Stephen, who is 26, said, "Sounds interesting. What's it about?"

I said, "It's about the four false values that drive most people's lives—fortune, fame, power, and pleasure. It's about how empty and unfulfilling those four things are."

"Fortune, fame, power, and pleasure, huh?" Stephen said. "Gee, that's me. That's the stuff I'm pursuing." He blinked. "And most of my friends, too."

"Steve," I said, "that's really what everybody's been after since the beginning of time. I'm not saying everybody wants all four, but most want at least two or three."

"I guess you're right," he said. "I mean, I want money, and I want to enjoy life—but I don't really care about fame."

"In that case," I said, "you're wiser than I was at your age, because when I was 26 and running the Spartanburg Phillies, I was chasing all four—and *especially* fame!"

I'm glad Stephen isn't interested in pursuing fame. Some people are fortunate enough to see through the deceptive façade of fame at an early age. One of those was child star and 1930s screen icon Shirley Temple. "I stopped believing in Santa Claus when I was six," she recalled. "Mother took me to see him in a department store and he asked for my autograph."[5] If only we could have stopped believing in fame at the same time we stopped believing in Santa Claus.

There is a hunger for love and affirmation in every human soul. But that deep inner hunger cannot be satisfied with fame, any more than it can be satisfied with money, power or pleasure. The human spirit longs for a sense of significance that transcends merely being known by faceless throngs of people.

Even though fame doesn't bring true satisfaction or significance, it is tragically habit-forming. Like having a heroin addiction, you have to keep going back and getting "just one more hit" of fame—not to get high on fame, but just to feel okay about yourself. As you continue to chase the applause of the crowds, and as you reach each new level of fame, you discover deeper and darker levels of emptiness. You find that you never get over feeling envious of the person who is just a few steps ahead of you in the race for fame.

Even if everyone around you thinks you have it all, *you* know that the hole in your soul is unfilled. You keep stuffing more and more fame into that hole, yet the emptiness just seems to grow and grow. Nothing satisfies. Nothing gives you peace. The promise of fame is an illusion.

There are many people who were world-famous a couple of years ago but are virtually unknown today. Do you remember who won the best actor and best actress Academy Awards two years ago, five years ago, ten years ago? How many Nobel or Pulitzer Prize winners can you name? Who was the Super Bowl MVP last year? The year before last? Five years ago?

Humorist and cartoonist James Thurber once observed, "The sound of a great name dies like an echo. The splendor of fame fades into nothing. But the grace of a fine spirit pervades the places through which it has passed."

AN EXILE OF MEANINGLESSNESS

There's no doubt that Napoleon Bonaparte was a famous man—but what does his fame consist of today? Unless you're a history buff, you probably know little about his life. You probably know that he was a French military leader and emperor around the turn of the nineteenth century. You probably know he was defeated at a place called Waterloo. You may even be able to mentally picture Napoleon with his hand tucked into his vest, thanks to a famous painting by Jacques-Louis David.

But for the most part, Napoleon's fame lies in tatters today. The life he lived has no effect on our lives today. Yet he lived his entire life in an obsessive quest for fame.

Napoleon was born on the island of Corsica, the son of an attorney. As a child, Napoleon suffered from chronic illness that may have hindered his physical growth. As an adult, he measured only 5 feet 2 inches tall, and his short stature is believed to have contributed to a lifelong sense of inferiority. He probably compensated for those feelings by plunging Europe into war for the sake of his own self-glorification.

Historians record that Napoleon spent the lives of at least 860,000 French soldiers (and countless enemy soldiers) in his quest for fame. At the height of his power, Emperor Napoleon controlled half of Europe and dominated 80 million human lives. Yet even as he was achieving all the fame any man could want, Napoleon remained haunted by the humiliation of his past. As a Bonaparte, he had a tinge of noble blood, but he was clearly not of royal birth like the rest of the crowned heads of Europe. The other royal families let Napoleon know they viewed him as an inferior.

Napoleon planned to overcome his own inferiority by marrying a European princess—preferably a princess of Russia. He considered Czar Alexander I of Russia to be a friend, so he proposed that the Czar permit Napoleon to marry his daughter, thereby creating a "blood pact" with Russia, the great European power to the east. Through this marriage, Napoleon hoped to legitimize himself as royalty and an equal to the other crowned heads of Europe.

When Czar Alexander rejected Napoleon's proposal, the French Emperor was humiliated. Outraged and offended, Napoleon launched his invasion of Russia in 1812, a disastrous military campaign that ultimately led to his undoing. Thousands of men died on both sides of the battlefront, sacrificed on the altar of Napoleon's ego. As Henry Blackaby and Richard Blackaby observed in their study of leadership, *Called to Be God's Leader*:

> It could be argued that hundreds of thousands of Europeans died in one man's vain attempt to achieve satisfaction through the brutal acquisition of power and fame. Ego-driven people become desensitized to the suffering of others. It is acknowledged that few commanders suffered military casualties with greater indifference than Napoleon. The Duke of Wellington lamented the loss of thousands, but Napoleon boasted he would readily sacrifice a million soldiers to attain his goals.[6]

Following Napoleon's defeat by Russia, a coalition of nations—Russia, Prussia, England, Spain, Portugal, Austria and Sweden—joined forces to drive Napoleon back into France. Napoleon's own marshals rose up against him and demanded that he abdicate, which he did in April 1814. Napoleon was allowed to go into exile on the tiny island of Elba. His enemies continued to call him Emperor, but they did so only to mock him. While in exile, Napoleon bemoaned the end of his fame, saying, "If I had succeeded, I would have been the greatest man known to history."

The ambition for fame leads inevitably to emptiness because fame cannot satisfy the hunger within the human soul. Those like Napoleon who chase after fame are destined to end their lives in an exile of meaninglessness. Along the way, they often leave a trail of destruction in their wake.[7]

The "Napoleon" of our era was Saddam Hussein, the strongman dictator of Iraq, who was executed in 2006. During a reign of more than three decades, he transformed his oil-rich country into a totalitarian police state, ruled by terror. He constantly invented ever-more-grandiose titles for himself, demanding that the people call him Glorious Leader, Descendant of the Prophet, the Anointed One, Chairman of the Revolutionary Command Council, Doctor of Laws, and Great Uncle to the People of Iraq. He attempted to reshape Iraq into a monument to his own ego.

He had a statue of himself erected at the entrance to every Iraqi village and a portrait of himself placed in every government office. The Iraqi people were required to have at least one framed portrait of Saddam displayed in their homes. A joke was told in Iraq (usually in nervous whispers) that the population of the country was 34 million—17 million Iraqi citizens and 17 million images of Saddam.

In the May 2002 issue of *The Atlantic Monthly* (published 18 months before Saddam was found hiding in a "spider hole" and taken prisoner by U.S. forces in Iraq), writer Mark Bowden offered this assessment of Saddam Hussein and his Napoleonic quest for lasting fame:

> What does Saddam want? . . . He seems far more interested in fame than in money, desiring above all to be admired, remembered, and revered. A nineteen-volume official biography is mandatory reading for Iraqi government officials, and Saddam has also commissioned a six-hour film about his life, called *The Long Days*, which was edited by Terence Young, best known for directing three James Bond films. Saddam told his official biographer that he isn't interested in what people think of him today, only in what they will think of him in five hundred years. The root of Saddam's bloody, single-minded pursuit of power appears to be simple vanity.
>
> But what extremes of vanity compel a man to . . . erect giant statues of himself to adorn the public spaces of his country? To commission romantic portraits, some of them twenty feet high, portraying the nation's Great Uncle as a desert horseman, a wheat-cutting peasant, or a construction worker carrying bags of cement? To have the nation's television, radio, film, and print devoted to celebrating his every word and deed? Can ego alone explain such displays? Might it be the opposite? What colossal insecurity and self-loathing would demand such compensation?[8]

Mark Bowden has put his finger on the exposed nerve of every wounded human soul who gets caught up in chasing this vapor called fame. Those with a pathetic and pathological need to glorify themselves are actually insecure beyond all measure. Whether or not they loathe themselves, there's no question that they struggle with intense self-doubt and a consuming sense of inadequacy.

And while Napoleon's pursuit of fame ended in exile, Saddam's ended in execution. He was buried in an unmarked grave in an undisclosed location. One Iraqi, whose father, brothers and many other family members were killed by Saddam's secret police, pronounced the dictator's epitaph: "Now, he is in the garbage heap of history."

As Sir John Sinclair, the Scottish politician and agriculturalist, once observed, "How men long for celebrity! Some would willingly sacrifice their lives for fame, and not a few would rather be known by their crimes than not known at all." How tragically true. We see this principle in the lives of famous tyrants like Napoleon and Saddam Hussein— and we see it in the desperate lives of our own young people.

"NOW I'LL BE FAMOUS"

At 1:43 P.M., on Wednesday, December 5, 2007, a 19-year-old youth emerged from the third-floor elevator of the Westroads Mall in Omaha, Nebraska. He pulled out an AK-47 semi-automatic rifle that he had concealed under his sweatshirt, along with two 30-round magazines of ammunition. He took aim at the unsuspecting Christmas shoppers below and opened fire. He continued shooting for about six minutes, the echo of gunshots and screams mingling grotesquely with the sound of Christmas carols.

When the shooting ended, six innocent people lay dead around the mall. Six others lay wounded. One later died in the ambulance on the way to the hospital, and another died in the emergency room. The gunman's final act was to turn the weapon on himself and take his own life.

The killer left a suicide note, explaining that the killings were revenge for his hurt over a breakup with his girlfriend and being fired from his job. He ended the note with the words, "Now I'll be famous."

The families of the dead will remember the killer as a pathetic loser who took the life of a loved one for no sane reason. But is he famous? Do you remember his name? A few years from now, will anyone?

At the same time, we have to examine ourselves and ask, "What am I willing to do to other people for the sake of a few moments of paltry fame? What are the insecurities and self-doubts that drive me to glorify myself at the expense of others? Am I guilty of hurting other people, then saying to myself, 'Now I'll be famous'?"

There are people in this world—and I know, because I've met them—who consider themselves good people, moral people, even devout and spiritual people. Yet you don't have to be around them long before you realize they are totally absorbed with their own self-glorification. They are little Napoleons, little Saddams, little mall shooters who will knock down anyone who gets in the way of their quest for fame—and it doesn't even occur to them that they are hurting other people. The only thought that glimmers in their minds is, "Now I'll be famous! Now I'll be popular! Now I'll be applauded! Now people will be impressed with me!"

What about you? Would you be willing to hurt another person's reputation in order to enlarge your own? Would you be willing to undermine a coworker to get that promotion? Would you spread gossip about a fellow Christian in order to secure a leadership position in your church? Would you steal someone else's limelight for a few moments of applause?

What would you do for a few moments of squalid fame?

TROPHIES IN THE TRASH

My friend Ernie Accorsi, former general manager of the New York Giants football team, recently told me a story about Vince Lombardi. Years after Coach Lombardi had left the Green Bay Packers, the city brought him back for a ceremony in his honor. The city was naming a street after him.

When Lombardi arrived for the ceremony, he was in a foul mood. Someone asked the legendary football coach what was wrong.

Standing by the sign that read "Lombardi Street," the coach replied, "They named a stadium after Curly Lambeau. I won five titles and they named an alley after me!"

Psychologist and broadcaster Dr. James Dobson tells the story of how, as a young man, he set a goal of grabbing a little fame for himself. He arrived at Pasadena College (now Point Loma Nazarene University) in

1954, an 18-year-old college freshman. He had come from south Texas, where he was able to play tennis 6 days a week, 11 months out of the year. He loved the game and he excelled at it.

Walking through the administration building soon after his arrival, young Dobson stopped at a display case filled with trophies. In the center of the case was a tennis trophy inscribed with the names of tournament winners going back to 1947. He was mesmerized. "Someday," he told himself, "my name will be on that trophy."

Today, Dr. Dobson finds it hard to believe that getting his name scratched onto a trophy was so important to him, but for the 18-year-old college freshman, it became the consuming goal of his life. He achieved that goal, winning the student tennis tournament in 1957 and 1958.

He graduated and moved on. Years passed. He forgot all about the trophy until he received a call from a friend. The friend said, "My son was at the campus where you used to go to school. He noticed a trophy in a trash can, and when he took it out, he saw that it was a tennis trophy. He noticed your name on the trophy, and he wondered if you'd like to have it."

That trophy sits on a shelf in the office of Dr. James Dobson today. But he doesn't keep it as a reminder of past fame and glory. Rather, he keeps it as a reminder that all ambition for fame is doomed to futility. As Dr. Dobson himself puts it, "If you live long enough, life will trash your trophies." Those who have found fame tend to agree: Fame's trophies eventually become trash. Those who seek their own glory invariably find that having fame is very different from what they expected.

Beatle George Harrison once recalled, "It made me nervous, the whole magnitude of our fame." The Beatles' first American tour, which included an appearance on *The Ed Sullivan Show* and concerts before screaming fans at the Washington Coliseum and Carnegie Hall, was viewed by the world as a triumph—but to Harrison and his fellow Beatles, the "triumph" rang hollow. On the plane back to England, Harrison moaned, "How [bleeping] stupid it all is! All that big hassle to make it, only to end up as performing fleas!"[9]

At a party for the release of his 1988 album *Cloud Nine*, Harrison recalled his early days as a Beatle. "At first we all thought we wanted the fame and that," he said. "After a bit, we realized that fame wasn't really what we were after, just the fruits of it. After the initial excitement and thrill had worn off, I, for one, became depressed. [I thought,] 'Is this all we have to look forward to in life? Being chased around by a crowd of hooting lunatics from one crappy hotel room to the next?' "[10]

In 1999, boxer Muhammad Ali was named "Sportsman of the Century" by *Sports Illustrated* in honor of his career as a three-time World Heavyweight Champion and Olympic gold medalist. Without doubt, there is no more famous sports figure in the world than Muhammad Ali. The Champ wanted to use his fame to do good in the world and especially to help the African-American community. After winning the gold medal in Rome, he said to himself, "I am the champ of the whole world, and now I'm going to be able to do something for my people. I'm really going to be able to get equality for my people!"[11]

Upon his triumphant return to his hometown, Louisville, Kentucky, the mayor welcomed him and told him that his Olympic gold medal was his key to the city. Soon afterward, Ali took his friend Ronnie to a little downtown restaurant. Ali wore his Olympic gold medal everywhere he went in those days, and he had it around his neck in the restaurant. The two men sat down and ordered cheeseburgers and vanilla milkshakes. The waitress didn't bother to take their order. Instead, she said, "We don't serve Negroes."

"That's okay," the Olympic champion said. "We don't eat them."

The joke fell flat. The waitress frowned.

Ali (who had not yet converted to Islam and was then going by his birth name, Cassius Clay) pointed to his medal and politely said, "I'm Cassius Clay, the Olympic boxing champion. I was told that this gold medal is the key to the city. So, ma'am, would you please get us those burgers and shakes?"

The waitress left, conferred with the restaurant manager, then returned. "I'm sorry," she said. "You're both going to have to leave."

The Champ walked out of the restaurant with his heart in his throat. "I wanted my medal to mean something," he later recalled. "It was supposed to mean freedom and equality. . . . I just wanted America to be America. I had won the gold medal for America, but I still couldn't eat in this restaurant in my hometown, the town where they all knew my name, where I was born in General Hospital only a few blocks away.

I couldn't eat in the town where I was raised, where I went to church and led a Christian life. Now I had won the gold medal. But it didn't mean anything, because I didn't have the right skin color."[12]

Ali left, went out to a bridge, took the gold medal from around his neck, and flung it out into the Ohio River. Thirty-six years later, he was presented with a replacement gold medal in Atlanta, when he lit the Olympic torch to start the 1996 games.

In the late 1980s, sports writer Gary Smith visited with Muhammad Ali at his home. This was about four years after the Champ had been diagnosed with Parkinson's disease, a neurological disorder that slowed his speech and his movements. Ali took Smith on a tour of his home, then led him out to the trophy room in the barn next to the house. In the trophy room were hundreds of mementos from Ali's boxing career. There was a large display board with photos from his many triumphant boxing matches.

Smith was surprised to see that many of the photos were ruined, curled by the dampness in the barn and stained and streaked with bird droppings. Looking up, Smith saw that there were pigeons roosting in the rafters of the barn. Smith looked at Ali, who was quietly turning the ruined photos to the wall. In a soft, raspy voice, the Champ said, "I had the world, and it wasn't nothin'. Look now."[13]

The lesson of Muhammad Ali's life is the same lesson that Dr. Dobson described: "If you live long enough, life will trash your trophies." The trophies of fame do not last. The glories of fame are destined to fade. If we spend our lives in pursuit of this vapor called fame, we will end our lives in tragic disappointment.

TESTED BY FAME

There is nothing wrong with being famous—as long as we learn to wear it well, use it to serve others and maintain our humility. When Nobel-winning chemist and physicist Marie Curie died on July 4, 1934, Albert Einstein remarked, "Marie Curie is, of all celebrated beings, the only one whom fame has not corrupted." To which Madame Curie's daughter Eva added, "She did not know how to be famous." Either of those statements would be a great epitaph for any famous person. As the great (and humble) retired basketball coach John Wooden has said, "Talent is God-given; be humble. Fame is man-given; be thankful. Conceit is self-given; be careful."

The Bible tells us that God uses fame to test our character. Silver is tested in a crucible, it says, and gold is tested in a fiery furnace, but our lives are tested by the praise, applause and fame we receive (see Prov. 27:21). If we respond to fame by becoming arrogant and self-centered, then we fail the test. But if we respond in humility, seeking to use our fame to do good for others and to glorify God, then the test of fame has proven that our hearts are pure, like silver and gold. As John Maxwell has observed, God is seeking people who will not pursue their own fame, but seek to make God famous.

If God has gifted you with the ability to do great things, and the public responds by offering you applause, praise and fame, you will be tempted. A little voice inside you will say, "Hey, I really am great! I'm entitled to be celebrated, served and pampered. I deserve it!" This is what happens to people when they achieve a little fame and start to believe their press clippings. Their heads swell, they start treating the people around them as "inferiors," and they fail the test of fame.

Artist and filmmaker Andy Warhol predicted that, in the age of television, everyone would eventually be famous for 15 minutes. What will you do with your 15 minutes of fame? How will you respond? Will you pass the character test and come through as silver and gold? Will you use your fame to serve God and others?

Or will you squander it all on your own ego? Will you use your fame to get your way and glorify yourself?

Broadcast journalist David Bloom of NBC News was a highly respected reporter and anchorman, and a Christian. He began his TV reporting career at a small station in LaCrosse, Wisconsin, and worked his way up in the news business, winning both the Peabody and the Edward R. Murrow awards along the way. In 1993, David Bloom joined the NBC News team, reporting from the White House. In 2003, he went to Iraq to cover the Gulf War, which ended the reign of Saddam Hussein. Embedded with the Third Infantry Division as it sped toward Baghdad, Bloom transmitted live hourly reports from atop the "Bloom-Mobile," an Army tank fitted with a satellite dish.

On April 6, 2003, while traveling in his tank about 25 miles south of Baghdad, David Bloom collapsed. The driver stopped the tank, and Bloom was taken out and airlifted to a field medical unit—but he died before he could receive medical attention. The cause of death: a deep vein thrombosis resulting in a pulmonary embolism. In layman's terms, a blood clot dislodged in his leg and blocked the pulmonary artery to his lungs, resulting in sudden death. Bloom died one month short of his fortieth birthday, leaving behind a wife, Melanie, and three daughters.[14]

The nation was stunned. We had been following David Bloom's reports from the battlefront. We were captivated by his courage and his enthusiasm for reporting the events of the war as they happened. I was personally challenged by a statement Bloom made shortly before leaving America to report his last, great story.

"It does not matter how famous you may think you are," he said, "or how often you are seen on the air. There is always someone more important. What matters is how you treat those you meet on a regular basis, no matter their stature or title. Fame and power are fleeting. Relationships, no matter how brief, are remembered and can last forever."

Those are the words of a man who understood fame and used it well. May you and I rise to the challenge of those words, accepting praise and fame with an attitude of gratitude and humility.

CHASING POWER

During my junior year at Wake Forest University, I had my own sports interview show, much like the three different weekly radio shows I have in Orlando today. I got to interview many of my sports idols, including Ted Williams, Arnold Palmer, Harmon Killebrew and Roger Maris.

But my favorite interview was with a man who was not a sports figure at all: Dr. Billy Graham. The evangelist was on the Wake Forest campus to speak at a chapel service, so I brought him into my studio to talk about sports. He turned out to be very knowledgeable and had played a lot of baseball in his youth. He was personally acquainted with quite a few athletes, and he gave me one of my best interviews ever.

Over the years, I have met and spoken with Dr. Graham a number of times, and I was honored to speak at two of his crusades in Chicago and Syracuse. My respect for him has deepened over the years. While working on this book, I was pleased to have as a guest on my Orlando radio show Michael Duffy, who coauthored a book with Nancy Gibbs, *The Preacher and the Presidents: Billy Graham in the White House*. The book explores Dr. Graham's unique place in history as a friend and adviser to 11 presidents, from Harry S. Truman to George W. Bush.

Dr. Graham counseled and prayed with presidents during times of crisis. He talked to President Eisenhower during the integration battles in the South—and he also answered Eisenhower's question, "How can I know that I'm going to heaven?" He knelt in prayer with both LBJ and Nixon during the era of Vietnam and campus unrest—and he dealt with Johnson's question, "Will I see my parents in heaven?" President Clinton even used Dr. Graham as a back-channel courier to convey a message to Kim Il Sung, urging the North Korean dictator to allow UN inspectors into his nuclear sites.

I asked Michael Duffy why Dr. Graham befriended the presidents. Duffy replied, "Billy Graham was not tempted by money. And he was not tempted to be unfaithful to his wife. But when Nancy Gibbs and I interviewed him, Dr. Graham told us very candidly that his weakness was *power*. We all have different areas of temptation and struggle, and that was Dr. Graham's weak spot. He was drawn to power and he enjoyed being around powerful people."

Duffy told me that Dr. Graham admitted crossing the line from spiritual adviser to political adviser in his friendship with Richard Nixon. This, Graham said, was a big mistake. When he realized that Nixon had been dishonest about the Watergate affair, Dr. Graham realized that he could be deceived and seduced by political power, and that this weakness threatened his witness as an evangelist. From then on, Dr. Graham made a commitment to serve purely as a spiritual counselor, and to leave politics to the politicians.

The fact that Dr. Graham recognized his susceptibility to the lure of power—and took steps to guard against it—only increased my longstanding respect for him. Few people have the strength of character to resist the seductive charms of power. Most people, given access to the most powerful man in the world, could not help being corrupted by it.

Power, like fire, is a very useful tool—and one that can easily be misused.

THE SWEET SMELL OF WHITE MARBLE

Power is the ability to influence or control other people so that they do what you want. In its most beneficial sense, power is one of the tools of leadership. A wise leader can use the personal power of persuasion to inspire a group of people to move together as one in order to achieve a lofty goal. But power can also take the form of raw force and intimidation, as in a totalitarian dictatorship.

Why do people chase power? The reasons behind our obsession with power are rooted in our common human needs and drives. Some of us seek power in order to inflate our egos and make us feel significant. Some seek power out of a desperate need to be known and admired by others. Some of us seek it because we are basically insecure, and controlling others makes us feel safe. Some seek power as a means of attaining the other three false values that people chase: money, fame and pleasure.

Political commentator Cal Thomas observed the following in his book *Blinded by Might*:

From the beginning, men and women have sought power. In the Garden of Eden, Adam and Eve wanted the power to be like God. China's Mao Zedong said power comes from the barrel of a gun. Lord Acton's often-quoted remark about power is that it is corrupting and when it becomes absolute, it corrupts absolutely. . . .

Power is the ultimate aphrodisiac. People may have wealth, position, and fame, but unless they have power, many of them believe their lives are incomplete. Power cannot only seduce, but can also affect judgment. It can be more addictive than any drug.[1]

Biographer Anne Edwards agrees. In her book *The Reagans: Portrait of a Marriage*, she observed, "Power is not only an aphrodisiac but also a hard-core addiction."[2]

John A. Huffman, Jr., senior pastor of St. Andrews Presbyterian Church in Newport Beach, California, recalls the time when he learned of a contagious disease that had spread throughout our nation's capital. The disease is called "Potomac fever." He learned about it from the late Admiral William Lukash, who served as White House physician under Presidents Johnson, Nixon, Ford and Carter. Once a person is infected with Potomac fever, he or she becomes a power addict.

Lukash explained how Potomac fever works. A young woman, fresh out of college, applies for a low-level White House job. Once hired, she's thrilled at the privilege of simply walking those white marble corridors where so much history has been shaped. She doesn't care about power. She is just happy to be there, carrying out even the most menial of duties in the White House.

Time passes. She acquires greater responsibilities—and as she is promoted, she begins to want more power. The first time she rides aboard Air Force One is a thrill. But soon, on future trips, she joins the competition for seats closer to the front, closer to the president and the seat of power. Eventually, the ambition for power becomes boundless and all-consuming.

That, Lukash told Huffman, is how Potomac fever gradually takes over a person. Huffman adds that another Washington insider, former

Senator Mark Hatfield, had another term for Potomac fever. He called it, "The sweet, sweet smell of white marble."

In his book *Getting Through the Tough Stuff*, pastor Charles Swindoll tells about a trip he took with his friend Charles Colson, the former chief counsel for President Richard M. Nixon. Colson was convicted of charges related to the Watergate scandal and spent time in federal prison. As they traveled together, Swindoll asked Colson, "Why would anyone want the burden of being president of the United States? I wouldn't want that job for all the money in the world!" Colson smiled knowingly and replied, "One word, my friend: *power*."

Charlemagne (Charles the Great, A.D. 742–814) was king of the Frankish Empire and the most powerful ruler of the Middle Ages. After conquering Italy, he was crowned Imperator Augustus by Pope Leo III on Christmas Day in 800. In January 814, after spending weeks in the forest on a hunting expedition, Charlemagne was stricken with pneumonia. On January 28, after taking Holy Communion, Charlemagne died at age 72, and was buried in Aachen Cathedral.

Two centuries later, Otho of Lomello, Count of the Palace at Aachen during the reign of Emperor Otto III, claimed that he and the Emperor had opened Charlemagne's tomb and found the late king's body. According to Otho, Charlemagne sat upon his throne, his crown upon his head, his scepter in one hand, and his other hand resting on the pages of an open Bible. Otho said that Charlemagne's finger pointed to a passage in the New Testament: "What good will it be for a man if he gains the whole world, yet forfeits his soul?" (Matt. 16:26).

I can't vouch for the accuracy of that story. I don't know if Otho of Lomello actually did find the body of Charlemagne as he claimed. But there are two features of the story that I know to be true: First, everyone who holds power today will someday be dead. Second, there is no amount of power that is worth the price of one's own soul.

POWER IS A TRAP

Saddam Hussein was born in the Iraqi village of Tikrit, the same village that, 900 years earlier, was the birthplace of Saladin, the renowned Muslim sultan who defeated the Christian crusaders and conquered Palestine. Saladin was, in fact, one of Saddam's two great heroes; the other was Soviet strongman Joseph Stalin. According to UN weapons inspector Charles Duelfer, Saddam saw himself as "the incarnation of the destiny of the Arab people." He believed that he had been chosen by Allah as a new Saladin, a man who would wield the limitless power of nuclear, chemical and biological weapons to, once again, defeat the "Crusaders" from the West (America), conquer Palestine and live forever as a hero of the Arab people.

Reporting for *Time* magazine, Johanna McGeary wrote that Saddam "appears to have not so much a strategy as a concept of grandeur. He is never satisfied with what he has. He operates by opportunity more than by plan and takes devastating risks if the gambles might expand his power. He believes in the ruthless use of force."[3]

Saddam Hussein's ruthless ambition for power, coupled with his country's vast petroleum resources, made him one of the most dominant and dangerous figures in the Middle East—but also one of the most pathetic. In a 2002 essay on Saddam Hussein for *The Atlantic Monthly*, Mark Bowden revealed a surprising picture of the dictator as a prisoner of his own enormous power:

Saddam is a loner by nature, and power increases isolation. . . . One might think that the most powerful man has the most choices, but in reality he has the fewest. Too much depends on his every move. The tyrant's choices are the narrowest of all. His life—the nation!—hangs in the balance. . . .

Power gradually shuts the tyrant off from the world. Everything comes to him second or third hand. He is deceived daily. He becomes ignorant of his land, his people, even his own family. He exists, finally, only to preserve his wealth and power, to build his legacy. Survival becomes his one overriding passion. So he regulates his diet, tests his food for poison, exercises behind well-patrolled walls, trusts no one, and tries to control everything.[4]

We are tempted to ignore the lessons of Saddam Hussein's power-grubbing existence. We think, "Well, Saddam Hussein was unhinged!

He was a dangerous madman! His life has nothing to teach me." But as pastor Rick Warren reminds us, "The world is full of little Saddams. Most people cannot handle power. It goes to their heads." Remember, power chasers come in all shapes and sizes. If the circumstances are right, if the temptation is great enough, anyone—including you, including me—can be seduced by the lure of power.

In his book *Jesus Loves Me*, pastor and author Calvin Miller describes the trap he calls "the power addiction":

> One of the hardest things to relinquish is our need to run things: power! We all seem to crave it at times. Why? It allows us to control others, but our appetite for power wars against Jesus' love. Desiring power we are most unlike Jesus! Power would allow us to avenge ourselves on those who mistreat us. How differently Jesus handled this appetite. Should *we* ever stand before Pilate, we would want to see how *he* would look in a crown of thorns. Let us put Herod on the cross and ask him how *he* likes it.
>
> Want power? Be careful! What horrors are bound up in the power addiction. . . . We break our addiction to power by relinquishing it. Thus we are kept from the perverted need to love ourselves.[5]

Leadership expert John Maxwell says that the lives of those who seek power tend to follow a predictable pattern. The power chasers may start out with good intentions and the desire to use their power for good. So they work hard to acquire power and in time they achieve a measure of it. But a little power is a dangerous thing. Attaining some power, they soon want more. They become obsessed with preserving and expanding their power—and they feel justified in using it. After all, the ends justify the means, don't they?

And that's when corruption sets in. A person who went into business, government, education, the arts or even the ministry with the best of intentions has become a person who pursues power for power's sake. He has become a person who is willing to step on people, to destroy careers and reputations, to do whatever it takes to maintain and expand his power.

And that is the downfall of the power chaser. His abuses are revealed for all the world to see. The corrupt CEO, politician or minister is exposed. His corruption may even land him in prison. He loses everything—his reputation, his family, his self-respect and especially his power. "Inevitably," Maxwell concludes, "anyone who abuses power, loses power."

THE LESSON OF THE RING

As Cal Thomas noted earlier, English historian Lord Acton (1834-1902) said, "Power tends to corrupt; absolute power corrupts absolutely." More recently, American novelist William Gaddis (author of *Agapē Agape*) replied, "Power doesn't corrupt people. People corrupt power." And American science fiction writer David Brin added, "It is said that power corrupts, but actually it's more true that power attracts the corruptible. The sane are usually attracted by other things than power."

This principle is illustrated in the fantasy trilogy *The Lord of the Rings*, by J. R. R. Tolkien. The tale revolves around an epic quest to destroy the Ring of Power before its evil force can be unleashed, resulting in destruction and enslavement throughout Middle Earth. In the story, we meet several characters who come in contact with the Ring of Power, and the way they respond to the Ring tells us a great deal about them.

When the wizard Gandalf is offered the Ring, he responds, "Do not tempt me! I dare not take it, even to keep it safe, unused. The wish to wield it would be too great for my strength!" Gandalf knows that even though his intentions are good, he is vulnerable to the seduction of power. He refuses the Ring so that he will not be corrupted by it.

The elf-lady Galadriel is also offered the power of the Ring—and she is greatly tempted. All she has to do is take the Ring and she would become infinitely powerful—"Dreadful as the Storm and the Lightning! Stronger than the foundations of the earth! All shall love me and despair!" But she wisely refuses the Ring and escapes its corrupting power.

Several characters in the book come under the spell of the Ring. Gollum, who once possessed it, is now possessed by it. The Ring is his obsession. It haunts him day and night. The power of the Ring has not only corrupted Gollum but has also truly driven him insane.

Another tragic character is Boromir, a noble and well-intentioned man who was tempted by the power of the Ring. He wants to use the power of the Ring to do good—but his obsession with power leads him astray and destroys him.

The only character who is fit to possess the Ring is Frodo, a humble hobbit of the Shire. He has no ambition to seize power. He has no desire to control the lives of others. To him, the power of the Ring is not a prize, but a weight—a crushing burden he wishes to rid himself of as soon as possible. Tolkien wants us to know that the responsibility of power is so heavy that only the backs of the humble can carry it.

It's true: Power corrupts—but it only corrupts the corruptible. It only corrupts those who are bent on chasing power. As Plato once warned, "He who seeks power is not fit to hold it." If we refuse to be seduced and corrupted by power, then we will avoid falling into its trap.

THE RIGHT USE OF POWER

Sir Winston Churchill served as the prime minister of the United Kingdom during World War II, England's darkest days. In mid-1940, the war was going badly. The Nazi forces under General Erwin Rommel were advancing, prompting the British Expeditionary Force to evacuate 300,000 troops from France. Another 13,000 troops were cut off and forced to surrender to the Nazis at St. Valery-en-Caux. The French government collapsed and the Germans marched into Paris. Churchill also knew (though the news was kept from the British public) that the Germans had sunk a British ship that was evacuating troops from France, killing 2,500.

These events weighed heavily on Churchill's mind, and the burdens of his office turned the once-jovial prime minister into an ill-tempered tyrant. A few lines from Churchill's speeches to the House of Commons in May and June of 1940 reveal his dark and depressed outlook. "I have nothing to offer you but blood, toil, tears, and sweat. . . . This nation must prepare itself for hard and heavy tidings. . . . The Battle of France is over. The Battle of Britain is about to begin." It was in the depths of these stressful days that the British prime minister opened a letter from his wife, Clementine. Dated 27 June 1940, the letter read:

My Darling,

I hope you will forgive me if I tell you something that I feel you ought to know.

One of the men in your entourage (a devoted friend) has been to me & told me that there is a danger of your being generally disliked by your colleagues & subordinates because of your rough sarcastic & overbearing manner. . . . I was told "No doubt it's the strain"—

My Darling Winston—I must confess that I have noticed a deterioration in your manner; & you are not so kind as you used to be.

It is for you to give the Orders. . . . With this terrific power you must combine urbanity, kindness and if possible Olympic calm. You used to quote: —"*On ne règne sur les âmes que par le calme.*" ["One can reign over hearts only by keeping one's composure."] . . .

You won't get the best results by irascibility & rudeness. They will breed either dislike or a slave mentality—(Rebellion in War time being out of the question!)

Please forgive your loving devoted & watchful
Clemmie[6]

Churchill took his wife's advice to heart and began treating his subordinates with more "urbanity, kindness, and . . . Olympic calm." Years later, reflecting on those dark days of mid-1940, just before the onslaught of the Battle of Britain, Churchill wrote in his memoirs, *Their Finest Hour*, "I readily admit that the post [of Prime Minister] was the one I liked the best. Power, for the sake of lording it over fellow-creatures or adding to personal pomp, is rightly judged base. But power in a national crisis, when a man believes he knows what orders should be given, is a blessing."[7] Winston Churchill learned that power, in order to do good, had to be used in a good way—not to intimidate, but to inspire and motivate.

At his inauguration as president on January 20, 1989, the senior President Bush, George Herbert Walker Bush, placed his hand on the Bible that had once been owned by George Washington himself, and he took the same oath of office, word for word, that Washington had taken 200 years earlier. Then Mr. Bush turned to the American people and said:

> We meet on democracy's front porch, a good place to talk as neighbors and as friends. For this is a day when our nation is made whole, when our differences, for a moment, are suspended. And my first act as President is a prayer. I ask you to bow your heads:
>
> Heavenly Father, we bow our heads and thank You for Your love. Accept our thanks for the peace that yields this day and the shared faith that makes its continuance likely. Make us strong to do Your work, willing to heed and hear Your will, and write on our hearts these words: "Use power to help people." For we are given power not to advance our own purposes, nor to make a great show in the world, nor a name. There is but one just use of power, and it is to serve people. Help us to remember it, Lord. Amen.

It was a beautiful expression of Mr. Bush's understanding of why he had been entrusted with so much power. And it was an expression of his commitment to use the power of his office for good, for God and for others—and not to serve or glorify himself.

John Maxwell once observed, "The best leaders feel motivated by love and compassion for their people." And Regina Brett, columnist for *The Plain Dealer* (Cleveland, Ohio), put it this way: "When the power of love overcomes the love of power, the world will know peace."

Lech Walesa is the former trade unionist and human rights activist who led Poland out from under the shadow of Soviet domination. By profession, he was a shipyard worker. On August 14, 1980, Lech Walesa scaled the wall of the Lenin Shipyard in Gdańsk, Poland, and led the shipyard workers' strike—a peaceful rebellion against Communist oppression. Out of that strike came the Solidarność (Solidarity) Free Trade Union. For his role in the formation of the union, Walesa spent nearly a year in prison, plus another four years under house arrest—but he was also awarded the Nobel Peace Prize. He donated the prize money to Solidarność.

Lech Walesa proved himself to be a man of power—and a man of peace. Before the Gdańsk Shipyard strike, he was an ordinary shipyard worker, with only a vocational school education. Yet he sparked the movement that brought down the Iron Curtain—and he rose to serve as president of Poland from 1990 to 1995. Looking back over those achievements, he reflected, "Power is only important as an instrument for service to the powerless."

Great leaders inspire and motivate; they do not terrorize and intimidate. They use their power *for* the people, not against them. That's why great leaders are so rare. Those who have the greatest skill at acquiring power do not always have the temperament and values for using power wisely and compassionately. Power chasers tend to be power abusers—and people abusers. A great leader uses power to serve the powerless, not to serve himself.

RELINQUISHING POWER

You may have seen a statue of Cincinnatus and wondered what it meant. Lucius Quinctius Cincinnatus was a Roman leader who lived five centuries before Christ. He is usually depicted with one outstretched hand, holding a bundle of rods surrounding an axe. These rods are called fasces, and they symbolize the power and authority of a Roman leader. With his other hand, Cincinnatus is grasping a farmer's plow. Cincinnatus is remembered by history as the only Roman dictator who willingly relinquished power, gave up the fasces of authority and returned to his private life as a citizen farmer.

One man who deeply admired Cincinnatus was President Harry S Truman. He once said, "If a man can accept a situation in a place of power with the thought that it is only temporary, he comes out all right. But when he thinks that he is the cause of the power, that can be his ruination."

On January 2, 1953, two weeks before the end of his presidency, Truman wrote a letter to his cousin, Ethel Noland, in which he reflected on the power he had wielded as president. He wrote, "Alexander the great, Augustus Caesar, Genghis Khan, Louis XIV, Napoleon, nor any other of the great historical figures have the power or the world influence of the President of the USA. It bears down on a country boy. But I'm coming home January 20, 1953, and will, I hope, pull a Cincinnatus, who was old G. Washington's ideal."

It's true. Cincinnatus was a role model for "old G. Washington." In fact, George Washington actually passed up a chance to be king of the United States.

Following the defeat of British forces under General Cornwallis at Yorktown, in October 1781, Washington established his headquarters in a house on the banks of the Hudson. There he awaited news from the peace conference in Paris. Though the negotiations were long and drawn out, Washington hoped Britain would agree to allow the 13 colonies to become a new nation, the United States of America, without further bloodshed. Meanwhile, he kept the Continental Army in readiness in case the British resumed hostilities.

In May 1782, Washington received a letter from one of his officers, Colonel Lewis Nicola, who wrote on behalf of himself and a number of high-ranking officers in the Continental Army. Nicola urged General Washington to consider what form of government the new American nation should adopt. Nicola argued that a democratic government would be weak and unstable—and he proposed that America should be governed by a British-style constitutional monarchy. He then suggested that America's first king should be "King George I"—that is, George Washington himself! All Washington had to do was say yes—and Colonel Nicola and his fellow officers would back him as king.

Washington's reply was swift and emphatic. He wrote back saying that he had read the colonel's letter "with a mixture of great surprise and astonishment," and he viewed the colonel's suggestion "with abhorrence." He added, "You could not have found a person to whom your schemes are more disagreeable." He strongly urged Colonel Nicola and his fellow officers to forget these ideas and never mention them again to anyone. "If you have any regard for your country, concern for yourself or posterity, or respect for me, banish these thoughts from your mind."

Had George Washington been a man obsessed with power, the history of this nation might have turned out very differently. In fact, we catch a glimpse of how tragically different America might have turned out by looking at another revolution—the French Revolution. The American Revolution produced an enduring democratic republic with George Washington as its first president. The French Revolution produced a new regime headed by Napoleon Bonaparte, a power-obsessed man who proclaimed himself Emperor. The era of Washington was marked by peace and prosperity. The era of Napoleon was a reign of terror, war and bloodshed.

General Washington used his status as a war hero to guide the nation toward democracy and representative government; then he served two terms as America's first president, running unopposed both times. When England's King George III received word that Washington refused to run for a third term, he was astonished. The king could not believe that any man who wielded such power would willingly relinquish it and return to his farm. King George said that if Washington was true to his word and walked away from the presidency, he would be "the greatest character of the age." And of course, King George was right about Washington.

George Washington relinquished power and is remembered as a hero. Napoleon Bonaparte abused power and is remembered as an egomaniacal tyrant. Shortly before his death, Napoleon reflected bitterly on the loss of his power and reputation. "They wanted me to be another Washington," he said.[8]

Our third president, Thomas Jefferson, served two terms in office. His eight years in the White House were often fraught with controversy and conflict. By the final year of his second term, the burdens of his powerful office had become a weight that he could no longer endure. In the final months of his presidency, Jefferson spent increasingly less time at the White House and increasingly more time at Monticello, his home in Virginia.

On March 2, 1809, just two days before his successor, James Madison, was inaugurated, Jefferson wrote a letter to a good friend in France, Pierre Samuel du Pont de Nemours, saying, "Never did a prisoner, released from his chains, feel such relief as I shall on shaking off the shackles of power."[9]

Sometimes wanting power is more attractive than actually wielding it.

THE POWER WITHIN US, THE POWER BEYOND US

In his book *Just Like Jesus*, Max Lucado relates the story of a wealthy old woman who lived more than a century ago, when electricity in homes was something of a novelty. This woman had a reputation for pinching pennies, so her friends and neighbors were surprised when she had her home wired for electricity. The first few times the man from the power company came to read her meter, he was surprised to see that she had hardly used any power. So he went to her front door and knocked.

She opened the door. "Yes?"

"Ma'am," he said, "are you using your electricity?"

"I certainly am," she said. "Those new electric lights are very handy."

"Your meter indicates that you hardly used any electricity at all. How often do you turn on your lights?"

"I turn them on every evening," the woman replied.

"How long do you leave the lights on?"

"Less than a minute," the woman said. "I turn the lights on long enough to light my candles, then I turn them off again."

The woman was connected to a source of enormous power, but she scarcely ever used it. Instead, she chose to rely on old-fashioned candles.

I think we are much like that wealthy old woman. We like to operate by human power—the power of our personalities, the power of intimidation, the power of persuasion, the power of position, the power of money, the power of political scheming and manipulation. But these forms of power are like flickering candles compared with the strong, steady power that is available to us.

The power I'm referring to, of course, is the power of God. His power created the universe and breathed life into our bodies. We have direct access to His power through prayer; and His power will motivate and energize us for service to God and others.

Oprah Winfrey once said, "It is possible to do whatever you choose, if you get to know who you are and are willing to work with a power greater than yourself to do it."[10] And in a speech to a graduating class at Salem College in Winston-Salem, North Carolina, Oprah said, "God can dream a bigger dream for you than you can dream for yourself. . . . You know what real power is? Real power is when you are doing exactly what you are supposed to be doing the best it can be done. Authentic power. There's a surge, there's a kind of energy field that says, 'I'm in my groove. I'm in my groove.' And nobody has to tell you, 'You go, girl,' because, you know, you're already gone."[11]

There is more power *within* us than we realize. And there is a far greater Power *beyond* us than we have even begun to tap into. At times it seems that this world is governed by the misuse and abuse of power— political power; economic power; military power; the power to intimidate, control, confuse and terrorize people. As Dr. Martin Luther King, Jr., once said, "Our scientific power has outrun our spiritual power. We have guided missiles and misguided men."

You and I are not willing to settle for such a world. We refuse to pursue power the way the rest of the world does. We seek a more lasting power, a purer and truer power, an infinitely higher Power. We want the power to do the right things in the right way.

We choose to live by the power of faith, the power of love and the power of God.

CHASING PLEASURE

True story:

He called himself "Prince of Joy." In an Internet chat room, he met a young lady whose screen name was "Sweetie."

Over the next few days, they spent hours chatting and flirting online, sharing their secrets and getting to know each other. They found they had a lot in common. They lived in the same city. He was 32; she was 27. Both were stuck in miserable marriages, though they had not yet talked to their spouses about divorce.

Though they had known each other for less than a week and had never met face to face, they felt that they were falling in love. So they arranged a date at a local restaurant.

When Prince of Joy arrived at the restaurant, he found Sweetie waiting for him and was surprised to discover—

Sweetie was his own wife!

So Prince of Joy and Sweetie ended up in divorce court, accusing each other of adultery—*even though they were unwittingly having an online affair with each other.*

Looking back on the embarrassing experience, Sweetie said, "We seemed to be stuck in the same kind of miserable marriage. How right that turned out to be!" Prince of Joy reflected, "I still find it hard to believe that Sweetie, who wrote such wonderful things, is actually the same woman I married and who has not said a nice word to me for years."[1]

This is what we've come to. We can find any guilty pleasure—and even be unfaithful to our marriage vows—with a few mouse clicks. And we never know who we might be flirting with in that online chat room.

We are a pleasure-chasing people. Our obsession with pleasure, sensuality and self-gratification is destroying our relationships and our souls.

A PRISON OF PLEASURE

Here's another true story, one you've undoubtedly heard—but this story is so instructive that it's worth hearing again.

Britney Spears was born in Mississippi and raised in a little town in Louisiana. Every Sunday, she attended a Southern Baptist church and Sunday School. As a little girl, she competed in gymnastics and performed in song and dance revues.

At age 11, she landed a regular spot on *The New Mickey Mouse Club* on The Disney Channel. When she left the show in 1994, she returned to her little Louisiana hometown and attended high school. A few years later, Britney was signed to a recording contract and became a solo opening act for the adenoidal boy-bands 'N Sync and The Backstreet Boys. Her image was that of a squeaky-clean pop princess.

But in the years since then, something has gone terribly wrong in her life. As I write these words, Britney Spears is in full-tilt self-destruct mode. In fact, there is a website called WhenIsBritneyGoingToDie.com, which is offering a Sony PlayStation3 video game system to the person who correctly predicts the pop star's day and time of death. "Use the form to guess Britney's final breath," the online form reads, "and be crowned Mr. or Mrs. Death."

Sick and ghoulish, you say? You bet.

It's also symptomatic of where we are as a society. Britney Spears is not just a pop music icon. She is a lost human soul. It's as if she's about to do a swan dive into an empty swimming pool in full view of the whole world, and no one is lifting a finger to save her.

The pop diva is literally killing herself in the pursuit of pleasure. Fame has been unkind to her, serving only to turn her personal problems into global headlines. The whole world knows about her problems with drugs and alcohol; her revolving-door trips through rehab; her 55-hour-long first marriage; her famous head-shaving incident in Tarzana; and a weird standoff with police and an ambulance ride to Cedars-Sinai Medical Center for a psychiatric evaluation.

In October 2007, Ms. Spears lost custody of her two toddler-aged children because of her habitual drug and alcohol abuse, and she was ordered to undergo random drug and alcohol testing and to undergo instruction from a parenting coach. The next two nights after losing custody of her kids, what did she do? She went on all-night partying binges.

She skipped out on another custody hearing in January 2008, going to church instead, because she had "no one to turn to, except God." I sincerely hope she made that connection with God that she was looking for.

Some people think that a pop star's descent into a living hell is something to joke about. Put up a Web page, let people bet on her death, give away prizes, lots of fun. But this young woman, for all her money and fame, is a mother of two little boys, a lost young woman who doesn't know anything about life except chasing pleasure, even if it kills her. She's trapped in one of the most lavish and pampered lifestyles imaginable. Her palace is her prison. By the time you read these words, it may well be her tomb.

And millions of other young people are following her example, cheapening themselves for the sake of pleasure. Writing in the *Los Angeles Times*, novelist Meghan Daum lamented the self-destructive ritual that our younger generation engages in every spring—the ritual known as "spring break." She observes:

> Around-the-clock binge drinking and lively cultural activities such as near-naked-girl-against-girl wrestling matches held in giant vats of pudding. . . . Spring break is now thought to be best experienced in places such as Cancun, Mexico, where the drinking age is eighteen and tour companies build packages almost exclusively around access to alcohol: $100 procures a wristband that grants admission to clubs offering unlimited free alcohol.

Ms. Daum cites a *Journal of American College Health* report that states that, during spring break pleasure orgies, young women consume, on average, 10 alcoholic drinks a day, while men average 18 drinks a day. The women who engage in these debaucheries, she points out, are college women, who supposedly want to achieve more with their lives than to simply become sex objects. Yet, these college women—most of whom would consider themselves "feminists"—willingly cheapen their own femininity by engaging in wet T-shirt contests and allowing strangers to lick tequila shots off their bodies. Why?

After traveling to Cancun in an attempt to unravel the twisted thinking of these women, Ms. Daum concluded that today's younger generation has decided that the true measure of adulthood is not emotional maturity or educational achievement. It's sexual desirability—otherwise known as "being hot." So these young women, in addition to studying sociology or feminist literature, are also spending hundreds of hours and thousands of dollars at the gym, the body wax salons, the tanning salons, and yes, the plastic surgeon (an amazing number of spring break bikinis are largely stuffed with silicone gel).

Ms. Daum describes one young woman who seemed to typify all the young spring breakers she met in Cancun. The young coed was clad in a bikini and high heels, sipping a stiff drink. "If I can be considered hot here, I'll be hot anywhere," she said rather sadly. "I'm here to get confident." Meghan Daum concluded, "The more women I talked to, the more it became clear that 'hotness' was, for them, the largest factor in the equation of their self-worth."[2]

We are witnessing an entire generation of young people, from pop stars to college coeds, becoming trapped in a prison of pleasure.

PRESSING THE PLEASURE LEVER

We've seen examples of this kind of self-destructive behavior before—people who are so obsessed with pleasure and sensuality that they don't seem to know or care that they are killing themselves. It's the kind of behavior we see in the cancer patient who, no longer able to breathe through his mouth and nose, smokes cigarettes through a trache tube in his throat. It's the kind of behavior we see in laboratory rats.

In the 1950s, two researchers, James Olds and Peter Milner, were experimenting on rats, trying to stimulate the pain center in the rats' brains with electrical current. Quite by accident, they discovered something they were not looking for: the brain's *pleasure center*. They inserted an electrode in the limbic system of the rats' brains, in a structure called the *nucleus accumbens*. They administered electrical current whenever the rat entered a certain part of its cage. They expected the rats to feel pain and learn to avoid that part of the cage. Instead, the rats enjoyed the electrical stimulation and kept returning to that part of the cage.

Olds and Milner constructed new experiments that allowed the rats to press a lever. Each time the lever was pressed, an electrical current stimulated the pleasure centers of the rats' brains. The rats would go into a pleasure-seeking frenzy, pressing the lever as many as 2,000 times an hour. They would ignore food and water, working themselves into a state of exhaustion and starvation. Eventually, they would die. They literally pleasured themselves to death.[3]

By now, you probably see an unsettling parallel between the rats' behavior and the behavior of many human beings, both celebrities and people you know. Perhaps you even see yourself in that laboratory box, endlessly pressing that pleasure lever.

Is pleasure an evil thing? Was pleasure set before us to tempt us, to derail our lives, to destroy us? No. We were designed by God to experience and appreciate pleasure. We were given five senses in order to experience the world around us, delight in it, and enjoy it. We were designed by God with the ability to receive pleasure from the beautiful world around us, from good food, from tantalizing fragrances, from the sound of birdsong and rushing water and delightful music. We were designed to experience pleasure in romantic intimacy and sex.

In the Bible, the psalmist wrote, "You have made known to me the path of life; you will fill me with joy in your presence, with eternal pleasures at your right hand" (Ps. 16:11). Pleasure is a gift from God.

But pleasure is like the waters of the river. As long as those waters are contained between the riverbanks, those waters are a source of life and blessing. But if those waters overflow the riverbanks, the resulting flood causes death and destruction. Those who chase pleasure have unleashed a deadly flood in their lives. Nothing good ever comes of such a flood.

Oscar Wilde (1854-1900) was an Irish playwright and novelist of the Victorian era, known for his biting wit and flamboyant lifestyle. He saw himself as belonging to a "Greek paederastic tradition" and engaged in so-called "man-boy love" with "rent boys," or underage male prostitutes. He openly and proudly admitted this fact in his famous 1895 morals trial. Convicted of the crime of "gross indecency," he was sentenced to two years of hard labor. He served out his sentence in a series of squalid English prisons.

While in prison, Wilde wrote a 50,000-word document that he kept with him in his cell until the end of his sentence. Upon his release, he gave the manuscript to a friend with instructions that it be published after his death. On November 30, 1900, just three years after his release from prison, Oscar Wilde died of cerebral meningitis, resulting either from a massive ear infection or from syphilis contracted during his wanton years before his trial and imprisonment. On his deathbed, Wilde was received into the church. Though too weak to take Holy Communion, he was baptized at his own request.

A little more than four years after his death, Wilde's prison manuscript was published under the title *De Profundis*. Here is an excerpt from his prison writings:

> I let myself be lured into long spells of senseless and sensual ease. I amused myself with being a *flaneur*, a dandy, a man of fashion. I surrounded myself with the smaller natures and the meaner minds. I became the spendthrift of my own genius, and to waste an eternal youth gave me a curious joy. Tired of being on the heights, I deliberately went to the depths in the search for new sensation. . . .
>
> I took pleasure where it pleased me, and passed on. I forgot that every little action of the common day makes or unmakes character, and that therefore what one has done in the secret chamber one has some day to cry aloud on the housetop. I ceased to be lord over myself. I was no longer the captain of my soul, and did not know it. I allowed pleasure to dominate me. I ended in horrible disgrace. There is only one thing for me now, absolute humility.
>
> I have lain in prison for nearly two years. Out of my nature has come wild despair; an abandonment to grief that was piteous even to look at; terrible and impotent rage; bitterness and scorn; anguish that wept aloud; misery that could find no voice; sorrow that was dumb. I have passed through every possible mood of suffering.[4]

Oscar Wilde learned what so many people—rich and poor, famous and anonymous—are still finding out today: The obsessive pursuit of pleasure always ends in some form of imprisonment, enslavement, despair and grief. Those who give themselves over to the obsessive pursuit of pleasure become like laboratory rats. They ultimately pleasure themselves to death.

THE PLEASURE PRINCIPLE VERSUS
THE REALITY PRINCIPLE

Mary Jane Ryan, author of *This Year I Will . . . : How to Finally Change a Habit, Keep a Resolution or Bring a Dream into Being*, observed that we human beings have "two brains—the brain that makes the resolution and says, 'I'll never smoke again,' and the brain we share with all mammals that wants pleasure. That pleasure-seeking side of the brain says: 'I want a cigarette; I want that chocolate doughnut.' And that brain is as smart as a bunny rabbit. That bunny rabbit brain is constantly scanning the environment with only two questions: Is this pleasurable or painful?"[5]

The father of psychoanalysis, Sigmund Freud, made a similar point when he coined two psychoanalytical terms, "the pleasure principle" and "the reality principle." The pleasure principle is what Mary Jane Ryan calls the "bunny rabbit brain." The pleasure principle is aware of only pleasure and pain. It constantly seeks to gratify the drive for pleasure while continually avoiding any sensation of discomfort or pain. It's the unthinking mammal part of us.

In contrast to the pleasure principle is the reality principle. The reality principle is an expression of our rational, spiritual, human side. It's the part of us that is able to think, reason, remember the past and anticipate the future. It's the emotionally and intellectually mature component of our personality. The reality principle understands that pleasure is not always good for us and that pain is not always bad. The reality principle can grasp the concept of "no pain, no gain." It can understand that we sometimes have to endure some pain in order to attain something more lasting and valuable than mere pleasure.

The reality principle still appreciates pleasure. But while the pleasure principle seeks sensory gratification through food, alcohol, drugs, thrill-seeking and sex, the reality principle seeks deeper and more lasting forms of pleasure: art, music, literature, drama, nature, relationships, spirituality and a sense of accomplishment. An emotionally mature person derives pleasure from reality by living a rich and rewarding life. But a person dominated by his or her "bunny rabbit brain" seeks only to press the pleasure lever and stimulate the pleasure center of the brain.

As the late sports medicine authority Dr. George Sheehan once observed, "Happiness is different from pleasure. Happiness has something to do with struggling and enduring and accomplishing." Anyone with a "bunny rabbit brain" can chase pleasure by gratifying the senses; but only an emotionally and intellectually mature human being can attain this elusive thing called happiness. We cannot experience true, lasting happiness until we become fully human, as God created us to be.

George Orwell (the pen name of Eric Blair, 1903-1950) was the author of *Animal Farm* and *1984*. Orwell understood that the mindless pursuit of pleasure erases our humanity and reduces us to the level of animals. In a 1946 essay titled "Pleasure Spots," he observed:

> Much of what goes by the name of pleasure is simply an effort to destroy consciousness. . . . Man needs warmth, society, leisure, comfort and security: he also needs solitude, creative work and the sense of wonder. . . . The highest happiness does not lie in relaxing, resting, playing poker, drinking and making love simultaneously. . . . Man only stays human by preserving large patches of simplicity in his life." He concluded that "modern inventions" like movies and radio programs served only "to weaken his consciousness, dull his curiosity, and, in general, drive him nearer to the animals."[6]

If Orwell thought that film and radio appealed to our animal side, what would he think about computers and the Internet (including Internet porn), iPods and iPhones, 999 channels of satellite television, *World of Warcraft* and *Final Fantasy*, Sony PlayStation and Nintendo Wii, and on and on, mindless entertainment and pleasure without end? The more high-tech and sophisticated our forms of pleasure become, the more like animals we become—endlessly pressing the pleasure lever, seeking one electronic stimulation after another.

We are becoming a society of people with bunny rabbit brains.

NO SATISFACTION

Pleasure is not as simple an experience as you might think. There are subtle and even unconscious ingredients that go into the making of a pleasurable experience. For example, it seems reasonable to assume that a $90 bottle of wine would provide a more pleasurable experience than a $2 bottle of wine. It only stands to reason that there would be something about the appearance, taste, fragrance, complexity, character and finish of the expensive wine that would enhance the pleasure of the wine drinker and justify the exorbitant price tag.

But is that always true?

A recent study conducted by Caltech and the Stanford Graduate School of Business suggests otherwise. The study participants were given an array of wines to taste. MRI images of the participants' brains showed the exact moments when the pleasure centers of their brains were stimulated so that the researchers knew exactly which wines were associated with the participants' pleasurable experiences. The wines were labeled according to their supposed price—but the labels lied. Some cheap wines were labeled as costing $90 a bottle. Some expensive wines were labeled as cheap. In some cases, three bottles bearing wildly different price tags contained identical wines.

The researchers found that the participants' pleasurable experience was determined not by the actual quality and price of the wine, but by the price tag on the bottle. If the wine taster was told that the wine was expensive (even if it was cheap), the taster's pleasure center registered a pleasurable experience on the MRI.

"People think high price means high quality," one of the researchers observed. "This placebo effect occurs very non-consciously."[7]

What can we conclude from this study? Perhaps one conclusion we can draw is that even our most refined and discriminating pleasures can be greatly influenced by unconscious forces that arise from the baser part of ourselves—from price snobbery, for example. We would like to think that, in a blind taste test, we could always tell a $90 Cabernet from a bottle of bargain-basement red wine. But the fact is that a peek at the price tag will probably have a bigger influence on our pleasure than the evidence of our own senses.

What's my point? Simply this: Perhaps the pursuit of pleasure is a bit overrated. Perhaps we could actually live richer and more genuinely pleasurable lives if we spent less money, time and effort chasing pleasure, and spent more time simply enjoying the richness of life's blessings. Most of the things that are truly enjoyable and pleasurable in life are very simple and cost little or nothing at all.

We easily forget how much simple pleasure there is in the fragrance of flowers or tomato vines in your garden; the sensation of cool, crisp bed sheets against your skin; a hot steamy shower on a cold brisk morning; an invigorating jog in the mountains or along the seashore; a long, leisurely phone call with a long-lost friend. Pleasures like these are free, or nearly so, and are so close at hand. So why pay a king's ransom and spend all your time and energy chasing pleasure when there are so many pleasures right within your grasp?

The Bible tells us that those who chase pleasure are never satisfied. Solomon, reputedly the wisest man who ever lived, observed, "He who loves pleasure will become poor; whoever loves wine and oil will never be rich" (Prov. 21:17). Solomon also wrote:

I denied myself nothing my eyes desired;
I refused my heart no pleasure.
My heart took delight in all my work,
and this was the reward for all my labor.
Yet when I surveyed all that my hands had done
and what I had toiled to achieve,
everything was meaningless, a chasing after the wind;
nothing was gained under the sun (Eccles. 2:10-11).

Or, as Mick Jagger of the Rolling Stones put it, "I can't get no satisfaction."

People confuse fun, thrills and pleasure with true happiness. They mistakenly think that if they can experience "enough" pleasure, then they will be happy, contented and satisfied in their lives. One obvious flaw with this view is that "enough" is never enough. Chasing fun, thrills and pleasure only increases our appetite for more. Like the laboratory rat pressing on the pleasure lever, human beings will keep chasing pleasure until it kills them. So the idea that pleasure brings happiness and contentment is nothing but a mirage. That's what Solomon is telling us.

Solomon, of course, spoke with authority. He was a king, and he had all of the things available to him that are supposed to make people happy and contented. He had wealth, fame, power and pleasure. And what was his conclusion? "Yet when I surveyed all that my hands had done . . . everything was meaningless, a chasing after the wind." After all, what good will our wealth, fame, power and pleasure do us in the grave?

It took a wise man like Solomon to state the essential problem of our mortality. Most of us spend our days trying to avoid thinking about death and the grave, because that kind of thinking leads to despair. It seems that most of those who think deeply about their own mortality have a tendency to end up trying to numb their despair with drugs, alcohol, entertainment, workaholism or some other anesthetic. Some even put an end to their despair by—

Well, let me tell you a story.

HUMAN JIGSAW PUZZLES

Novelist Ernest Hemingway lived the kind of life most people only dream of. In his early twenties, Hemingway lived in Paris as part of an eclectic circle of influential writers, which included Ezra Pound, Gertrude Stein, and F. Scott Fitzgerald. He traveled the world, hunting big game in Africa and watching bullfights in Madrid. He had wealth, fame and every pleasure money could buy, including an endless supply of women and whiskey. Yet he continually questioned the meaning of his own life and suffered frequent bouts of depression.

On the morning of July 2, 1961, Hemingway took down a double-barreled shotgun from the wall of his home in Ketchum, Idaho, stood the gun butt against the floor of his hallway, rested his forehead against the twin muzzles, put his thumbs over the twin triggers and ended his life in the most bloody and gruesome way imaginable. He did not leave a suicide note.

A seemingly endless supply of money, fame and pleasure was not enough for Ernest Hemingway. Pleasure does not give meaning and significance to life. Fun and thrills and enjoyable experiences can help us forget for a while that we are mortal beings, doomed to death and despair. Alcohol and drugs can dull the pain. Wealth and fame can mask the pain. But the underlying pain of the human condition never goes away—

Until we learn how to resolve the pain once and for all.

As the prophet Isaiah once said, "But see, there is joy and revelry, slaughtering of cattle and killing of sheep, eating of meat and drinking of wine! 'Let us eat and drink,' you say, 'for tomorrow we die!'" (Isa. 22:13). For most of his life, Hemingway tried to live as one of the people Isaiah spoke of, eating and drinking and living for pleasure, avoiding the reality of the grave. Finally, just three weeks short of his sixty-second birthday, he leaned over a double-barreled shotgun and surrendered to the inevitable.

There is no salvation in any of the things people turn to as an escape from their own mortality. There's certainly no salvation in pleasure. Alcohol leaves you hung over. Drugs leave you broke and addicted. Promiscuous sex brings guilt, shame, pregnancy, abortion and sexually transmitted diseases. In the end, the obsessive pursuit of pleasure leaves us worse off than we were before. As Thomas Jefferson once said, "Do not bite at the bait of pleasure until you know there is no hook beneath it."

The ironic truth about pleasure is this: If you stop chasing pleasure and start pursuing God, you'll gain God *and* a rich, rewarding, pleasurable life as well. You won't find your life being poisoned by the false pleasures of drugs, alcohol and promiscuous sex. Instead, you'll drink deeply of the life of God's Spirit, and you'll know the ecstatic experience of being loved unconditionally by God. As Jesus Himself said, "I have come that they may have life, and that they may have it more abundantly" (John 10:10, *NKJV*).

God designed us to live a lie of abundance and significance—and we were created to find that abundance in Him. As St. Augustine said in a prayer to God, "You have created us for yourself, O Lord, and our hearts are restless until they rest in you." And the seventeenth-century philosopher and mathematician Blaise Pascal observed in his *Pensées* that our craving for pleasure is a vain attempt to fill an "infinite abyss" in our lives, and that "this infinite abyss can be filled only with an infinite and immutable object; in other words by God himself."[8] Even the atheist philosopher Jean-Paul Sartre (1856-1939) recognized that we all have a "God-shaped hole" within that we constantly try to fill with material things, fame, power and pleasure. Though he himself thought God was a myth, Sartre correctly understood that human beings need faith in God in order to be fulfilled.[9]

We human beings are like jigsaw puzzles with a piece missing—and that missing piece is shaped like God. We can try to fill that hole with other things, with every sort of pleasure and thrill imaginable, but none of those things are the right size and shape to fill the hole. Our only hope of finding lasting happiness and meaning is by giving up the pursuit of pleasure and taking up the pursuit of God.

WE WERE MADE FOR HAPPINESS

I'm not saying that we must give up pleasure. I'm saying that the greatest, deepest, richest pleasures of all are to be found in God. There's no question that we are naturally attracted to food, drink, sex and thrills. These are the pleasures that our bunny rabbit brains understand best. These pleasures are intensely appealing to our lower mammal brains.

But I personally want more out of life than spending hour after hour of mindlessly pressing the pleasure lever, slowly committing suicide with a vacant smile on my face. I want more out of life than simply gratifying my bunny rabbit brain. I want to enlarge my mind, enrich my soul, and elevate my spirit. I want to experience all the joys of knowing God. And I believe you want that too.

God has promised that a relationship with Him is the key to a life that is truly rich, rewarding and pleasurable in the deepest sense. As the psalmist has written, "Delight yourself in the LORD and he will give you the desires of your heart" (Ps. 37:4).

In the Old Testament, the prophet Nehemiah led his people out of exile and back to the ruins of Jerusalem. Working quickly, they rebuilt the city walls. Once the walls had been rebuilt and the city was secure against enemies, Nehemiah called the people together and told them, "Go and enjoy choice food and sweet drinks, and send some to those who have nothing prepared. This day is sacred to our Lord. Do not grieve, *for the joy of the LORD is your strength*" (Neh. 8:10, emphasis added).

The joy of the Lord is your strength, and my strength as well. We were not put upon this earth merely to chase after food, sex and cheap thrills. We were put here to build lives that are strong, secure and enduring, like the walls of Jerusalem. And as we build according to God's plan for our lives, He gives us true pleasures that satisfy not only our rabbit brains but also our souls—choice food and sweet drinks. And He gives us true joy. *The joy of the Lord is our strength.*

The joy of the Lord is the strength we need to live courageously, to resist self-destructive temptation, to live wisely and well. It's the strength to die at peace and leave a legacy that endures after we are gone. It's the strength to live forever with Him in eternity. This, my friend, is the abundant life that Jesus spoke of. The God of the universe is the Lord of true pleasure and joy. Only by knowing Him can we experience true satisfaction.

Beginning in the 1640s, thousands of children in England and Scotland were instructed in the Christian faith by a series of 107 questions and answers called "The Shorter Catechism." The first of these questions and answers was:

Q. What is the chief end of man?
A. Man's chief end is to glorify God, and to enjoy Him forever.

That is the source of our deepest and most enduring happiness and pleasure: to know and glorify God, and to enjoy Him forever. This is the happiness that can never be taken away from us. This is the pleasure that endures throughout our life and into the life to come.

"WHO AM I?"

For each of the four false values that people pursue to their own destruction, there is an antidote, a cure.

As we saw in chapter 2, the cure for chasing after money is to adopt a lifestyle of generosity, a willingness to use our possessions in service to God and others. The more we give and experience the joy of giving, the less we want to spend on our own selfish wants. Every time we give, we loosen the grip of selfishness upon our life. Every time we use our wealth and material possessions to serve someone other than ourselves, we strengthen the armor around our soul, making it harder for greed and materialism to infiltrate our life.

As we saw in chapter 3, the cure for chasing after fame is to adopt a mindset of humility. This means that we make a deliberate, volitional choice to elevate others, to share credit with others and to stop trying to get noticed and feed our own egos. Above all, the antidote to chasing fame involves a decision to stop trying to make ourselves famous and seek instead to make God famous.

As we saw in chapter 4, the cure for chasing after power is to adopt the mindset of a servant. Those who do not know how to serve are not fit to lead. We need to commit to using whatever power we may attain for the good of others and to serve God. Instead of seeking to acquire power for ourselves, we need to commit to relying upon God's power, which He makes available to us to do His will.

Here, in chapter 5, we conclude that the cure for chasing after pleasure is to recognize that God has created us to desire happiness—and He has made us to seek our happiness in Him. The pleasures most people chase after, the bunny rabbit brain pleasures of gratifying our most basic appetites, have a tendency to get out of hand, to dominate our life and to enslave us in a prison of addiction. Ultimately, those pleasures will kill us.

But the pleasures that God sets before us—the pleasures that come from knowing and enjoying Him—serve only to heal us, never to hurt us. The more we develop a taste for the pleasures of God, the less important the bunny rabbit brain pleasures become. As we move deeper into an enjoyment of God, the destructive pleasures lose their grip on us. We stop being like laboratory rats that mindlessly press the pleasure lever. We become complete, mature human beings. More important, we become *spiritual* beings, intimately connected to the Spirit of God.

Actress Grace Lee Whitney was seven years old when she lost her identity. It happened when her mother—the only mother she had ever known—sat her down and told her that she was adopted. "When you were a baby," Grace's mother said, "your father and I chose you to be our very own. Another woman gave birth to you, but we chose you to be our little girl."

Little Grace looked up at her mother in disbelief. "You mean, you are not my mother?"

"No, I'm not."

Hearing those words, Grace felt that the bottom had dropped out of her world. She no longer knew who she was or where she belonged. She didn't know who her "real" mother and father were, nor where they might be. It was the first of many times she would ask herself, "Who am I?"

For years she wondered how her birth mother could have given her up for adoption. *Is there something wrong with me?* she wondered. *Am I defective and unlovable? If my own mother didn't love me, who will?*

Looking back, Grace now understands that her birth mother actually loved her enough to want her to have a good home. She understands that her adoptive mother truly did love her. But she couldn't understand that as a 7-year-old, or as a 27-year-old, or even as a 37-year-old. Her life was dominated by a search for love.

At around the same time that she learned she was adopted, Grace discovered that Santa Claus doesn't exist. She recalled, "I began to feel that everything I had ever trusted and believed in was a myth. I didn't know what was real or what was unreal. My parents weren't my parents. Santa Claus was a lie. What's next? Immediately, I thought of all the things I had learned in Sunday School about God, about Jesus. *So it's all a myth*, I concluded. And that's why, at a very early age, I ceased to believe in God."

"IF YOU DON'T STOP DRINKING, YOU'RE GOING TO DIE"

Soon, Grace began filling the God-shaped hole in her soul with addictive behaviors, including compulsive overeating, smoking (which she began at age 13), and drinking (which she began at age 14). "I drank Southern Comfort," she recalled, "to get rid of the voices in my head that told me, *You're no good! Your mother gave you up because you're not good enough! . . .* When that first splash of Southern Comfort hit the back of my throat and started going down, I couldn't imagine ever living without it again. It fixed me. It filled all the holes where the wind was blowing through and causing me so much pain. As soon as that first drink hit bottom, the pain stopped—and that's all I cared about."

It was around this same time that she lost her virginity and got caught up in chasing after pleasure. And money. And power. And fame—especially fame. "I was hungry for applause and attention," she recalled.[10]

It was the hole in her soul that drove her to Hollywood to become a star. Soon after she arrived, she started getting movie roles. She became acquainted with legendary director Billy Wilder and landed roles in his films *Some like It Hot* and *Irma la Douce*, appearing opposite such stars as Marilyn Monroe, Jack Lemmon, Tony Curtis and Shirley MacLaine. She became a busy working actress, appearing in numerous films and television series, and finally landed a major role in Gene Roddenberry's classic TV space opera *Star Trek*. She was cast as Yeoman Janice Rand, the smart and sexy aide to Captain Kirk (William Shatner). It was a dream come true for Grace Lee Whitney—a continuing TV role, and all the money, fame and unlimited pleasure that go with it.

But midway through the first season, something went horribly wrong. Following a Friday night cast party on the studio set, a production executive took Grace aside and invited her to his office to chat. Once they were alone in his office, he told her he had big plans for her future—but he also needed some favors from her. Sexual favors.

Grace refused. The executive became violent and forced himself on her. Knowing that her acting career would be over if she made trouble for the executive, Grace chose not to report the sexual assault.

The following week, when she was getting ready to film the next episode, Grace learned that she was being written out of the TV show. Apparently, the studio executive who sexually assaulted Grace didn't want her around as a reminder—so he fired her.

Grace's humiliating ejection from the show plunged her into a deep depression. In her desperation, she tried to fill the huge gulf in her life with drugs, alcohol and sexual promiscuity. During the next 10 years, she went into a tailspin of alcoholism and addiction that left her sitting on a curb in downtown L.A., drinking cheap gin straight from a bottle in a paper bag.

In 1981, Grace ended up in a hospital, suffering from delirium tremens. The emergency room doctor examined her and said, "Your liver is enlarged, and there's a hole in your esophagus, probably due to all the alcohol you've consumed. Lady, if you don't stop drinking, you're going to die."

This news scared Grace. She couldn't imagine not drinking. "I'll die?" she asked. "When? How many months do I have?"

"Not months," the doctor said. "Days."

After she got out of the hospital, a friend took Grace to a 12-step recovery group. There, she heard other alcoholics tell how they were able to stay sober by relying on a Higher Power. The Power they spoke of, Grace realized, was the only thing that could fill the God-shaped hole in her soul. She remained in recovery and never touched a drink after that day. Two years into her recovery, Grace gave her life to Jesus Christ, and He has been the Lord of her life ever since.

Today, Grace Lee Whitney travels the world, attending *Star Trek* conventions, speaking in women's prisons and giving radio and TV interviews. She also shares her strength and hope at 12-step recovery meetings. The God-shaped hole in her soul, which she once tried to fill with wealth, fame, alcohol, drugs, sex and every form of pleasure, is now filled with God Himself.

She knows who she is. She knows where she belongs. She knows that she is loved. And the rich and rewarding life she now lives is available to you and me as well.

God designed us to be happy and He wants us to be happy; and He made us in such a way that we can only find true happiness in Him. Our longing for happiness comes from the God-shaped hole within us. There is only one thing in the universe that is shaped like God and as big as God, and that is God Himself. When we discover that He is the "missing piece" that perfectly fits that hole, then the jigsaw puzzle of our life will finally be complete.

PURSUE GOOD CHARACTER

Tony Dungy holds a weird distinction.

As a Pittsburgh Steelers safety, he became the only football player in the modern NFL era to both intercept a pass and throw an interception in the same game. During an October 30, 1977, game against the Houston Oilers, Dungy (who had already intercepted a pass on defense) was called in as an emergency quarterback after starter Terry Bradshaw and backup Mike Kruczek were both carried off the field.

Dungy is undoubtedly more proud of another distinction he holds, that of being the first African-American coach to win a Super Bowl. He coached the Indianapolis Colts to a 29-17 victory over the Chicago Bears in Super Bowl XLI at Dolphin Stadium in Miami, February 4, 2007. (It was the second Super Bowl victory for Dungy who, as part of the Steelers "Steel Curtain" defense, collected his first championship ring in Super Bowl XIII, also in Miami.)

But I think that the most important distinction Tony Dungy holds is that he is a person of outstanding character. He is widely respected both on and off the field as a coach and a community leader. He's active in many community organizations, including Mentors for Life (which he founded), Big Brothers and Big Sisters, Prison Crusade Ministry, Family First, Fellowship of Christian Athletes, and Athletes in Action. A committed Christian, he once considered retiring from football and going into full-time prison ministry. His 2007 memoir, *Quiet Strength: The Principles, Practices, and Priorities of a Winning Life*, is a *New York Times* bestseller that has had a powerful impact on coaches and players at all levels.

The title *Quiet Strength* comes from the fact that, as a coach, Dungy is a teacher and a role model, not a dictator and a screamer. His coaching style is a blend of principles he learned from some of the greatest coaches in the NFL and of his own Christian values and beliefs system. He believes coaches should inspire and motivate, not intimidate.

After winning Super Bowl XLI, Dungy paid tribute to the Bears' head coach, Lovie Smith, a fellow African-American and fellow Christian who coaches in the "quiet strength" mode much like Dungy. He said, "I really wanted to show people you can win all kinds of ways. I always coached the way I've wanted to be coached. I know Lovie has done the same thing. . . . For your faith to be more important than your job, for your family to be more important than that job—we all know that's the way it should be, but we're afraid to say that sometimes. Lovie's not afraid to say it and I'm not afraid to say it."[1]

Strong ethical character has always been the foundation of Tony Dungy's football career, both as a player and a coach. After retiring as a player, he served as the Steelers' defensive coordinator under coach Chuck Noll throughout much of the 1980s. An incident that took place during those years illustrates how Tony Dungy's character governed his decision-making as a coach.

A friend in the media once shared with him a surprise offensive play that an opponent planned to use against the Steelers in an upcoming game. Unlike some coaches who feel "all's fair in war and football," Tony Dungy doesn't believe in using ill-gotten information to win games. So he refused to use the information to defend against the trick play. He didn't share the information with his players or with Coach Noll.

On game day, Dungy was on the Steelers sidelines when he saw the opposing team line up in the formation for the surprise play. The Steelers' opponent was in the "red zone," in easy scoring position, and the game was close. His competitive nature was screaming within him to shout a warning to his players—but his ethical character kept his mouth clenched shut.

Sure enough, the opposing team ran the play and the Steelers defense was caught flat-footed—

Touchdown.

Dungy was miserable. He knew he had done the right thing, but his silence had given the opposing team a touchdown. His silence might have even cost the Steelers the game.

Then he saw an official throw a yellow flag. The play and the touchdown were called back on a penalty.

"I guess the moral of that story," he later reflected, "is that if you're honest and do things the right way, it'll all work out in the end."[2]

In a world that seems obsessed with chasing money, fame, power and pleasure, there are tragically few inspirational role models who pursue good character. If you want to live a life that truly matters, if you want to leave a legacy that never dies, then watch how Tony Dungy does it.

Pursue character.

DOES CHARACTER REALLY MATTER?

The late basketball point guard Ralph Beard led the University of Kentucky Wildcats to two consecutive NCAA championships in the late 1940s. In his four seasons as a star in the Wildcats' "Fabulous Five" lineup, he scored a total of 1,517 points. He was drafted into the NBA by the Chicago Stags, where he played alongside the great Hall of Fame guard Bob Cousy (who later went to the Boston Celtics). As a member of the United States basketball team, Ralph Beard won a gold medal at the 1948 Summer Olympics in London. Those are all great accomplishments.

But Ralph Beard isn't remembered primarily for his accomplishments on the basketball court. He is remembered for a scandal. When he died in November 2007, the tragic headline on his *New York Times* obituary read, "Ralph Beard, a Star Tarnished by Point Shaving, Is Dead at 79."

His old teammate Bob Cousy remembered him as a "lightning fast" talent who, if not for the scandal, "would have been a Hall of Famer."

Growing up poor and fatherless in Louisville, Kentucky, Ralph Beard dreamed of stardom in the NBA. He got to live his dream and even played in the NBA's first All-Star Game. But in October 1951, he and other players were accused of having taken money from gamblers during his college years. The following April, Ralph Beard pleaded guilty to point shaving and received a suspended sentence. The NBA barred him for life.

How much money did he take? A mere $700. And he insisted throughout his life that, though he took the money, he never fixed a game, never shaved a single point. Why did he do it? In his youth, he said, he "never had two dimes to rub together. My mother cleaned six apartments so we could have one to live in. I took the money, and that was it. I always gave 101 percent on the court."

It was a youthful error in moral judgment—yet the scandal became the headline of Ralph Beard's obituary. He knew it would be that way. In a 1999 interview with *The Tampa Tribune*, he said that the painful effects of the scandal would "be with me until they hit me in the face with that first spade full of dirt—because basketball was my life."[3]

It doesn't take much to destroy a legacy. It might be as little as a $700 youthful indiscretion. That's why character is so important. To live a life that matters, to leave behind an enduring legacy, we must guard our character. We must leave no gaps in the armor of our soul.

This is a message that goes against the grain of the culture we live in, especially in today's youth culture. A 2007 online survey conducted by Junior Achievement and Deloitte & Touche USA shows that 40 percent of today's young people believe they have to break the rules and cut ethical corners in order to get ahead in today's world. Almost a quarter of teens think it's acceptable to cheat on tests, and 15 percent think plagiarizing written assignments is okay, especially if a student is in a deadline crunch.

Young people today have absorbed an attitude of moral relativism. Their values shift and change according to their immediate wants and needs. As this generation moves into the workplace, the companies and organizations they work for will increasingly reflect their worldview. A society that is already reeling from a series of corporate scandals can expect more to come. Imagine the result when our governmental agencies, financial institutions, drug companies and healthcare corporations are run by a generation of people with a fluid sense of ethics, morality and character. Imagine having your next surgery performed by a doctor who cheated his or her way through med school.

"This way of thinking," warns David Miller of the Yale Center for Faith and Culture, "will inevitably lead to unethical if not illegal actions that will damage individual lives and ruin corporate reputations."[4]

Does character really matter? You bet it does. It matters to each of us as individuals. It matters to the legacy we leave behind. It matters to relationships and to social institutions. When the time comes that character no longer matters, we are finished as a society.

WHAT IS CHARACTER?

Gail Blanke is founder and CEO of Lifedesigns, LLC, and author of *Between Trapezes* and *In My Wildest Dreams*, a *New York Times* business bestseller. One of the top motivational speakers in the nation, she has appeared on *Oprah*, CNN, the Fox News Channel, and other news and interview shows. The issue of good character is a recurring theme in her speaking, writing and executive coaching.

I recently interviewed Gail, and she told me, "My parents always encouraged me to believe that I could be anything I wanted to be. They taught me the importance of being a person of good character who makes good decisions. They used athletic competition to teach me lessons about life, good character and good sportsmanship. My family was extremely athletic and my father actually beat Jesse Owens in the hurdles. I was a near Olympic qualifier myself in swimming.

"My parents instilled sayings in my mind throughout my youth. 'You've got to stand for something, or you'll fall for anything,' they said. And, 'Stand up for people and your ideas.' I was encouraged and expected to take the high road in every situation. Whenever I faced adversity or problems, my dad wouldn't let me whine or give up. He'd say, 'Well, Gail, here's a great opportunity to build some character.'

"When I was in the ninth grade, our family moved from Cleveland to Toledo, Ohio. The move was tough on me, because at the same time that I lost all my old friends, I was enrolled in a more advanced school. I was used to getting straight *A*s in my old school, but in my new classes, I quickly fell behind—especially in Latin. I desperately wanted to excel in Latin in the new school, and I was trying hard, but I just wasn't getting the grades I was used to.

"One day, during a Latin test, I compromised my character. I looked at the test paper of the girl in front of me and copied some of her answers. I went home that night and was a complete wreck. I was so miserable about having cheated that I went to my mother in tears and told her what I had done.

"My mother wisely decided to use that situation as a teaching moment. She said, 'What do you think you ought to do?' She wanted me to think about what I had done and about what I needed to do to make it right.

"I said, 'I'll tell my Latin teacher what I did. I'll do it tomorrow.'

"Mom said, 'That sounds like a good idea.'

"So the next day, I went to school and confessed. The teacher said, 'Gail, I'm going to have to fail you on this test. But something good has come out of this: I now know that I can trust you.'

"Looking back, I realize that the teacher's solution was the perfect balance of consequences and affirmation. I felt better because my conscience was cleansed—and I had done the right thing. My mother didn't punish me because I had shown character in confessing what I had done and accepting the consequences.

"Today, I have two daughters of my own. When my older daughter was going off to college, my 11-year-old asked her if she had any advice. My college-bound daughter told my 11-year-old, 'Just don't do anything to disappoint Mom and Dad. They think the world of you.' I thought that was a truly amazing answer, because it was an answer about building good character and making good choices."

What is character? We might define character as a commitment to do what is wise, honest and right, regardless of the cost or circumstances. For example, a person of good character will not steal or cheat, even in times of great need. A person of good character will speak the truth even if there is a price to pay for doing so. A person of good character will demonstrate courage even when the cause appears to be lost.

You can be a person of exceptional character even if you do not possess exceptional talent, intellect, skills or education. Good character is an equal opportunity personality trait. It is something anyone can develop whether rich or poor; advantaged or disadvantaged; white or black or any shade in between; liberal or conservative or middle-of-the-road. Character is for everyone. Those who have strong character have everything they need to live an effective and rewarding life.

People of character do not need rules and laws to tell them not to lie or steal. They have an innate understanding that unethical behavior would violate their character. As my friend and writing partner, Jim Denney, wrote in *Answers to Satisfy the Soul*, a person of strong character "could not lie and say, 'I'm a person of character who happened to tell a lie.' He would know that in the act of lying he had become a liar. A lie wouldn't just break a rule, it would stain his character."[5]

Let's take a look at some of the specific traits and qualities that make up this thing called *character*.

Integrity

General Richard B. Myers USAF (Ret.) served as Chairman of the Joint Chiefs of Staff (the nation's highest-ranking military officer) from 2001 to 2005. When I interviewed him for a previous book, *Coaching Your Kids to Be Leaders*, the general told me, "One of the many leadership lessons I learned early in my Air Force career was that you must have high credibility in your primary field of expertise first before anyone will want to follow you. Credibility comes from character—and especially from the character trait called integrity."

I asked him where he learned the importance of integrity. "I grew up in America's heartland, in Kansas," he replied. "My teachers and coaches were part of the 'greatest generation.' Many of them served in World War II and Korea. They were not boastful about their service; they were simply men and women of quiet integrity. By their actions and through their words, they taught me that integrity means being true to one's values and standards. It means saying what we mean, and meaning what we say. It means holding fast to our honor so that we are trustworthy and incorruptible. To be a leader and a role model, you must be a person of integrity."

Integrity may be defined as a pattern of consistency and congruence between your words and your actions. A person of authentic character and integrity will behave in exactly the same way, whether he or she is in public or in private. That person's behavior will be just as honorable, ethical and moral when no one is watching as when he or she is being observed by others.

To be a person of integrity, you must be whole and uncompartmentalized. If you are a different person in different situations—for example, if you are a saint on Sunday and a sinner the rest of the week—then you are fragmented and compartmentalized. If part of you is fraudulent, then *all* of you lacks integrity—and you can't consider yourself a person of character.

A number of years ago, *The Washington Post* published a profile of a politician who was widely described by both friends and foes as "compartmentalized." The newspaper writer described this political leader's "tendency to block things out, to compartmentalize different aspects of his life, to deny reality at times," as well as his "lack of normal standards of self-control, an addiction to the privileges of public office and a reliance on aides to shield him from public scrutiny of private behavior."

The tragedy of this man is that he is probably the most gifted leader and persuasive communicator of our lifetime. Yet the compartmentalization that he practiced between his private life and his public image proved corrosive to his own reputation, his public legacy and the political and social causes that he championed.

As *The Washington Post* writer went on to say, this politician's ability to compartmentalize paradoxically fueled his amazing rise to power while also threatening his power and position: "In his cycle of loss and recovery, the traits that account for his success are inseparable from the ones that provoke failure—the drives and impulses seem one and the same."[6]

As a general rule, the most successful and effective leaders are those whose public image and private reality are one and the same, those who are truly people of integrity. But there are always a few politicians, business leaders, religious leaders and others who hide who they *really* are behind a false façade. The very impulses that make them so amazingly successful also make them vulnerable to being found out and toppled by scandal. And I wonder if a compartmentalized person, in the privacy of his or her own thoughts, doesn't often wonder, "Who is the real me?"

Honesty

People of honesty are sincere, genuine and 1,000 percent committed to living out the truth. Honest people admit their mistakes and refuse to cut ethical corners. If they find a wallet in the street, they look for the owner. When they come home from the office, you won't find a purloined postage stamp or paperclip in their pocket. They never cheat on expense accounts or tax forms.

Brian Roquemore is president and CEO of America's All Stars, Inc. (www.4allstars.org), an Orlando-based organization devoted to developing strong character in students from K through 12. Brian recently told me a story about the importance of honesty in everyday life.

"In 1966, when I was 19," he told me, "I took a trip to Europe and had the time of my life. Soon after arriving, I bought an old BMW police motorcycle from another American for $250, and I had a blast, just going wherever that bike would take me.

"One day, while in Holland, I arrived at the ferry to cross the estuary from Vlissingen to Breskens, only to learn that I had missed the last ferry. I camped out overnight and took the first boat the next morning at 5:00. After the half-hour ferry ride, I climbed onto the motorcycle and puttered off toward Belgium, unaware that my wallet had fallen out of the back pocket of my blue jeans. The wallet contained my passport, the title to my motorcycle and my entire bankroll for the trip, $700 in American money plus some local currency.

"A man saw me lose my wallet. He was a butcher who took the ferry every day to work. He climbed into his panel truck and tried to catch me, but was no match for my motorcycle. Finally, he gave up and went on to his job.

"I discovered that my wallet was missing when I reached the border crossing between Holland and Belgium. I had a big problem. I had no money to continue my trip, no money to buy a ticket home and no passport. Long story short, I retraced my steps back to the ferry terminal. No one had turned my wallet in there. Someone directed me to the constable's office. The constable spoke no English, I spoke no Dutch, but somehow he got the picture.

"The constable called around to several police stations and—Eureka! A butcher had reported finding a lost wallet. The constable wrote down the address of the butcher's shop and gave it to me. I got on my bike and went to that address. I walked inside and the butcher came to the counter with my wallet in his hands.

"I didn't insult the man by opening the wallet and counting the money—I have no doubt that it was all there. I shook his hand, and gave him a big hug, not caring if his blood-spattered apron stained my clothes. I tried to give him a cash reward, but he refused to take it. Then I remembered I had a few Kennedy half-dollars in my pocket. This was 1966, and they had only started minting these coins in 1964. So those coins were quite a memento. The butcher accepted the Kennedy coin with pride and taped it up in the front window of the butcher shop.

"In the years that followed," Brian concluded, "I made several return trips to Europe, and I made it a point to visit my friend the butcher. He welcomed me into his home and introduced me to his wife. On my last visit to the butcher's home, his wife answered the door. The moment she saw me, she started to cry. I knew my friend had passed away. But his wonderful act of honesty impacted my life at a deep level and taught me more than words can say about the importance of character."

Brian's story shows that the character quality of honesty is the foundation upon which to build not only enduring friendships, but also enduring legacies. Back in 1966, a Dutch butcher picked up a wallet off the ground, and more than 40 years later his good character is still being praised in this book!

The character quality of honesty is also crucial to overcoming addiction. Bill Denehy was a Major League Baseball pitcher in the late 1960s and early 1970s. He recently shared his story with me.

"I'll admit that I didn't spend much of my early and middle years thinking about character issues," Bill told me. "The first time I realized that character really does matter was on June 15, 1992. That was the day I checked into a clinic for drug and alcohol abuse. While in rehab and recovery, my recovery group taught me about my character defects and my need to build character. Recovery programs like Alcoholics Anonymous expose your flaws and show you the changes you need to make.

"Addiction makes you selfish. I was no exception to that rule. Not long before I went into rehab, our family was on vacation in Connecticut. My daughter Heather asked me if we could play catch, but being the selfish addict that I was, I put it off. We never played catch during that vacation.

"On June 14, the day before I went into rehab, I was at one of Heather's softball games, chatting with the other parents. Heather came up as we were talking, and I said to her, 'Is there something we haven't done that you'd really like to do?' She looked at me with sad eyes and said, 'Let's play catch sometime, Dad.' You'd think that, with me being a former pro ball player, the least I could do is play catch with my daughter—but I had never done it.

"In November 1992, I was out of rehab—and Heather and I finally played catch. We had a great time, and I finally discovered what I'd been missing because of my selfishness.

"So you can see what I mean about honesty. You can't overcome addiction without total honesty. I'm not talking about honesty in terms of not stealing or shoplifting. I'm talking about *being honest with yourself.* You can't lie to yourself and pretend that everything is all right when it isn't. You have to address your destructive behavior, your wrong attitudes, your character flaws. It's like when someone says, 'How're ya doing?' and you say, 'Great!' when in reality you are dying inside. You have to admit that you are not okay, that your life is falling apart, and that you can't go on like this.

"Going into recovery opened my eyes to the defects in my character. I had sponsors who mentored me and took me through the Twelve Steps of Alcoholics Anonymous. The fourth step required me to take a 'searching and fearless moral inventory' of myself. A lot of my character defects came out at this point, and I had to address them. My sponsors helped me fit back into society and overcome the anger and blaming I had developed growing up.

"The twelfth step is that you become a sponsor and a mentor, and you carry the message you've received to other alcoholics who need direction and help. Since I went into recovery, I've sponsored dozens of people. I keep my sobriety by giving it away."

Humility

Humility is the ability to keep one's ego in check. It has been said that a humble person does not think less of himself; he simply thinks of himself less. Genuinely humble people are not wimpy or passive. In fact, some of the most powerful and impressive people I've met have also been amazingly humble. Genuine humility is an amazing character strength. When you come into the presence of a truly humble person, you are instantly impressed by the power of his or her personality.

An authentically humble person is always comfortable in his or her own skin. A humble person's self-appraisal doesn't rise or fall based on what others think. His ego cannot be inflated by flattery or deflated by insult. As Mother Teresa wisely observed, "If you are humble nothing can touch you, neither praise nor disgrace, because you know who you are."

Humble people treat everyone as equals, because they genuinely don't view anyone as an inferior. About five years after the death of Diana, Princess of Wales, I had dinner with Graham Lacey, an English businessman who had personally known her. I said, "If Princess Diana were with us at dinner tonight, what would she be like?"

"For one thing," Graham said, "I know that the princess would have been fascinated with all of your 19 children. In fact, she would have eagerly insisted on going to your house so she could meet them all. She'd have been down on the floor playing with the younger ones. When she got back home to England, she would have sent each of them a handwritten note. At Christmas she would have mailed each one a card."

No wonder everyone who met her was enchanted by her, especially the "common people." Her warm and elegant humility made her by far the most beloved member of the British royal family.

John R. W. Stott, the great Anglican evangelical clergyman, once observed, "Leaders have power, but power is safe only in the hands of those who humble themselves to serve." One leader who exemplified that statement was General Omar Bradley (1893-1981), who served as the first Chairman of the Joint Chiefs of Staff. Bradley spent nearly seven decades on active duty—longer than any other soldier in U.S. military history. Because of his great rapport with the foot soldiers of World War II, he was called "The G.I.'s General."

Long after the war, General Bradley encountered a veteran who had served under him in Europe during World War II. "General," the man said, "it's an honor to shake your hand. We won that war because of you."

"No, sir," Bradley replied with genuine emotion, "we won that war because of you." That's the power and strength of true humility.

Responsibility

Fred Claire, the retired Los Angeles Dodgers general manager, once said to me, "You can't possibly take a leadership position unless you are ready to take responsibility for your own actions. Leadership starts with taking responsibility and being accountable." It's true. One of the most important of all the character traits is a strong sense of personal responsibility.

Responsible people are self-starters. No one has to stand over them with a whip to make sure they get their work done. They take their duties seriously and carry them out without having to be monitored. Responsible people also take personal responsibility for their own actions. If they make a mistake, they don't make excuses or shift the blame to others. They own up to their mistakes—and correct them.

I interviewed Dr. Vincent Mumford, director of the Sports Leadership Graduate Program at the University of Central Florida, for my book *Coaching Your Kids to Be Leaders*. "No one taught responsibility and accountability like my mother," he told me. "I was the team captain and starting guard on my junior varsity basketball team. One night my mother told me to do the dishes. I was tired, so I figured I'd do it later. I fell asleep and didn't get to the dishes.

"The next day, my mother informed me that I was punished and couldn't play basketball. It was embarrassing! I went to school and told my coach what happened. He came to my house after school and spoke to my mother, but she wouldn't budge. Not only did I miss a game, but I was ridiculed by my teammates. She let me join the team after that one-game suspension—and I learned a valuable lesson: A leader is responsible and accountable to the team."

Compassion

People of compassion show kindness, mercy and benevolence to all people, regardless of any distinctions. Genuine compassion does not arise from the emotions, but from an act of the will—a conscious and volitional decision to do good to other people. Compassionate people willingly sacrifice their own comfort and convenience in order to reach out and help other people. They are motivated by genuine caring, not by a desire for self-promotion and public recognition.

If you are familiar with *The Book of One Thousand and One Nights*, then you may recall reading stories about Haroun al-Rashid, the famed caliph who, from A.D. 786 to 809, ruled an empire that included much

of modern-day Iran and Iraq. Though many of the deeds and exploits of
Haroun have been wildly exaggerated, he was an actual historical leader
of ancient Persia. He was noted for his wisdom and compassion (his
name in English would be "Aaron the Just"), and his reign was marked
by great scientific and cultural advances.

Because of his deep compassion for his people, Haroun took great
pains to make sure that government officials treated his citizens fairly,
especially those who were poor and powerless. Haroun sometimes disguised himself as a simple peasant and walked through the streets and
marketplaces, talking to the common people. This way, he always knew
whether the people were happy and well treated—and he also knew
which officials to punish if the people were mistreated.

Today, in the Middle Eastern country of Jordan, there is a ruler who
has patterned his life after Haroun al-Rashid. His name is King Abdullah. He became king of Jordan in 1999, following the death of his
father, King Hussein. When Abdullah ascended to the throne, the people of Jordan had doubts about him: Would King Abdullah be as kind
and compassionate as his late father? Would he be a strong enough
leader to fill his father's shoes? Many doubted whether the American-
educated Abdullah was serious enough and wise enough to lead the
nation. He was, after all, famed for his fondness for Tex-Mex food and
Star Trek (as prince, he had appeared as a starship crewman in a 1995
episode of *Star Trek: Voyager*).

But King Abdullah silenced his critics by emulating the legendary
Haroun al-Rashid. Numerous times after becoming king of Jordan,
Abdullah disguised himself as a taxi driver or marketplace vendor. This
way, he could go out among the people, question them, listen to them
and find out what they needed from their government and their king.

For example, he once worked as an orderly in a government hospital in Zarqa, the Jordanian industrial center northeast of Amman. Working in disguise, he was able to see for himself how doctors treated (or
mistreated) their patients. Upon his return to the palace, he ordered
numerous reforms to improve conditions in all government hospitals
throughout Jordan.

King Abdullah faces many difficult challenges as the ruler of a nation in a turbulent part of the world. As a reformer, he is often criticized

on the one hand for pushing reforms too quickly, and on the other for not reforming quickly enough. It's a delicate balancing act. But King Abdullah has maintained that balance and has proven himself to be a leader of great character and compassion.

Love

General Tommy Franks (U.S. Army, retired) led the United States Central Command and was responsible for combined military operations in a 25-nation region, including the Middle East. He was the chief architect of the War on Terror in Afghanistan and Iraq following the terrorist attacks of September 11, 2001. I recently had the privilege of interviewing him by telephone. In the course of our conversation, I told General Franks that my son David is a Marine and was in combat at the start of the Iraq invasion in 2003.

"You tell your son," the general replied, "that someone else loves him besides you." Both of us had a lump in our throat when he said that.

Like General Franks, all great leaders seem to understand that love is essential to life and to leadership. General Eric K. Shinseki, former Army Chief of Staff, once said, "You must love those you lead before you can be an effective leader. You can certainly command without that sense of commitment, but you cannot lead without it."

Eddie Robinson (1919-2007) coached football at Grambling State University, Louisiana, for 56 years, from 1941 through 1997. He retired as the winningest coach in college football history. He said, "Coaching is the profession of love. You can't coach people unless you love them." Legendary UCLA basketball coach John Wooden agrees: "The coach's most powerful tool is love."

Hunter Smith is a punter for Tony Dungy's world champion Indianapolis Colts. Smith once said, "I don't believe that the mean old S.O.B.-style of coaching works. I've played for both types and I'll tell you this: When you treat players like men and you have expectations of them, but you love them, they will go to war for you. People play better when they are respected."

Dick Vermeil, who coached the St. Louis Rams to a 1999 NFL world championship in Super Bowl XXXIV, says that love is not just something you show. It's something you put into words. "My coaches know how I feel," he says. "You know why? Because I tell them I love them. . . . You surround yourself with good people and work hard and be unselfish and care and don't be embarrassed to say, 'I love you,' and 'I appreciate it' because if you say it, someone else will say it back to you." He added that he learned the importance of love in coaching from his mentor, Sid Gilman, a great coach of the Rams and Chargers. Vermeil recalled, "I don't think I've ever had a phone call from Sid that didn't finish with him saying, 'Hey, I love you, Dick.'"

When I say that love is a character quality, I'm not talking about love as a feeling of attraction or fondness. The character trait of love is not an emotion; it's a decision. It's an act of the will. It's a commitment to do good to others regardless of any distinctions (race, gender, creed, relationship), regardless of their actions, regardless of whether or not they deserve to be loved. A person who possesses the character quality of love makes a decision to love even people who are unloving, unlovable and unlovely. This is the radically new kind of love that Jesus taught in His Sermon on the Mount. He said:

> You have heard that it was said, "Love your neighbor and hate your enemy." But I tell you: Love your enemies and pray for those who persecute you, that you may be sons of your Father in heaven. He causes his sun to rise on the evil and the good, and sends rain on the righteous and the unrighteous. If you love those who love you, what reward will you get? Are not even the tax collectors doing that? And if you greet only your brothers, what are you doing more than others? Do not even pagans do that? (Matt. 5:43-47).

Jesus isn't talking about love as an emotion. He doesn't expect us to have warm, fuzzy feelings about our enemies. He's talking about love as a decision of the will. In your emotions, you may feel nothing but hurt or rage toward your enemy. But in your will and your intentions, you can choose to do good toward your enemy and pray for your enemy. In time, positive feelings may follow your deliberate actions of love.

This kind of deliberate love is inclusive and it loves all people the same. It enables us to love those we've never met and even those who drive us crazy with their disagreeable behavior. Add this kind of committed love to your romantic relationship and it will enable you to love that person as long as you live. Add this kind of love to your family relationships and it will get you through all the rough patches and hard times.

This kind of love is the ultimate in unselfishness. We can't control our feelings, but we can always control our choices. Feelings may change, but a *commitment* to love is as durable as you choose to make it. That's why the apostle Paul, in his famous New Testament "Love Chapter," said:

> Love is patient, love is kind. It does not envy, it does not boast, it is not proud. It is not rude, it is not self-seeking, it is not easily angered, it keeps no record of wrongs. Love does not delight in evil but rejoices with the truth. It always protects, always trusts, always hopes, always perseveres. Love never fails. . . . And now these three remain: faith, hope and love. But the greatest of these is love (1 Cor. 13:4-8,13).

These words don't describe a feeling or emotion. They describe a volitional *choice* and a *character quality*.

Fred Rogers (1928–2003) was a Presbyterian minister, educator and host of the children's TV show *Mister Rogers' Neighborhood* from 1968 to 2001. In addition to being a TV icon, Mister Rogers was an advocate for children. He died in 2003, not long after retiring from his television series. Fred Rogers knew a lot about the true nature of love, and he constantly taught love to children and grown-ups. "Love," he once said, "is an active noun like 'struggle.' To love someone is to strive to accept that person exactly the way he or she is, right here and now."[7] Take it from Mister Rogers. Authentic love isn't easy. It's a struggle to love people who aren't easy to love.

A memorial collection of Fred Rogers's wisdom, *The World According to Mister Rogers: Important Things to Remember*, was published in 2003. In the foreword to the book, Mister Rogers's wife, Joanne, wrote, "A quote he loved especially—and carried around with him—was from Mary Lou Kownacki: 'There isn't anyone you couldn't love once you've heard their story.' There were many times I wanted to be angry at someone and

Fred would say, 'But I wonder what was going on in that person's day.' His capacity for understanding always amazed me."[8]

When we choose to love our fellow human beings, even when it is not easy to love, we become people of character like Mister Rogers—and we make the world a much more beautiful, caring and forgiving place. Pastor and author Charles Swindoll has formulated a simple definition of authentic love. His "ABCs of love" are:

> I *Accept* you as you are.
> I *Believe* you are valuable.
> I *Care* when you hurt.
> I *Desire* only what is best for you.
> I *Erase* all offenses.

While this book was being written, I interviewed author Hal Urban on my Orlando radio show. Hal had come to talk about his latest book, *The 10 Commandments of Common Sense: Wisdom from the Scriptures for People of All Beliefs*. The book is a practical handbook on how to apply the wisdom of Scripture to everyday life.

"As I was getting ready to start out on a lengthy speaking tour," Hal told me, "I came across a verse of Scripture that I had read many times before. This time, however, it spoke to me in a brand-new way. The verse said, 'Do everything in love.' I thought, 'Everything? What would my life look like if I did *everything* in love?' So I decided to try it and find out. As I set out on my trip, I made up my mind that in all my interactions with people along the way—with airline attendants, hotel clerks, waiters and waitresses, everybody—I would do everything in love."

So, Hal went on his speaking tour and when he returned home, he said to his wife, "That's the best week I've ever had!"

Well, as Hal told me his experience of doing everything in love, I felt inspired! I had a three-day trip of my own coming up, so I did the same experiment. In all my interactions with the people I met along the way, I tried to do something to serve them in love. And it was amazing the difference it made on my trip.

I talked to people and found out about their families, their interests, their plans and dreams. While people were assisting me in my travels or my hotel stay, I tried to find some little way to repay their kindness.

In some cases, my interaction with a waiter or a clerk was so brief that there was little that I could do or say—but at the very least I could always pray for that person, and I did. And when I returned home, I told my wife, Ruth, "That was the best three-day trip I've ever had!"

It occurred to me that this wonderful insight that Hal Urban shared was not exactly new. Jesus told us, "Love one another," some 20 centuries ago. And Paul's command, "Do everything in love" (1 Cor. 16:14), has been around almost as long. The problem is that we tend to read these words, nod in agreement, and then promptly forget them in real-life situations. So I'm grateful to Hal Urban for reminding me that people of character do everything in love.

Courage and More

We've really only scratched the surface of the subject of character. In fact, I've written an entire book on character, which may interest you: *Souls of Steel: How to Build Character in Ourselves and Our Kids* (FaithWords 2008). There are so many other character qualities that we could explore—self-reliance, generosity, fairness, self-control, patience, diligence, respect, tolerance, and more. In fact, you could probably think of enough additional character qualities to expand that list many times over. But we have to end this chapter somewhere, so let me end it with the character quality of courage.

I would define courage as the willingness to take risks to achieve great goals, the willingness to withstand opposition and face obstacles for a great cause, and the willingness to face suffering and death with dignity in order to set an example of character for others to follow. Let me tell you about two people of character and courage who had a profound impact on my life.

Back in the 1970s, when I was the general manager of the Philadelphia 76ers, I met a man named Arthur S. DeMoss and we became good friends. Art DeMoss came from a tough background. He started in business as a bookie in his early twenties, becoming very wealthy by running a couple of horse rooms in Albany, New York. At age 25, he committed his life to Jesus Christ in a revival meeting and completely turned his life around. After marrying his wife, Nancy, he started a life insurance company that grew to become a financial empire. He used his considerable resources as a means of sharing his faith with others.

Art DeMoss was not a polished man. He was a diamond in the rough—tough, hardheaded and plainspoken. But he had as big a heart as any man I've ever known. His number-one goal in life was to reach people for Jesus Christ. Art would hold huge outreach dinners in his home, inviting some of the most influential people in the nation to his home. Then he would share the gospel with them over dinner. There would often be as many as 200 people attending, which gives you some idea of the size of his home. He'd bring in a guest speaker (I spoke at several of these dinners), then Art himself would speak. He was not a polished speaker, but when he talked, people responded.

Art also hosted smaller group Bible studies in his home. At one of these meetings in his living room, he said, "Tonight I want to hear everybody's testimony. We'll go around the room and each of you can tell us how you met Jesus Christ." So we went around the room, and different people told their story. There was one young man named Doug who said, "I don't have a testimony."

"Come with me," Art said. He took Doug into another room and they were gone for about 20 minutes. Finally they returned, and Art said, "Doug will now share his testimony." And Doug told us all how Art DeMoss, just moments earlier, had introduced him to Jesus Christ.

When our daughter Karyn was born on July 28, 1979, in New Jersey, Art called us, extended his congratulations and led us in a prayer for God's blessing on the lives of our children. That was the last conversation I had with Art DeMoss. On September 1, he was playing tennis. He threw the ball up to serve and suffered a massive heart attack. He was dead before the ball hit the ground. He was only 53.

When we got the news that day, we rushed over to Art's home to see the family. When we arrived, I asked one of his daughters how they were doing. "We're pretty rejoicing," she said with a sad smile. I knew exactly what she meant. It's painful to lose someone you love, but when you believe you'll see that loved one again in eternity, you can still be "pretty rejoicing," even in your grief.

The next morning, all of Art's family went to church. They entered the church as the great hymn of assurance, "It Is Well with My Soul," was being played:

When peace like a river attendeth my way,
When sorrows like sea billows roll;
Whatever my lot, Thou hast taught me to say,
It is well, it is well, with my soul.

Bill Bright, the founder of Campus Crusade for Christ, officiated at Art's funeral. The church was packed with mourners. Bill looked around and said, "Would everyone here who is going to heaven because of Arthur DeMoss please raise your hand?"

There was a lump in my throat as I saw half the people in the audience raise their hand. I thought, *Wow! What a life Art lived! What a legacy he left!* It occurred to me that, in the grand scheme of things, there are really only two things that last: God's Word and the souls of people. As in the words of missionary pioneer C. T. Studd, "Only one life, 'twill soon be past. / Only what's done for Christ will last."

That brings me to the second man of character and courage I want to tell you about: Dr. Bill Bright. You may know that Bill is responsible for a little booklet, published by Campus Crusade for Christ, entitled *Have You Heard of the Four Spiritual Laws?* Later in this book, I'll tell you the story of how Bill Bright, by means of that little booklet, changed my life.

In 1988, Bill came to Orlando, where I had begun working to start a new NBA franchise called the Orlando Magic. Bill was looking for a good place to relocate his headquarters from Southern California, and a group of us worked hard to sell him on the benefits of Central Florida. We must have helped convince him, because he eventually moved his entire organization to Orlando.

Bill suffered for years from pulmonary fibrosis, a chronic and progressive lung disease. Breathing became a difficult struggle for him. I remember going to see him at Florida Hospital in Orlando. When I arrived, his wife, Vonette, was pushing him in a wheelchair along the hospital crosswalk. I remember the date quite clearly—September 10, 2001—because it was the day before the September 11 terrorist attacks.

I greeted him and said, "Bill, how are you doing?"

Smiling behind his oxygen mask, he said, "Praising the Lord."

I recently visited with Vonette Bright. As we reminisced about Bill, she told me of a phone call he received shortly before his death. The call was from President George W. Bush. The evangelist and the leader of the Free World chatted for a few minutes. Then, near the end of the call, Bill thanked the president and said, "I'm honored, Mr. President, to receive a call from the most powerful man in the world—but soon I'm going to meet Someone far greater."

On July 19, 2003, he did.

Vonette told me about a conversation she had with Bill shortly before he went into the presence of his Lord. She asked him why God allowed him to go through such suffering, and Bill immediately replied, "What I'm going through is very minor. I'm here in a bed of ease. I'm surrounded by people who love me. Suffering is a matter of perspective. It's not pleasant, but God allows only so much. I'm so blessed."

That's courage and character talking. Courage is not fearlessness. I'm sure Bill felt his share of fear as he faced his own mortality. But fear and death could not overcome his trust in his Lord.

When I think of the legacy that continues to live on after Arthur DeMoss and Bill Bright, I'm a bit envious! That's the way I want to live—and the way I want to die. I want hundreds and even thousands of people to be able to raise their hands and say, "I know Jesus because of this man! I will live forever because of this man! I am a part of his legacy that will never die."

May that be your legacy of character as well.

PURSUE INFLUENCE

Mom Burgher, Bill Durney, Bill Veeck and Mr. R. E. Littlejohn are not around anymore. But if not for them, you wouldn't be reading this book. Each of them had a profound impact on my life. I am who I am because of them.

I met Mom Burgher in the fall of 1962, while I was working on my master's degree in physical education at Indiana University in Bloomington. She and her husband, Bob, owned Burgher's Grill on Main Street in the center of town. It was one of those great American eateries that you hardly ever see anymore, like something out of a Norman Rockwell painting. Not only were the Burghers' burgers great, but the Burghers themselves took a personal interest in the lives of their customers. When the lunch-hour rush was over, they'd come over to your booth and chat with you about your hopes and dreams for the future.

Though we all called her "Mom," she had no children of her own. Yet, in a real sense, Mom Burgher had many sons. She called all the athletes and coaches at Indiana University "my boys," and it was true. She came to all the football and basketball games, decked out in Hoosier crimson. She was a friend, mentor and counselor, and we all knew we could come by her house at any time of the day or night for some sound advice or a bite to eat. Anytime I faced a big problem in my school life or personal life, all I had to do was talk it over with Mom and I was ready to take on the world.

My most vivid impression of the Burgher home was the walls covered with framed pictures. These were photos that "Mom's boys" would send her over the years after they left Indiana University. Long after Bob Burgher passed away, Mom kept mentoring and mothering these young men who passed through Bloomington. I exchanged notes and cards with her long after I left Indiana, and well into my career with the

NBA. Whenever I was back in Indiana, I went out of my way to visit Mom Burgher.

When Mom Burgher died in her eighties, she left behind a legacy of influence in hundreds of lives, including my own. I used to think that every college town must have a Mom Burgher. But over the years, I've come to realize that people like Mom are rare. The world is crying out for more people like Mom Burgher, people who are willing to pursue a life of influence.

A FEW OF MY INFLUENCERS

During my two years playing minor league baseball in Miami, I got to know a man named Bill Durney. Bill had been around college and professional sports for many years, and was at that time serving as general manager of the Miami Marlins, an A club in the Phillies system. After two undistinguished seasons behind the plate, I moved into the Marlins front office, and Bill showed me the ropes of running a minor league team. I was an eager student, and I told Bill, "I need an education in pro baseball, and I'd like you to be my mentor."

Bill could have told me to get lost. After all, there was no percentage for him in taking me under his wing. But Bill Durney was a person who pursued influence. He agreed to coach me on the business side of baseball. I eagerly absorbed every scrap of wisdom he could share with me. Every major principle I absorbed about sports management, I learned from Bill Durney. He had an enormous impact on my life—and he also introduced me to another great influencer, Bill Veeck.

In his heyday, William Louis Veeck, Jr., was the most famous promoter, innovator and franchise owner in Major League Baseball. He was especially famous for his wild publicity stunts. During his career, he owned the Cleveland Indians, the St. Louis Browns and the Chicago White Sox. It would not be an overstatement to say that Veeck (whose name rhymes with "wreck") profoundly changed the business of baseball. In 2001, I wrote a book (with Michael Weinreb) called *Marketing Your Dreams: Business and Life Lessons from Bill Veeck*.

I met Bill Veeck for the first time when I was 22 years old, and he mentored me throughout my career as a minor league baseball general manager, and on into my career in the NBA. I continued to seek his advice and encouragement right up until his death in 1986. I particularly remember one conversation I had with Bill after a disappointing season as manager of the Spartanburg Phillies. I had spent six months working 16-hour days, but the team had racked up a losing record, and I was down in the dumps.

After listening to my tale of woe, Bill said, "Pat, how many people did you draw to the ballpark this season?"

I told him: 114,000, a very good attendance record for minor-league baseball.

"Well, Pat, how many of those people had a good time?"

"All of them. I never had one complaint."

"What else could you have done this summer that would have given that much fun to so many people?"

"Not a thing."

"Then, Pat, you had a good season. You never have to apologize for giving people a good time."

Over my years in sports management, I've had great seasons, good seasons, and some not-so-good seasons. Through it all, I have thought of Bill Veeck's advice a few thousand times, and I've been endlessly grateful for Bill's influence in my life. His influence continues to live on through my mentoring influence on others.

WHAT WOULD MR. LITTLEJOHN DO?

In previous chapters, I've mentioned the impact that Mr. R. E. Littlejohn had on me. When I arrived in Spartanburg, South Carolina, to take over as general manager of the Spartanburg Phillies, the owner, Mr. Littlejohn, was out of town. When I stopped by his house to introduce myself, I was met at the door by his wife. During our conversation, she told me, "You'll never meet another man like Mr. R. E." She was absolutely right. Mr. R. E. Littlejohn was definitely one of a kind.

As I got to know him, I found him to be a man of immense wisdom. I had lost my own father a short time earlier, and I was fortunate that Mr. Littlejohn practically adopted me as the son he never had. Mr. Littlejohn had such a profound influence on my life that, years later, my firstborn son was named James Littlejohn Williams.

During my years in Spartanburg, I had four great ambitions—the same four ambitions we've been talking about in this book. I was ambitious for money, for fame, for power and for the pleasures of the good things in life. Even as a young man in my twenties, those good things were already coming my way. I drove an expensive car, I wore expensive clothes, I was respected in the community and I had the freedom and the funds to live pretty much the way I wanted.

Yet, when I went home to my apartment at night, I often asked myself, "Is this all there is to life?"

During those days, I watched Mr. Littlejohn very closely, paying careful attention to the way he lived and the choices he made. I found him to be the most exemplary human being I have ever known. I admired him and wanted to be like him; and God used Mr. Littlejohn to alter the course of my life. I can authentically say that it's primarily because of Mr. Littlejohn's influence that I ceased living for money, fame, power and pleasure, and I began living for God.

His longtime friend, Robert Odom, once told me that Mr. Littlejohn "always had time for others. He was always moved by the needs of others. He was always influencing others for the better." The reason that Mr. R. E. Littlejohn influenced so many people was that he was consciously *aware* of his influence on others. Let me give you an example of this.

The Spartanburg ballpark I managed for Mr. R. E. was a rarity in the baseball world: It was "dry." That's right, we didn't sell beer. When I first arrived in Spartanburg, I didn't understand that this was Mr. Littlejohn's policy. So I went to Mr. Littlejohn and said, "We could make a lot of money if we sold beer at the park."

He looked up in astonishment. "Before I sell beer at those games," he said, "I'd sell the team."

That's when I found out that Mr. R. E. was very conscious of the impression his organization made on the young people of the community. He strongly believed that alcoholic beverages were a corrupting influence, and he wouldn't even allow ads for beer to be posted on the ballpark walls or printed in our programs. I never brought the subject up again.

He taught me a lesson that has stuck with me to this day: Always be aware of your influence on others. Even now, whenever I face a tough decision, I always ask myself, "What would Mr. Littlejohn do?" At that point, the solution to my problem usually becomes clear.

"I WON'T CHEAT"

Your influence is your ability to affect and shape the lives, thoughts and beliefs of other people. We all have an influence on the people around us. That influence will be positive or negative, but it is never neutral. Other people are watching our behavior, listening to our words and taking note of the choices we make. We can't escape the fact that our lives have an impact on those around us, so we have an obligation to make sure that we influence others for the better.

In the course of my years in the sports world, I have heard many sports figures say, "I never asked to be anyone's hero. I never asked to be a role model. I don't want anyone to look up to me. I just want to live my life as I please." Sorry, the world doesn't work that way. Everyone has influence, like it or not, and the more visible and famous you are, the wider your sphere of influence.

Dale Murphy was a catcher and outfielder in Major League Baseball from 1976 to 1993, and has been widely hailed as one of the outstanding players of the 1980s. Though he played with the Phillies and Rockies before he retired, Murph is remembered for his long career with the Atlanta Braves. He appeared in the all-star game seven times, twice led the National League in home runs and RBIs and won five consecutive Gold Gloves and back-to-back MVPs. With 398 career home runs to his credit, Dale Murphy outranks such legendary sluggers as Ralph Kiner, Joe DiMaggio and Johnny Bench.

But when I think of Dale Murphy's influence, it's not his athletic prowess or his player stats I'm thinking of. It's the choices he made and the example he set.

Back in the late 1980s, when his batting prowess was fading and his career had begun to wane, Dale Murphy became aware that something new was coming into the league: steroids. Today Murph says that he was never offered steroids and never saw them in the Atlanta Braves clubhouse. But he knew that steroids were being used around the league and could have easily gotten them if he'd wanted them. Some players were using steroids to add a few years to their playing careers. But Murph wasn't willing to cheat in order to extend his career or pump up his stats. Why? He was intensely conscious of his influence on others.

Dale Murphy was known during his career for clean living. He would not smoke or drink or endorse tobacco or alcohol products. Dale appeared in commercials for ice cream and cameras, but turned down $25,000 to endorse a car after test-driving it and deciding he didn't like the car. He wouldn't allow himself to be photographed with scantily clad women. His language was notoriously clean, and he donated countless hours to help the March of Dimes, the American Heart Association, and the Make-a-Wish Foundation.

Before a home game against San Francisco on June 12, 1983, Murph went into the stands and visited with six-year-old Elizabeth Smith, who had lost a leg and both hands when she stepped on a downed power line. As Murph gave the girl a Braves cap and T-shirt, the girl's nurse asked, "Could you please hit a home run for Elizabeth?"

Caught off guard, Dale Murphy replied, "Okay, sure," though he knew there was no way he could guarantee such a promise. That night, he hit two homers and drove in all three runs in the Braves' 3–2 win over the Giants.

Since his retirement, Dale Murphy has campaigned hard against drugs in sports—both mind-altering drugs like cocaine and performance-enhancing drugs like steroids. He loves baseball, and he wants to see the game played cleanly. He goes so far as to advocate a lifetime ban from the game for any player who fails even one drug test. When it comes to the game's influence on the next generation, Murph leaves no room for compromise. "The guys using this stuff are messing with the integrity of the game," he once said. "Let's kick them out."

Murph started the I Won't Cheat Foundation, with its website at www.iwontcheat.com. His goal is to keep young people from trying mind-altering or performance-enhancing drugs. Visitors to the website are presented with the medical facts about steroids, plus an online sign-up form that invites young people to take a pledge "not to cheat in sports, in the classroom, or in life."

Murph also speaks at schools and youth rallies, urging young people to stay away from drugs and cheating—not to avoid getting caught, but because it's right, it's healthy and it's smart to stay away from drugs. He also underscores the need for young people to care about their reputation and their influence. "It will matter in your life," he tells them. "It will matter to you and the respect people give you."[1]

WHAT IS YOUR PLATFORM?

Dale Murphy is a sports celebrity who seeks to leverage his achievements on the playing field into a positive influence on the lives of others, especially young people. People in the sports world who are conscious of their influence often speak of their "platform." In the literal sense, a platform is an elevated stage from which a person can speak and be heard by the crowd below. A sports celebrity has a platform of fame, which he or she can use to influence fans, young people and society at large.

Quarterback Kurt Warner earned two NFL MVP awards (1999 and 2001) and won his championship ring by leading the St. Louis Rams to victory over the Titans in Super Bowl XXXIV. He is intensely aware of his influence as a sports star. "God has given me an unbelievable platform that reaches an enormous amount of people," he says. "We've got our family background with our son who was injured at a young age and has some physical and mental disabilities. My wife lost her parents in a tornado. We've had difficult times financially—and then we had success. We can touch an unbelievable amount of people and speak to them on a lot of different levels. The Lord's blessed us with the opportunity to reach out to lots of people. . . . It's not just about stepping on the football field. It's about affecting people's lives for Jesus, and that's my platform."[2]

Hockey defenseman Glen Wesley of the Carolina Hurricanes is another sports star who is aware of his influence. He once said, "The Lord has given me a great platform to speak to young kids and neighbors and friends. I give them an opportunity to look at themselves and see what life is all about, knowing that we're here on Earth, but this is temporary. Heaven is eternity. I know that puts things in perspective for me. I know that one day I will get to drink from the Lord's Cup, if not the Stanley Cup."[3] When he said those words, Wesley had spent nearly two decades in the NHL, playing for four different teams, without winning a championship.

But on June 19, 2006, the Carolina Hurricanes defeated the Edmonton Oilers in seven games—and Wesley won his Stanley Cup. Instead of using this achievement to glorify himself, he used it as an opportunity for influence.

When a hockey team wins the Stanley Cup, each member of the team gets to keep the cup for a day. For his day with the Cup, Glen Wesley chose to take the Cup to Marine Corps Base Camp Lejeune, near Jacksonville, North Carolina. His first priority in using his influence was to set an example for his three children. He loaded his family in the car along with the Cup and together they visited the Wounded Warriors Center at Camp Lejeune.

At the Wounded Warriors Center, Glen Wesley carried out his second priority, using his sports platform to bring a positive influence and a message of gratitude to the Marines who had been severely wounded while serving their country in Afghanistan and Iraq. These Marines were recovering from both physical and mental injuries they had received in the War on Terror. When Glen walked into the center, holding the Stanley Cup above his head, the Marines shouted and applauded. Wesley showed a video with highlights from the championship game, then he spoke, thanking the warriors for their service and sacrifice, and sharing his faith in Jesus Christ. Then the wounded Marines had their pictures taken with the hockey star.[4]

Glen Wesley understands the importance of influence. In the end, God allowed Glen Wesley to drink from both the Lord's Cup *and* the Stanley Cup.

You may not have the platform of a sports star. But there are people who look up to you, watch your life and listen to your words. Like it or not, my friend, you have a platform and you are responsible for your influence. How are you using your platform?

THE SALT OF THE EARTH

No human being ever had a greater influence than Jesus of Nazareth. Read His Sermon on the Mount and you will see that it is all about influence. Jesus begins with the Beatitudes, which describe the kind of people we should be. He tells us that we are truly blessed when we demonstrate humility, patience, contentment, mercy, compassion, integrity, a hunger for righteousness and good works, and a love for God. He says that we are blessed if we courageously persevere in doing good, even though we are mistreated by evil people. If you are the kind of person Jesus describes in the Beatitudes, then God can use you as an agent of change and influence in society.

After the Beatitudes, Jesus talks about being "salt" and "light." He says, "You are the salt of the earth" (Matt. 5:13). Salt is a preservative. In Jesus' day, before the invention of refrigeration, meat and fish were preserved by salting and drying, much as beef jerky is made today. Meat that would quickly spoil can be kept for weeks when it is dried and salted. You and I are "the salt of the earth" if we help to preserve our society by having a positive influence on the people around us. Our influence fights the moral decay and spiritual corruption that destroys so many lives all around us.

Salt is also a seasoning. As "salt," you and I influence our society by enhancing the flavor of life. All around us, people are chasing after false values—and they are discovering that money, fame, power and pleasure do not satisfy. We come along, living lives that are based on eternal values, filled with the joy of life. When people learn that the Source of our joy is God Himself, the "seasoning salt" of our life triggers their hunger for God.

"You are the salt of the earth," Jesus said—and then He added this strange thought: "But if the salt loses its saltiness, how can it be made salty again? It is no longer good for anything, except to be thrown out and trampled by men" (Matt. 5:13). What does Jesus mean? Can salt lose its saltiness? Well, if you buy a box of good old Morton's Salt and store it in a dry place, it will still be salty a year from now or a hundred years from now. Why? Because the table salt you buy at the store is a stable, crystalline compound—sodium chloride ($NaCl$).

But in Jesus' day, you couldn't get nice, pure table salt. In those days, salt was collected from salt marshes around the edge of the Dead Sea. The salt crystals were contaminated with crystals or granules of magnesium chloride, calcium chloride, potassium chloride and other impurities. People would purchase salt in the marketplace and store it in earthen jars or leather pouches. Rain from a leaky roof or steam from cooking pots could sometimes cause moisture to form in the salt containers. When salt gets wet, it can dissolve, leaving behind the worthless, tasteless crystals of its impurities. The stuff would look like salt, but it would have lost its saltiness. It was fit only to be tossed out—not in the field, where it would harm the crops, but in the road, where it would be trampled.

Jesus is saying that we need to guard our distinctiveness, our saltiness. We need to be on guard that we don't allow anything into our life that would dilute our character and integrity, our humility and contentment, our courage and endurance, our mercy and good works, our love for God and our caring for others. If we lose our saltiness—those unique traits that Jesus described in the Beatitudes—then we have lost our influence in the world. We can no longer act as a preservative in our society. We can no longer act as seasoning, awakening a hunger for God in the souls around us.

What does it mean to be distinct from the world? Does it mean that we walk around with beatific smiles and with our eyes cast heavenward? No. We don't have to be "weird" in order to be distinct. We can enjoy life and all the good things life has to offer. We can work, laugh, watch TV, work out at the gym, shop at the mall, go out to dinner, take in a movie, go on a cruise, and all the other things that people love to do.

So how do we become distinct? We live out a different set of values than the people around us. We live for a different purpose. Instead of chasing fortune, fame, power and pleasure, we pursue good character and influence. We "do everything in love." We live out the values of the Beatitudes.

Once we start living by the Beatitudes, it's a lot harder to be rude, demanding and impatient toward the people around us. Instead of walking past the lonely old man on the park bench, we stop to chat with him. Instead of ogling the waitress, we notice that she's having a hard day and we give her a word of encouragement. Instead of rolling our eyes at the noisy kids in the dentist's office, we put down the magazine and chat with them about their favorite TV show or their trip to Disney World. It's all about influence.

As people of the Beatitudes, we make a commitment to stop speaking negatively about other people. We stop gossiping behind their backs. We start affirming them to their faces. Imagine the influence we would have if we made a point of speaking well of our bosses, our coworkers, our employees and our customers. It's all about influence.

What kind of influence would we have if we would simply do everything—*everything!*—in love? What would the world around us look like if the people we meet started to imitate our example, if they started doing everything in love? Imagine how the salt and light would spread!

THE LIGHT OF THE WORLD

Jesus also said, "You are the light of the world" (Matt. 5:14). Light illuminates. It chases away shadows of sin and evil. It highlights beauty. It enables us to see the path ahead. As we become the kind of people Jesus describes in the Beatitudes, we become lamps of influence and illumination, shedding His light into the lives of the people around us and casting a radiance throughout society.

Throughout the Sermon on the Mount, Jesus issues a call that could be summarized this way: "Don't be like the rest of the world. Stand out by taking a stand. Don't live for yourself, for money, fame, power and pleasure. Live for God. Serve others. Be the salt that preserves your society and saves it from corruption. Be a light to illuminate the path of life for the people around you. Be distinct from the world around you. Be an influence and an agent of change."

Clearly, Jesus is not telling us that we should go hide our light in a cave or a monastery somewhere. He wants the light of our influence to shine throughout our homes, our neighborhoods and our world. He said, "A city on a hill cannot be hidden. Neither do people light a lamp and put it under a bowl. Instead they put it on its stand, and it gives light to everyone in the house. In the same way, let your light shine before men, that they may see your good deeds and praise your Father in heaven" (Matt. 5:14-16).

When our light shines brightly into the world, our influence for God becomes irresistible. So here is a three-step process for becoming people of influence, as God intended us to be:

- *Step One:* Become people of character, godliness and integrity—the kind of people Jesus described in the Beatitudes. Be distinct—don't be bland. Don't blend in to the world around you. Maintain your saltiness.

- *Step Two:* Go out into the world—into the streets and malls, the offices and factories, the university campuses and military bases, wherever the people are—and let your light shine for everyone to see. Be a role model. Live a distinct and exemplary life so that everyone around you can see the character of God living in you.

- *Step Three:* When people notice that you are different, and they ask why you live such a different kind of life, give them an answer that reflects well on God. Say, for example, "My goal in life is to become more and more like Jesus Christ every day. I often fall short of that goal, but when I fail, I just pick myself up off the ground and keep pursuing that goal."

Former Arkansas governor Mike Huckabee recalls attending a life-changing event the summer before his senior year in high school. That event was Explo '72, a Campus Crusade for Christ conference that drew 100,000 students from the U.S. and 75 other nations to the Cotton Bowl in Dallas, in June 1972. The event featured inspirational speakers, plus concerts by Love Song, Larry Norman, Children of the Day, Johnny Cash and other artists. Dr. Billy Graham spoke on the final night, and his theme was, "You can touch the world. One person can make a difference."

Dr. Graham ended his message by asking that the stadium lights be extinguished. Instantly, the crowd was plunged into darkness. Then Dr. Graham did a simple yet startling thing: He lit a candle. Huckabee was at the far end of the stadium, yet even at that distance, he clearly saw the light from the lone candle in the evangelist's hand.

Dr. Graham held out his candle and lit another held by Dr. Bill Bright, Campus Crusade's founder. Then those two men lit the candles of two other people on the stage. Then all of them lit still more candles held by others. In this way, the flame from that first candle spread from person to person, all around the stadium.

Within minutes, the light of 100,000 candles shone across the stadium, lighting up the night sky. Huckabee recalls that the light of all of those candles was so bright that people who lived near the stadium called the fire department and reported a fire at the Cotton Bowl!

Huckabee says he carried the lesson of that demonstration with him throughout his life: "I realized, more than anything, that the darker things are, the more difference even the tiniest light will make. . . . We live in a dark spiritual age—all the more reason for you to hold your candle high and hold it out to others! The darker the world gets, the brighter your light will shine."[5]

Those who live out the values of the Beatitudes will influence our world for the better. They will become agents of change and transformation. They will be the salt of the earth, the light of the world. They will bring healing to our troubled and dysfunctional society.

When people think of the influence of Jesus, they probably think first of how He preached to the masses. But far more important than His preaching to the masses was the influence he had on a few individuals. He spent the bulk of His time investing in the lives of 12 men. He poured His life into them, and He changed the world through them.

Jesus started with a dozen of the most ordinary people you can imagine. Most were uneducated fishermen. One was a despised tax collector. Another was a political radical. There wasn't one man among the Twelve who seemed destined for greatness. None were great leaders or great communicators or great strategic thinkers. But Jesus spent three years teaching them and mentoring them—in short, *influencing* them at a deep and profound level.

When He wanted to teach them how to pray, He didn't merely give them a set of instructions. He led them out into an olive grove, got down on His knees, and prayed with them through the night. When He wanted to teach the Twelve about servanthood, He didn't preach a sermon. He took a basin of water and a towel, and then He went around to each of them and washed their feet. His influence was expressed in His active example. His message was not, "Do what I say," but "Do as I do." His call to them was not, "Hear me," but "Follow me."

If you want to be a person of influence, then follow the Ultimate Example. Follow Jesus, and do as He did. Jesus took a bunch of uneducated underachievers and, in just three years, He molded them into a force to be reckoned with. And after He left them, they spread His message, expanded His church and shook the world to its foundations. Even while the young Christian Church was being persecuted, and Christians were being imprisoned, tortured and killed, the Church grew at an astounding rate. Within a few decades, that tiny handful of followers became a movement of hundreds of thousands of believers spread from one end of the Roman Empire to the other.

Those early followers of Jesus changed the world—and the world is still changing because of Jesus and His followers. Columnist Philip Yancey wrote the following in *Christianity Today*:

> Sociologists in Latin America have documented how the act of conversion can lead to significant social change. A man goes forward to receive Christ at an evangelistic meeting. He joins a local church, which counsels him to stop getting drunk on weekends. . . . He starts showing up at work on Monday mornings, and eventually gets promoted to foreman. With new faith and a renewed sense of worth, he stops beating his wife and becomes a better father to his children. Newly empowered, his wife takes a job that allows her to afford education for her children. Multiply that by several scores of converted citizens, and soon the economic base of the entire village rises.[6]

That is how salt and light transform lives—and transform society. That's the power of influence.

HOW TO BE A PERSON OF INFLUENCE

My friend Dr. David Uth, senior pastor of the First Baptist Church in Orlando, recently told me the following:

> I have always said that it's too bad that dying is the last thing you do, because it teaches you so much about living. The Swedish

chemist Alfred Nobel was shaken by a glimpse of his own death
when a French newspaper accidentally published his obituary
in 1888, while he was still alive.

Nobel had made a fortune—hundreds of millions of dollars—from the invention of dynamite and from his business as
a manufacturer of armaments. The obituary read, "The mer-
chant of death is dead. Dr. Alfred Nobel, who became rich by
finding ways to kill more people faster than ever before, died
yesterday." Nobel decided he was living for the wrong reasons
and he was leaving a legacy that would make him a hated man.
So he founded the Nobel Prize as his legacy, a reminder of the
turning point in his life.

Nobel was fortunate because he got to read his own obituary. Most of us will never get to read our own obituary, but at
least we can live our lives so that when our obituary is written,
it will be a legacy we can be at peace with.

Acquiring fortune, achieving fame, pursuing power, chasing pleasure—if these are your life goals, my friend, then you are busily frittering
away your life. Why waste your life on such meaningless goals when you
could invest your life in making a lasting difference in the lives of others
and in the world around you? Let me suggest some practical ways that
you can become involved in having an eternal influence on your world.

1. *Be careful what you say.* Think of the effect your words have on the
people around you, especially young people. Jamie Brown is formerly
the Special Assistant to the U.S. President for Legislative Affairs. Her
duties included helping prepare Supreme Court nominees for their
confirmation hearings. She was recently hired for a senior position in
Google's Washington office. She once told me that we adults need to
be aware of our influence on the next generation—and we need to consider the impact of our words on impressionable young minds.

"A casual throwaway comment about a young person's potential,"
she said, "could severely, permanently limit that boy or girl. So be careful what you say! When we talk to young people, our message should always be, 'I believe in you! I know you can do it! I'm proud of you!'" It's
true. We easily forget that words have the power to cut to the core of the

human soul. We need to wield that power for the purpose of healing others, using our words as a surgeon's scalpel, not a butcher's knife.

2. *Be aware that others are watching your example.* People are watching you all the time. Your children take notice when you break the speed limit or sneak home office supplies from work. Your employees take notice when you fudge on your taxes or mistreat customers. Your co-workers notice when you cheat on your expense account.

You have a platform, and you are continually influencing the people around you for better or worse. So live your life as if you are under a microscope, even in your private moments. Make sure there is no conflict between your words and the way you live your life. Practice total integrity and you will have an enduring influence.

3. *Use your accomplishments and your influence to inspire the next generation.* Florence Griffith-Joyner, better known as Flo-Jo, was an African-American track and field athlete who attained world records in the 100- and 200-meter events. She won three gold medals and one silver at the 1988 Olympic Games in Seoul, Korea. In September 1998, the world was stunned to learn that Flo-Jo had died in her sleep. Her life was cut short by a previously undiagnosed brain abnormality that caused a massive seizure, which stopped her breathing.

I met Flo-Jo at an awards dinner in 1995, and she told me her story of growing up poor in South Central Los Angeles. When she was eight years old, she met the great boxing champ Sugar Ray Robinson. "Sugar Ray looked me in the eye," she said, "and he told me, 'It doesn't matter where you come from, what your color is, or what the odds are against you. All that matters is that you have a dream, that you believe you can do it, and that you commit yourself to that dream. Do that, and it *can* happen—and it *will* happen.' Right then and there, I was sold. I was just eight years old, but I was all fired up about what my future could be."

Sugar Ray Robinson was a man of influence, and he changed that little girl's life. There are young people around you, within your sphere of influence. They are hungry for affirmation and inspiration. Wouldn't *you* like to be the "Sugar Ray Robinson" in the life of a young person?

4. *Take advantage of every "moment of influence."* When you go to the movies with friends, don't just sit back and be entertained. Think about the message of the movie; and when you go out for coffee afterwards,

discuss the film you just watched in terms of your faith and your values. When you watch the news or a TV show with your child, press the mute button during the commercials and talk about the events or themes you've just viewed. Find out what your children think, and let them hear your views. Seize those "moments of influence" and use them to impact the lives of the people around you.

5. *When you make a mistake, admit it.* Nobody's perfect, so when you blow it, turn your errors into object lessons that others can learn from. Professional golfer Lee Janzen, who twice won the U.S. Open, once said, "We have a perfect God, but we are imperfect people. God is always willing to use a willing heart."

What's the point of pretending you're perfect when it's plain for all to see that you are not? Show people that you are humble and honest enough to admit your mistakes. You'll be amazed to discover that people respect you even more when they hear you say, "I was wrong." Most important of all, you'll set a positive example for the people around you.

6. *Be generous with your time and resources.* People of influence consciously invest their time and money in the people around them, and especially in young people. When I think of influence expressed through generosity, I think of basketball coach Paul Westphal.

After a stellar career as a player for the Celtics, Suns and Super-Sonics, Paul Westphal went into coaching (he is currently an assistant coach with the NBA's Dallas Mavericks). Paul is consciously and intensely committed to being a positive influence on young people. While serving as head coach of the Phoenix Suns, he also volunteered as an unpaid basketball coach at Scottsdale Chaparral High, where his son, Michael, was a player. He once said, "I got the same thrills at Chaparral as I did coaching the Suns."

For Coach Westphal, his role as a dad and as a positive influence on his kids always trumped his role as an NBA coach. During one NBA game, Paul Westphal called a timeout, called his team to the bench and began diagramming a crucial play. He felt a tug at his arm. Looking down, he saw seven-year-old Michael looking up at him. Westphal took a dollar bill from his pocket, handed it to the boy without a word and Michael dashed off for the concession stand to buy a soda. Westphal turned his attention back to the clipboard and the team. Many coaches would have blown a gasket in such a situation. Paul Westphal is more than a coach. He's a man of influence.

Another way Paul Westphal and his wife, Cindy, use their influence is by promoting adoption. During Paul's years as head coach of the Phoenix Suns, he and Cindy were actively involved in the work of a Phoenix-based adoption agency, Christian Family Care. In 1989, the Suns decided to retire the jersey Westphal wore in his playing days and display it on the Suns' "Ring of Honor." Jerry Colangelo, the Suns' owner, had planned a halftime ceremony at which Westphal would be named a "Phoenix Suns Legend" and would be given gifts valued in the tens of thousands of dollars.

When told of Colangelo's plans, Paul Westphal asked the team owner to donate all that money to an education fund administered by Christian Family Care, with the fund to be named in honor of Paul's late father. As usual, Paul's number-one priority was influence.

7. *Make all of your decisions on the basis of ethics and integrity, not personal advantage.* Whenever you make a decision, consider how that decision will impact your influence on others. Think of all the people who look up to you as a role model and then ask yourself, "What will they think of my decision? Will they see an example they want to follow? Or will they be disillusioned?"

In *The Power of Ethical Management*, authors Ken Blanchard and Norman Vincent Peale give us a wise template for making principled decisions that enhance our positive influence with others. This template is a quiz called "The Ethics Check" and consists of three simple questions:

1. *Is it legal?* Will I be violating either civil law or company policy?
2. *Is it balanced?* Is it fair to all concerned?
3. *How will it make me feel about myself?* Would I feel good if my decision was published in the newspaper? Would I feel good if my family knew about it?[7]

As we set a good example through the decisions we make, we must also use our influence in helping young people learn to make good, ethical decisions. I once heard a story about a young man at college who wrote a letter to his dad. The son wrote, "Hey, Dad! The stamp wasn't canceled on your last letter, so I peeled it off and reused it. I'm sending you this letter for free!" A few days later, the young man received a reply from his father. A brand-new, unused stamp was pasted at the top of the page—but his father had scrawled a big black X across the stamp. Underneath it, the father wrote, "Dear son, your debt to the United States government has been paid. Love, Dad."

This father was a person of influence. He seized an opportunity to teach his son an important lesson: If you maintain your integrity in the small things, the big things will take care of themselves.

The future history of our world will be written by the next generation. And the future of that generation will be shaped by our influence. There are few things in this world more important than the example we set for our kids and the people around us.

Florida financier Jimmy Hewitt is the man who talked me into coming to Orlando to start a new NBA franchise. He's a big fan of Florida State football, and he recently told me about a conversation he had with Bobby Bowden, head football coach of the Florida State Seminoles. Bobby is in his late seventies and still coaching. He could have retired long ago as one of the winningest coaches in college football history, but he continues to coach players and influence young lives. Jimmy asked Coach Bowden why he continues to coach the Seminoles.

"You can't take a trophy to heaven," Coach Bowden replied. He went on to say that he's not interested in becoming a *former* coach. He still has lives to influence and work to do. He can't influence young lives from an easy chair.

I love that spirit. Coach Bowden knows what he's talking about. You can't take a trophy to heaven, but your influence is a legacy that never dies. When you and I face God in eternity, He's not going to ask to see our trophies. He's going to ask how our lives affected the people around us, especially the young people.

A TROUBLING DREAM

Martin Niemöller was a German U-boat commander in World War I. Known as "the Scourge of Malta," he was awarded the Iron Cross for sending an untold number of Allied ships to the bottom of the Mediterranean Sea. After the war, he studied theology at Münster Seminary and was ordained an Evangelical Lutheran pastor.

Shortly after Adolf Hitler came to power in 1934, Niemöller, as a representative of the Protestant church, met personally with the Nazi leader. Hitler promised that the Nazi government would not interfere with the church, nor would it institute restrictions or persecution against the Jews. To his lasting regret, Niemöller believed Hitler's assurances. By the mid-1930s, Niemöller realized that Hitler had lied to him. He saw danger looming for both the Jews and the Christian church, so he joined with fellow churchmen (including Dietrich Bonhoeffer and Karl Barth) in founding the Confessing Church, which opposed the policies of the Nazi government.

As a result of his anti-Nazi activities, Martin Niemöller was arrested on July 1, 1937. Convicted the following year, he spent eight years in the Sachsenhausen and Dachau concentration camps. Niemöller was actually scheduled for execution when, in mid-1945, Allied forces liberated him and his fellow prisoners. After the war, Niemöller confessed that he had not done enough to oppose the murderous Nazi regime when he had the chance. Out of that sense of regret, he wrote these famous lines:

> First they came for the Communists,
> —but I was not a Communist so I did not speak out.
> Then they came for the Socialists and the Trade Unionists,
> —but I was neither, so I did not speak out.
> Then they came for the Jews,
> —but I was not a Jew so I did not speak out.
> And when they came for me, there was no one left to speak out
> for me.

Niemöller died in 1984 at age 92. Shortly before his death, he shared with a few friends that he had been having a troubling, recurring dream. In it, he saw the day of the final judgment of the human race by the Lord Jesus Christ. To his surprise, Niemöller recognized Adolf Hitler standing alongside Jesus, weeping uncontrollably. The Lord had His arm around Hitler, and He said to one of the most murderous men known to history, "Why did you do it, Adolf? Why did you create the concentration camps? What drove you to murder so many innocent people?"

"I didn't know!" Hitler replied. "No one ever told me about Your love for me."

And Niemöller related that at this point in the dream, he always awoke with a start, drenched in cold sweat and consumed with guilt. He remembered his face-to-face meeting with Adolf Hitler, and it occurred to him that what Hitler said in the dream was true. He, Martin Niemöller, had met with Hitler as a representative of the Church—yet he had never said a word to Hitler about the love of Jesus Christ. He never once said, "God loves you, Herr Hitler. He sent His Son to die for you. If You will simply accept the free gift of His forgiveness, you can have peace with God."

Could World War II have been averted? Could the Holocaust have been stopped before it began? Martin Niemöller went to his grave wondering whether history might have been different if he had only said to Hitler, "Jesus loves you."

There is someone in your life who desperately needs your influence. A few caring, compassionate words could make all the difference in that person's life. Don't risk being haunted by regret: "If only I had spoken up; if only I had used my influence . . ." Speak up! Be a role model to some young person who needs your influence.

Don't waste your life chasing fortune, fame, power and pleasure. Make an eternal difference in someone's life. Pursue influence.

PURSUE PARENTHOOD

I have 19 sons and daughters. That's right: 19.

I'm "Dad" to 4 birth children, 14 kids by international adoption and 1 by remarriage. They've all left home and gone off to college or the Marine Corps or the wedding chapel—but there was a time, not so long ago, when I had 16 teenagers living under one roof. And let me tell you, that roof was rocking!

To me, parenthood is not merely a matter of producing biological offspring. After all, the vast majority of the children I raised were connected to me by love, not DNA. Whenever people ask how many children I have, I say, "Nineteen, 14 of which are adopted—but I forget which 14." Every kid needs to be parented—but sometimes, because of death, divorce or abandonment, a child may be deprived of one or both biological parents. Does that mean that he or she has to go through life unparented? Not if you and I have anything to say about it!

There are many ways to "pursue parenthood." A "parent" could be a birth parent, a step-parent, an adoptive parent, a grandparent, a godparent, an aunt or uncle, a parental figure like a coach or mentor, or anyone else with the capacity to love and nurture a young person. So even if you never have birth children of your own, you can pursue parenthood.

Everyone can. And everyone should.

THE FOUNDATION OF MY LIFE

There are few joys in the world that compare with being in the delivery room, watching a child being born. I have welcomed four birth-children into our family, and I held each of them in my hands as the doctor cut their umbilical cord. I kissed them, blessed them and helped name each one. I looked into their faces, prayed for them and told them that God had set a wonderful, wide-open future before them. Without question, that is one of the most profound worship experiences any parent can have.

I have also welcomed 14 adopted children into our family. Instead of a hospital delivery room, I stood in an airport, my insides swarming with butterflies, my heart in my throat, waiting to see that big jet plane arriving from South Korea, the Philippines, Romania or Brazil. Those planes have brought 14 amazing children swooping into my life. I didn't get to cut their umbilical cords, but just as I did with my birth kids, I have kissed them, blessed them and helped give them new American names. I have looked into their faces, prayed for them and told them about the wonderful, wide-open future God has for them.

Welcoming those 14 children into our home was every bit as touching and unforgettable as watching my birth-children being born. Each of those experiences is indelibly etched in my memory.

Perhaps the reason I'm so fervent and fanatical on the subject of parenting kids is that I have such a deep appreciation for all the advantages and blessings my own parents gave me. I have truly had a wonderful life, and I can look back and see that so much of who I am today is the result of the foundation my parents laid for me during my childhood.

I was born in Philadelphia in 1940, and my father named me Patrick Livingston Murphy Williams. He probably would've given me even more Scotch-Irish names, but there was only room for four names on my birth certificate. I discovered what an advantage it was to have so many names the first time my mother hollered at me for getting into mischief. I don't remember what I did, but I remember those words: "Patrick Livingston Murphy Williams, come here this instant!" But by the time she had finished, my Keds sneakers had carried me two blocks from home.

My dad, Jim Williams, gave me a baseball glove to play with when I was three, and he took me to my first baseball game when I was seven—Cleveland at Philadelphia in a double-header at Shibe Park. I yelled my head off and downed hot dogs until I was sick, and had the time of my life. That day, I knew I would make my career in professional sports. Of course, I thought I would be a baseball player—and for two years in the minors, I was. But I spent the rest of my career in sports management, and that one special day at the ballpark was the catalyst for it all. So thanks, Dad.

Though I usually played catch with Dad, my mother, Ellen Williams, also encouraged my baseball dreams. We had positioned two rocks in our backyard—a "home plate" rock and a "pitcher's mound" rock. Mom would pitch to me and I would practice my swing, then we'd trade places and I would pitch to her.

One time, when I was seven, I hurled my best fastball, and Mom took a swing. The bat connected like a thunderclap, and she lined that ball straight into my eye. I dropped to the ground like a sack of flour—out cold. Mom thought she'd killed me. Moments later, when I came to, I had the most agonizing headache imaginable. I also had a huge shiner. I wore that black eye as a badge of honor—an honest-to-goodness baseball wound!

My single-minded passion for sports dominated my young life. I lived and breathed sports, especially baseball. I had closets and filing cabinets filled with sports memorabilia, including a collection of players' autographs. Because I wanted to be a ballplayer one day, I imitated the habits of my heroes.

I once read a magazine article about Rogers Hornsby, the hard-hitting second baseman for the St. Louis Browns and Cardinals. The article said that Hornsby never went to the movies because the flickering light might damage his eyes. I figured if it's good enough for Rogers "The Rajah" Hornsby, it was good enough for Kid Williams! I avoided movie theaters after that.

Mom made sure I knew there was more to life than baseball. She got me involved with Cub Scouts and took me to museums, the zoo, concerts and Broadway shows. The arts were very much a part of our family life, and I enjoyed a well-rounded upbringing. So thanks, Mom.

MY MANY PARENTS

My birth parents weren't the only ones who "parented" me and helped chart the course of my life. Mom's younger brother, Bill Parsons, was a teacher and coach. He had a major influence on my life by taking me to professional and college baseball games. He taught me to keep score on a scorecard, and I learned how to do arithmetic by checking box scores and batting averages.

Uncle Bill idolized Ted Williams, the great Red Sox leftfielder and legendary hitter. And because Ted Williams was Uncle Bill's hero, he was my hero too. If I refused to eat my Brussels sprouts, he'd say, "You know, Ted would have eaten his Brussels sprouts. You think maybe that's why he's such a great hitter?" Well, then I'd have *two* helpings of Brussels sprouts! So thanks, Uncle Bill, for your influence on my life.

One day, when I was seven, our family was visiting at my grandparents' home in Ardmore, Pennsylvania. I was sitting on the front porch, a scorecard balanced on my knees, listening to a radio broadcast of a game between the Philadelphia A's and the Washington Senators. As the game progressed, I marked the boxes on the scorecard and I realized that the A's Bill McCahn was pitching a no-hitter. In fact, an error by first baseman Ferris Fain was all that kept McCahn from having a perfect game.

When the game was over, I ran into the house and dashed upstairs to my grandfather's room. His health had been declining for a long time, and he was sick in bed. Being so young, I didn't understand how sick he was. As I ran into the room, I called out, "Grandpop! Bill McCahn just pitched a no-hitter!"

I think he smiled faintly, but he was too weak to reply. To my knowledge, those were the last words my grandfather heard. Within hours, he was gone.

Looking back, I realize that while my mom and dad laid the foundation for my life, there were many other family members who built on that foundation and helped make me who I am today. They encouraged my obsession with sports. They affirmed me and strengthened my self-confidence. They taught me values and exemplified character. In a real sense, I was parented not only by my birth parents, but by my Uncle Bill, my grandparents and many other caring people in my family.

But the "parenting" of young Pat Williams didn't end with my family. When my father died in a car accident shortly after my graduation from college, Mr. Littlejohn, the owner of the Spartanburg Phillies, became a surrogate father to me. When I was in my twenties, all the questions and problems I would've taken to my dad, I took to Mr. Littlejohn. He always had a wise, fatherly answer. Mr. Littlejohn had two daughters, but no sons, and I believe I became the son he never had.

He invested in me, affirmed me, mentored me and loved me as much as any parent could. I felt blessed to know him.

So when I say, "pursue parenthood," I'm not saying you should go out and have a lot of kids! I'm really saying that you should look around and see if there are any kids in your sphere of influence who need a parent's love, a parent's guidance, a parent's affirmation and a parent's blessing. There are so many kids with so many needs, and so few parents to go around. When you think of the joy that comes from filling that need in a child's life, false values like chasing money, fame, power and pleasure just don't stack up!

If you want your life to truly matter, if you want to leave a legacy that never dies, then pursue parenthood. Ask yourself, "What can I do to fill that hole in the life of a child?"

PARENTING, MENTORING AND COACHING KIDS

Kids need a lot of things in order to grow strong, healthy, and confident about their future. They need good nutrition, a good education, exercise, fresh air and sunshine. But above all, kids need parents. According to the U.S. Department of Health and Human Services, children who are deprived of one or both parents are significantly more prone to emotional and psychiatric problems, substance abuse, early sexual activity, suicide, poor school performance and antisocial behavior.[1] So whenever we see a child at risk, a child who lacks a mom or dad or both parents, we need to ask ourselves: "What can I do to fill that gap in this child's life?"

Nathan Baker, a coach at Campbell University in North Carolina, told me, "I grew up in a little town with one stoplight. My younger brother and I were raised in a single-parent home. Mom worked hard to provide for us, but it was hard for her. My high school basketball coach, Gary Williams, befriended me and mentored me and became almost a substitute father. He and his family took me places I couldn't afford to go to, and they invited me to church. By my junior year, I was 6' 6" and I played on Coach Williams's varsity team.

"I attended a revival at their church, and I felt the Lord dealing with me, urging me to give my life to Him. I didn't go forward in the meeting. Instead, I got up and drove around for a while, and finally stopped at Coach Williams's house. I went in and he knew right away that there was a struggle going on inside me. We talked about it—and then the greatest thing in my life happened. I gave my life to Jesus Christ. I have loved and served Him ever since.

"I look back on that day and wonder: What if Coach Williams hadn't been a part of my life? What if I had not had Coach Williams there as my friend, someone I could talk to about my spiritual struggle? He made all the difference in my life, and he inspired me to become a coach and use my God-given leadership abilities in working with young athletes."

There are many ways to have a positive impact on a young person's life. You can volunteer at your church's youth group, an after-school tutoring program, a youth sports program, a young people's arts program, the local shelter for abused women and children, Big Brothers and Big Sisters, Child Evangelism Fellowship, the soccer-and-literacy program America SCORES, the Points of Light Foundation, MENTOR/ National Mentoring Partnership, and more. One especially effective way to get involved in affecting and improving the lives of children is through Scouts.

Todd Shaw is president of On-Track Ministry and a chaplain in the popular motor sport of karting (formerly known as "go-cart" racing). He told me that when he was a boy, his Scout troop needed an adult leader. "I appointed my dad without his knowledge," Todd recalls, "and he accepted the job (with a little coaxing)." Did Todd's dad quit Scouting when his own kids outgrew it? No way! "Twenty years later," Todd says, "Dad's still very involved in Scouting, and he loves every moment."

Don't you need to be an expert outdoorsman to be a Scout leader? No way! "My dad knew nothing about Scouting," Todd told me, "but that didn't stop him. He took courses, recruited great help, and the end result was a great troop. That experience had a big part in shaping who I am today."

Todd's dad had a positive impact on many other lives besides Todd's. "Of all the memorable things we did in Scouting," Todd told me, "the most meaningful were the service projects our troop did. Every Christmas, we delivered fruit and care baskets to the needy. My father made sure we didn't just drop off the baskets. He showed us how to talk to people and truly listen to them. That was a big factor in the development of my people skills—my ability to strike up a conversation with people I didn't know, and my ability to really reach out and care about people and their needs."

When I was researching and writing two previous books, *Coaching Your Kids to Be Leaders* and *Souls of Steel: How to Build Character in Ourselves and Our Kids*, I interviewed more than 1,600 people from all walks of life. I asked such questions as, "What were the most important factors that influenced you to become a leader or a person of integrity and character?" The two most frequent responses were "My parents" and "Scouting." That should come as no surprise. After all, to be a Scout, young people must make this pledge:

On my honor, I will do my best
To do my duty to God and my country
And to obey the Scout Law;
To help other people at all times;
To keep myself physically strong,
Mentally awake and morally straight.

There was a time when the Boy Scouts of America were considered the most iconic and prototypically American institution in our society. There was no organization that said "mom and apple pie" and "Norman Rockwell's America" like the Boy Scouts. As the moral fabric of our society has begun to unravel, Scouting has come under increasing attack. The organization has been attacked for being "intolerant." Well, it's true that Scouting is intolerant of things that our society has begun to embrace: dishonor and dishonesty, disloyalty and disrespect, impurity and irreligiousness, indifference and ignorance. Scouting teaches respect for God and country, good citizenship, morality and virtue, character and leadership.

The federal government, under pressure from special-interest groups, has sometimes denied Scouts the right to use our national parks for Boy Scout jamborees. A number of United Way chapters and the Pew Charitable Trust have cut off funding for the Scouts. The *Philadelphia Daily*

News ran an outrageous editorial in June 2003, comparing the Boy Scouts to the terror-supporting Taliban.

Since 2003, the city of Philadelphia has been using legal strong-arm tactics to evict the Cradle of Liberty Council of the Boy Scouts from their Philly headquarters at 22nd and Winter Streets, even though the city gave the Scouts that site "in perpetuity" back in 1929. One tactic the city employed was to raise the Scouts' annual rent on the building from $1 to $200,000. These kinds of attacks from the forces of so-called "political correctness" are increasing in frequency and ferocity.

An editorial in *Investor's Business Daily* cited a survey that found that "63 percent of U.S. Air Force Academy graduates, 68 percent of West Point graduates, 70 percent of Annapolis graduates and 85 percent of FBI agents, not to mention 26 of the first 29 astronauts, were all Scouts." In view of those statistics, the editorial writer asked, "How is it that an organization that has done immeasurable good for tens of millions of boys [is now viewed by some as] one of America's most notorious and dangerous hate groups?"[2]

In the past 100 years, Scouting hasn't changed, but our society has—and not for the better. Scouting builds character and leadership skills in young people—and it provides substitute parental figures in the lives of many kids who do not have a mom or dad in their everyday lives. I urge you to consider Scouting as a place where you can "pursue substitute parenthood."

TIPS FROM A PARENTING VETERAN

I recently had former NBA player Allan Houston as a guest on my local radio show. The former Knicks and Pistons shooting guard now travels the country, speaking on subjects from fatherhood to faith to entrepreneurship. On my show, he told me what he's learned about fatherhood from his own dad—and from his son.

"Every son wants to be like his father," Allan told me. "My seven-year-old son has a toy shaving kit he brings into the bathroom when I'm shaving. He takes off his shirt and stands in front of the sink next to me, and pretends to shave. And that's a reminder that he's watching me and learning from me what it means to be a man. And it also reminds me where I learned what being a man is all about: my father.

"My dad was a basketball coach, and he's not shy to let people know where I got my jump shot from! In fact, he still believes he can out-shoot me. As a coach, he taught me the fundamentals of the game of basketball. He knew I'd have an advantage against my opponents if I was prepared and I knew what to expect out on the court. In the same way, he taught me the fundamentals of life so that I would be equipped to deal with every situation life might throw at me.

"My father not only taught me how to shoot a jump shot, but how to gain trust by always being honest, how to take responsibility for my actions and how to show respect for others. He taught me that making money is not as important as how you treat people while you're making it. He taught me the fundamentals of life, and now I'm teaching them to my son." That's sound parenting advice from Allan Houston, who is both a great father and a grateful son.

A few years ago, I was in Boston to promote *How to Be Like Mike: Life Lessons about Basketball's Best*, my book on the life of legendary NBA star Michael Jordan. In the morning, I did an interview on a local TV talk show. That evening, I went to the Fleet Center, where Michael and the Washington Wizards were playing the Boston Celtics. I got to visit with Mike in the locker room before the game.

"Hey, Williams," he said, "I saw you on TV this morning, talking about the book. You know, you're telling all my stories!"

I grinned and said, "You know, Mike, your stories are getting raves from readers all over the country. People write and tell me, 'When you see Mike, thank him for being a role model for the next generation.'"

"Well," Mike replied, "I'm just a product of my mom and dad. Everything I am today is a result of the way James and Deloris Jordan raised me and all the things they taught me."

What a tribute to his parents! And it's true: So much of what a child becomes in life is a result of the foundation parents lay through their words and example.

I certainly don't claim to have been a perfect dad, and I don't claim to have 19 perfect kids. We've had our share of problems, conflict and trials in the Williams mega-household. But I have learned a lot from both my triumphs and mistakes as a father. These children came from a variety of backgrounds, experiences and even languages and cultures. Yet our little mini-United Nations has succeeded pretty well, and I believe this is due to some principles we learned and employed in our rather unusual family system.

Let me share a few tips from a parenting veteran.

Tip 1: Give Kids the Gift of Your Time

When you spend time with your kids, you show them they are important to you and that you value them. Take time to talk to them, look them in the eye, listen to them, hug them, play games with them, share meals with them, help them with their homework, guide them and affirm them. Kids especially need the gift of your time when there is stress and upheaval in their life—for example, when their world is being rocked by divorce.

Bryan Davis, director of All-Pro Dad, a Tampa-based ministry of encouragement for fathers, sent me this email with 10 practical ways we can make more time for our children:

1. Commit to a family mealtime each day.
2. Write your children's activities into your schedule book—in ink!
3. Identify one thing on your weekly schedule that you can do without and replace it with "kid time."
4. Take one of your children along when you run errands.
5. Volunteer to participate in a regularly scheduled child activity, such as coaching a softball team or helping out with a school activity.
6. Identify one children's show on TV that you secretly like to watch and make a point of watching it with your child.
7. Develop an interest in a hobby you and your child can enjoy together.
8. If your work requires that you travel, take one of your children with you when your business trip can be extended into a long weekend.
9. If your work schedule is flexible, start your workday earlier so that you can get home earlier in the afternoon to be with your family.

10. Leave your work, cellular phone and pager at home when you go on family vacations and outings.

The great Boston Celtics center Bill Russell, who was named to the NBA's 50th Anniversary All-Time Team in 1996, was once asked by an interviewer to name his proudest accomplishment. Now this is a man with a long list of accomplishments to choose from. During his 13-year career in the NBA, he was the linchpin of a Celtics dynasty that won 11 NBA championships. Five times, he was named the NBA's Most Valuable Player. What did he name as the achievement he was proudest of? Raising his 12-year-old daughter.

After his 1973 divorce, he became a single parent with custody of his daughter. He recalls, "I asked her the first morning we were together, 'Are you sure you want to do this? 'Cause you're 12 years old and I don't know anything about 12-year-old girls. . . . I can only make you two promises: One, I will love you until I die. The other is, when you leave here to go into the world, you will be better able to take care of yourself than any man you'll meet anywhere.'"

Bill Russell devoted himself to his new role as a single parent. He gave his daughter the gift of his time, attention, caring, affection, advice and encouragement. The result? "That young lady," he recalls, "was an honor student at Mercer Island High School and went to Georgetown and then graduated from Harvard Law School. And there's only one thing wrong with her going to Harvard law school: she now thinks she's certified to tell me what to do."[3]

Tip 2: Affirm Unstintingly

Always convey unconditional acceptance and affirmation of youngsters, whether they win or lose, succeed or fail. Even if the child doesn't perform as well as you'd hoped, never let your disappointment show. If you only affirm and praise a kid when he succeeds, he'll sense that your acceptance is conditional—and when he fails, he'll feel condemned and devalued.

In their book *Raising Cain: Protecting the Emotional Life of Boys*, child psychologists Dan Kindlon and Michael Thompson tell the story of a dad, Raul, who took his six-year-old son on a ski vacation. The boy had a hard time getting the hang of skiing, and he spent more time falling on his face and picking himself up than he spent schussing the slopes. But no matter how poorly the boy did on his skis, his dad encouraged him and cheered him on. At the end of the day, Raul asked his son what he liked best about their day on the slopes. The boy's enthusiastic reply: "Watching you watch me ski!"

Kindlon and Thompson conclude, "What really mattered to the boy was not how well or poorly he skied but what his dad thought of him. So it is with most boys in middle childhood: their opinion about whether they are competent depends on how they think their father sees them."[4]

In her book *Balcony People*, Joyce Landorf Heatherley suggests that there are two kinds of people in the world: *evaluators* and *affirmers*. Evaluators look only at the performance of other people. They are focused on finding and correcting the faults and mistakes of other people. Evaluators are focused on the past and love to tell us how miserably we failed.

But affirmers love to build other people up by encouraging them. Affirmers are focused on the future. They love to tell us, "Just pick yourself up and keep going! I know you can do it! I believe in you! I see greatness in you!"

Joyce Landorf Heatherley has a name for those who continually affirm other people. She calls them "balcony people," because they are always in our balcony, applauding us and cheering us on. The world has more than enough evaluators to go around. But there are all too few balcony people in the world.

As parents, mentors, teachers and coaches, we need to become balcony people for our kids. We need to affirm them unstintingly. We need to invest time in their lives, letting them know they are important to us. So we go to their games, recitals, concerts and school plays—all the key moments of their lives. We make a point of always being in the balcony, applauding and cheering wildly, letting them know we are on their side, not on their backs.

Affirmation, Heatherley says, "is based not on what we are, or what we've accomplished, but just on the fact that we are *who* we are. For instance, there is an incredible bonding which happens almost instantaneously when a doctor puts a newborn infant, still wet from the birth canal, upon the mother's bare breast. The mother affirms her baby *not* for what the infant has accomplished or achieved but simply because the baby *is*."[5]

That's how we should affirm the children in our life—both our own children and the children we teach, coach and mentor. We need to tell them, regardless of their performance, "I'm proud of you. I believe in you. I'm on your side whether you make a touchdown or a fumble, whether you break the tape or finish last." We are their balcony people, and we affirm them simply because they are *here*.

Tip 3: Listen to Your Kids

Stop, look and listen: That's shorthand for "*Stop* what you're doing, *look* your kids in the eye and *listen* to what they're really saying to you." All too often, we pretend that we are listening to our kids, but we are really just waiting for the interruption to be over. We say, "Uh-huh. . . . Yeah. . . . That's nice." And we don't hear a word they're saying. Kids aren't stupid. They know when they're being patronized—and being patronized makes them feel devalued and unimportant.

When your kids talk to you, look them square in the eye (with little kids, bend down to their level) and really *listen*. Give your children your full attention. Interact with what they tell you. Take a genuine interest. Let your children know that you enjoy their company and you value the time you spend with them.

And there's another advantage to truly listening to kids with your full attention: They will reciprocate. Harry Rhoads, president of the Washington Speakers Bureau, once told me, "Adults, and particularly parents, must be willing to listen to youngsters in order to build a foundation of two-way communication and trust. Kids listen better when they feel listened to."

Another important facet of listening is *listening for what kids don't say*. Many young people have trouble verbalizing emotions. Sometimes it's because they lack the fully formed verbal skills to put their feelings into words. Or they may fear that if they say what they really feel, they'll be criticized or made to feel foolish or incompetent. So parents, teachers, coaches and mentors must sometimes probe (with care and sensitivity) and find out what kids are feeling beneath the surface of their words.

In the book *Raising Cain*, child psychologist Michael Thompson shares an incident from his own experience as a parent. He and his six-year-old son, Will, were driving through the Green Mountains of Vermont, on their way to visit Will's older sister at camp. As they drove the winding mountain road, a powerful storm whipped up, replete with blinding explosions of lightning and thunder, and a wind-driven downpour that made it hard to see the road.

Thompson slowed the car and concentrated anxiously on his driving. He wondered, *If the storm makes me nervous, how must Will feel?* He checked the rearview mirror. His little boy was wide-eyed and obviously frightened in the back seat.

The storm, though violent, didn't last long. When it ended, Thompson considered different ways to ask his boy about his fears. He considered asking, *You weren't scared, were you, buddy?* But he realized that such a question would only invite his son to deny his feelings. So Thompson asked, "That was a little scary, wasn't it, Will?"

"No, Dad," the boy replied, "that was *very* scary."[6]

Like this father, we need to listen to our kids' feelings, not just their words. We need to give them permission to express their fears, hurts and other emotions, and let them know that their feelings will be heard and accepted.

Tip 4: Focus on Being Real, Not Perfect

We parents make mistakes. When we do, kids know it. So when you mess up, 'fess up. Admit that you were wrong and ask forgiveness. Many parents seem to feel that saying "I'm sorry" to their children will cause them to be diminished in their kids' eyes. Not so! Your kids need to see that you are big enough to admit mistakes—and by doing so, you set a good example for them.

In *Raising Cain*, Dan Kindlon and Michael Thompson point out the need for parents, especially fathers, to be honest and authentic with their kids instead of pretending to be perfect. "Whether conscious or unconscious," they write, "a father's emotional façades don't fool his son past the age of about eight or nine years old. A man who . . . can't admit mistakes, teaches his son a defective model of manhood."[7]

Tip 5: Be Consistent and Dependable

When we keep our promises, we build a sense of security in our kids' lives. When we are consistent and dependable, kids know they can expect us to keep our word—and to follow through on our warnings. Kids need to know that we mean what we say and say what we mean, whether it's a promise to take them to Disney World or a promise to ground them if they break curfew. When we keep our word on a consistent basis, our children learn to see us as reasonable people who behave in predictable ways. That helps them know where the boundary lines are and increases their sense of safety and security.

When it's necessary to correct our kids, we should do so calmly and reasonably—and we should remind them that the consequences they are about to receive are precisely what we told them to expect. Kids—and especially teenagers—will gripe and moan about how unfair you're being. But whether they realize it consciously or not, there is a part of them, deep inside, that is glad you love them enough to be consistent. They feel protected by the dependable guardrails and boundary lines that you have put in place.

Take it from a father of 19: Kids need structure and limits. They need set times for doing homework. They need set limits on TV and other entertainment. And they need a set bedtime. They will fight your rules and test them at every opportunity, but you have to be the parent and maintain your rules, your structure and your authority.

Tip 6: Always Discipline in Love, Not Anger

If a blow-up happens and you're angry with your kids, it's time for a "time-out"—for you and for them. Take a break for 5 to 10 minutes to calm down, reflect and think rationally and constructively about your next move. When you're calm and collected, talk to your kids—and don't let them provoke you into getting mad. If you lose control of your emotions, you lose control of the situation—and your kids get the upper hand. As long as you remain calm and rational—no matter how hysterical the child becomes—you demonstrate that you are in control.

When you get stopped for speeding, does the officer blow his top and start ranting at you? No. He is unfailingly polite. He calls you "Sir" or "Ma'am," as the case may be. He writes the ticket in a businesslike matter, hands it to you, and says, "Have a nice day." Why? Because the police are trained to maintain a firm but calm professionalism. By doing so, they convey to you that they are in control of the situation. So when you have to "arrest" the behavior of your kids, take a cue from the traffic cop. Keep your voice firm and low. Keep your emotions in check. Show your kids who's in control. And tell them to have a nice day.

When you have to discipline your kids, avoid using the word "punishment." You don't want your kids to be "punished." You want them to be authentically, lovingly *disciplined*. It will transform the way we administer consequences to our kids if we remember that the words "discipline" and "disciple" are both derived from the Latin root word *discipulus* (a disciple, a person who has been well trained and instructed). So, instead of punishing our kids, let's make disciples of them.

Tip 7: Set a Good Example

One of the most important duties you have as a parent (or parent substitute) is to be an inspirational role model for that child. Remember, those kids are watching your every move. They are learning what it means to be a responsible and effective adult by watching how you live your life. They are checking to see if what you say matches what you do. When you make ethical decisions and respond to pressures and crises, they are taking mental notes and filing them away for future reference.

In December 2007, Club Libby Lu, the Chicago-based retail chain that sells clothing and accessories for young girls, announced the winner of its nationwide Hannah Montana essay contest. (*Hannah Montana* is a Disney Channel sitcom for kids.) A six-year-old girl from a town near Dallas, Texas, won the grand prize, which included airfare and tickets to a sold-out Hannah Montana concert in Albany, New York. The winning essay began with this heartbreaking sentence: "My daddy died this year in Iraq."

According to the child's mother, the soldier, identified as Sgt. Jonathon Menjivar, had been killed six months earlier in a roadside bombing. After the winner was announced, however, contest organizers learned that the Defense Department had no record of anyone by that name having died in Iraq. The essay was a lie.

Questioned by contest officials and the media, the mother admitted to the deception. "We wrote the essay, and that's what we did to win," she said. "We did whatever we could do to win."[8]

What a tragic legacy to leave to your child: "We did whatever we could do to win." Another way to put that: "I'm willing to do anything—including lying and cheating—to get money, fame, power and pleasure." With parents like that, is it any wonder that the world is in moral and spiritual free fall? As someone once observed, "Our kids will become what we are, so we'd better become what we want them to be."

But what if we've already ruined our good example? What if we have stumbled badly in life—and our kids know it? At that point, we have to be very clear with our kids, admit our sins and point out the crucial life lessons of our failures. In April 2008, I received a letter from Jerry, an inmate in a California prison. He had received two of my books, *The Warrior Within* and *Coaching Your Kids to Be Leaders*, and he was in the process of reading them. He wrote:

> God is good and He's watching over me. He's continuing His work in and through me. Please pray for me that God would shine His light into the dark areas of my heart. And also please pray for my son as he struggles to process what I've done—the sins of his father, the disappointment over my failure to be there for him when he needs me most. Please pray that the lines of communication become very clear as I try to teach him to take a different path than the one I've taken.

I do pray for Jerry, and for the tough challenge he has of being a dad to his son while he's in prison. And I pray for all the moms and dads who have taken a wrong turn in life, leaving their kids to struggle with feelings of disappointment and disillusionment. I hope you'll join me in praying for them and learning from their experience.

My friend, set a good example for your kids.

Tip 8: Don't Give Up on Teens

The toughest year of my life was the year I had 16 teenagers under one roof at the same time. I got through it. Whatever you're going through with teenagers right now, I think you can get through it too.

Here's how I define teenagers: A teenage boy is an iPod-toting space alien who oozes testosterone and continually asks for the car keys. A teenage girl is a continuous loop of unintelligible chatter who wanders the mall with a cell phone stuck to the side of her head. But somewhere behind the nostril and eyebrow piercings, the rainbow-hued hair, the freakazoid attire and the thrashcore music, you can still catch a glimpse of the image of God.

I know it's scary to watch teens make poor choices, reject your values and rebel against your authority. But even though their sense of style comes from another solar system, and even though their music makes The Who and The Doors sound like Lawrence Welk, their rebellion is really no worse than what you did at their age. You were a teenager once, right? And you survived. If you keep praying for them, loving them and accepting them, odds are they'll survive too.

Rebellion is normal at this stage of their life. In fact, up to a point, it's desirable. Teenagers are still kids, but they think they are adults and they want all the stuff that adults have—except the responsibility that goes with it. They want freedom, money and cars. To top it off, their hormones are raging. They're going through a process called "individuation," a time of separating themselves from their parents and discovering who they are as individuals. They are figuring out their own values, their own view of the world and their own sense of what is right and wrong, what is true and false. Not only is this normal, but it's also healthy.

Obviously, you don't want your kids to throw out everything you taught them—your values, your ethics and your faith. But you want to let them know that you respect their individuality and you want them to think for themselves. Let them know you're not threatened by their questions or ideas. Pick your battles with care. If your teen chooses a fairly harmless form of rebellion, tolerate it. Save the heavy ammunition for the big battles involving dangerous or immoral behavior. If you give teenagers some freedom to be themselves and express their individuality, you'll give them a zone of safety in which to express their rebellious impulses.

No matter what happens, keep telling your kids you love them. Tell them that you make the rules and enforce the rules because you love them. You give them as much freedom as you can because you love them; and when they abuse the freedom, you impose consequences because you love them. Love, love, love! Keep saying it until they're sick of hearing it, then say it some more.

Don't say anything you can't take back. Don't do anything you'll regret later. Teens often say, "Leave me alone!" But deep down, every child fears abandonment, and teens are still children at heart. They may reject your values and push you away, but they don't want to lose you completely. They still want to be connected, even if they refuse to admit it. Take a step back and give your teens some space, but let them know that you'll always be there and you'll always love them.

Tip 9: Encourage Kids to Invest Their Lives in What Truly Matters

As you raise, train and coach those kids, give them opportunities to build character and have a positive influence on the world around them. Teach them not to chase after false values—money, fame, power and pleasure. Inspire them through your words and your example to pursue those things that have lasting significance.

The next time you see your kids looking bored, wasting time in front of the TV or zoning out at the computer, pull the plug and sit them down for a heart-to-heart. Tell them, "Look around you. There's important work to be done. Not just around our house, but around our neighborhood, around our community. Instead of sitting bug-eyed in front of that flatscreen while your brain turns to Jell-O, why not use your time to make a difference in the world?"

At this point, the kid will probably stare at you slack-jawed. "Like, uh, what do you want me to do?"

You reply: "Make a difference in someone's life. Get some friends together and go visit a convalescent home. Find a senior citizen whose house needs a little care. Volunteer to wash windows and weed flower-beds. Find an overgrown lawn and volunteer to mow it and edge it for free. Get the names of some guys in the Armed Forces and write to them and thank them for the job that they're doing. Make friends with some elderly neighbors and ask them what life was like when they were young. Serve meals at a homeless shelter or rescue mission. Help build houses with Habitat for Humanity. Go out to the park or the mall and talk to people about your faith. The sky's the limit. Use your imagination. Be a servant to someone else and see how it makes you feel."

This is a new concept for most kids. Allow a few moments for the idea to sink in. Likely as not, they'll ask you, "What do I get out of it?"

Answer: "You will get a sense of accomplishment and satisfaction in knowing that you have made a difference in someone else's life. You'll test your character, you'll grow more mature and you'll increase your confidence. You'll know that you are doing the work God put you on Earth to do."

And here's another suggestion: Offer to go with them. Volunteer your own time. Gandhi once said, "Be the change you want to see in the world." In other words, if we want to change our world, if we want to change our kids, let's start by changing ourselves. Let's teach our kids to be servants the same way Jesus taught His disciples: by *example*.

Wise old Solomon once wrote, "Sons are a heritage from the LORD, children a reward from him" (Ps. 127:3). Children are not a burden or an obligation. Children are a reward! Whether you are a biological parent, an adoptive parent, a step-parent, a godparent, a scoutmaster, a den mother, a coach, a soccer mom or soccer dad, a youth worker or a mentor, those kids are a reward from God. The job of working with kids isn't always easy, but the rewards are eternal.

You may not see immediate results in their life. They may not think to say thank you for your sacrifices. At times, you may wonder if all the heartache and hassle of raising kids is really worth it. Keep loving them anyway. Keep sacrificing for them anyway. Keep investing in their life. I guarantee the day will come when you will be glad that you invested wisely.

In his book *The Legacy*, Steven J. Lawson, senior pastor of Dauphin Way Baptist Church in Mobile, Alabama, wrote, "Long after whatever personal investments you may leave your children are spent, a spiritual legacy will only compound daily and pay rich dividends throughout all eternity. The man who leaves only a financial inheritance for his children leaves them poor. But the man who leaves a spiritual legacy for his family, whatever size his financial inheritance may be, leaves them rich."[9]

FIGHT FOR THESE KIDS!

Jeff Myers, Ph.D., is president of the Myers Institute for Communication and Leadership, headquartered in Dayton, Tennessee. The mission of the Myers Institute is to equip people to influence our culture through leadership and communication skills. Jeff is a speaker and the author of numerous books and video coaching systems. He shared with me a story of a life-and-death situation he faced with his son Graham.

For Graham's ninth birthday, Jeff decided to take his son on an ocean adventure—kayaking to an island, then hiking to a swimming hole that was tucked away in a hidden part of the island. They had river kayaked many times, but ocean kayaking would be a new challenge. So before setting out on their trip, they practiced ocean kayaking a few times to get used to it.

The day they set off for the island was a perfect day with a slight breeze and gentle waves. As they went, the waves grew stronger. Nearing the island, they found that the contour of the island and a nearby reef caused the waves to overlap at right angles near their landing site. Jeff realized that the chaotic waves would be difficult to navigate, but he felt they could make it by paddling fast and furiously. So Jeff and Graham made for the beach.

They never saw the wave that slammed into them, rolling their kayaks.

When Jeff surfaced, he saw Graham's overturned kayak. The boy couldn't right himself. Graham reached his son and pulled his head above water—

And another wave hit them, slamming the hull of the kayak into the boy's head.

"Are you all right?" Jeff yelled.

"I'm okay," the boy spluttered.

Father and son pulled their kayaks ashore. Then they climbed the rocky strand between the sea and the stone cliffs, headed for the secret swimming hole. The waves rose and washed the rocks where Jeff and Graham stood, threatening to dislodge them. Then Jeff saw the biggest wave of all—

"Graham!" he shouted. "The wave—!"

There was no time for the boy to react.

Jeff reached out and grabbed Graham's life jacket, yanking him up hard just as the sea smashed over the rock where the boy had been perched. The water receded, sucking everything away. If Jeff hadn't snatched his son, the sea would have taken him.

Clearly, conditions were worse than Jeff had expected. He decided to call off the trip to the swimming hole and seek an alternate route back to the kayaks. He placed Graham on a high promontory, out of reach of the waves. "I'm going to find a way out," he told his son. "I'll be gone for a few minutes, but I'll come back for you."

But Graham didn't want to be left alone with the waves crashing just below him. As Jeff left him, the boy called out, "Dad! Wait!"

"I'll be right back!" Jeff answered—but his voice was drowned out by the thundering waves. Graham couldn't hear his father's voice.

Jeff scouted ahead, looking for another path back to the beach, but couldn't find one. When he returned to the place where he'd left Graham, he had only been gone about three minutes—but Graham was shaking in terror, afraid his dad wouldn't come back.

Jeff looked his son in the eyes and said, "Graham, I will do everything in my power to protect you! You believe that, don't you?"

The boy nodded, shivering.

"But," Jeff continued, "we both know that only God can keep us completely safe from harm, right? Son, let's pray together and ask Him to watch over us."

So Graham and Jeff prayed together—the most heartfelt prayer Jeff had ever heard his son pray. Then they started back the way they came.

As they went, Jeff had only one thought: *Fight for this boy!*

And he did fight. Again, they were pounded by the waves. Jeff repeatedly placed himself between the sea and his boy so that his body absorbed the brunt of the waves. The sharp volcanic rock cut into the flesh of Jeff's hands, arms and legs, leaving wounds that are visible today as permanent scars.

Finally, they reached their kayaks, pushed out into the waves, and made for the open sea.

Jeff later reflected, "This wasn't just a fight for my son's physical life. It was a fight for his very spirit. I wasn't just battling the ocean waves. I was battling the waves of fear within him—and within me."

My friend, you and I are engaged in the very same fight. We are fighting for our kids—and not just for their physical lives, but for the spirit within them. We are battling the forces of a corrosive society. We are battling the forces of fear and doubt. It's a worthwhile fight—and our kids are counting on us to fight hard, and never give up.

Pursue parenthood, my friend, and by God's grace be the best parent to your kids that you can possibly be. No kids of your own? No problem! There are plenty of kids in this world who need a surrogate parent, a stand-in father, a substitute mother, a caring coach, a wise and involved mentor. Pursue parenthood with those kids.

They are huddled and shivering inside. Look out! Here come the waves!

Fight for those kids!

PURSUE FAITH

I wasn't even 25 years old yet, and I was in charge of a minor league baseball team, the Spartanburg Phillies. I was accountable to the owner, Mr. R. E. Littlejohn, but he gave me a lot of freedom to run the show as I saw fit. So I fixed up the ballpark, hired an announcer and an assistant and dreamed up a bunch of eye-popping promotions.

From boyhood through my college career, my one and only dream had been to be a Major League Baseball player. My two lackluster seasons as a catcher with the Miami Marlins had decisively written *"finis"* to that dream. But in Spartanburg, I had found a new dream: being general manager of a baseball team. And I knew that if I played my cards right, I could parlay a few seasons of success in the minors into a front office career in Major League Baseball. Once I made it to the majors, everything I wanted would be mine: fortune, fame, power and all the pleasures a big league exec could wish for.

During my first season in Spartanburg, our team played poorly, but we drew 114,000 fans to the ballpark for 60 home dates. I was named Executive of the Year in the Western Carolinas League, and our success was trumpeted in sports pages across the country. The Phillies head office in Philadelphia took notice. I looked in the mirror and saw a whiz kid, a boy genius.

The next season was an even bigger success. We attracted 173,000 fans to the ballpark—and we had a winning team. The town went crazy as the Phillies went on a 25-game winning streak and beat our archrivals, the Greenville Mets, for the pennant.

I reveled in my success. I had a fat bank account, everyone in town knew my name and I was getting attention from the national sports media. I dressed in tailored suits and drove a big Oldsmobile Toronado. The Spartanburg Jaycees named me Outstanding Young Man of the Year, and again I was named Executive of the Year by the league. I had arrived!

And I was *empty*.

It was a baffling feeling, achieving so much yet still feeling restless and unfulfilled. For years, I had primed myself for success. I had envisioned what it would feel like to achieve my goals—and I expected that success would bring me a sense of happiness that would last the rest of my life. I couldn't understand why, in the midst of my success, my life seemed hollow and without purpose.

Sure, when the team won a big game, or I got my name in the paper, I experienced a momentary thrill. But I soon discovered that the excitement quickly faded—not in months or days, but within minutes. In my headlong pursuit of money, fame, power and pleasure, I was really chasing happiness—but I could never catch it.

HEART TROUBLE

At the same time, I saw that my boss, Mr. Littlejohn, seemed to have already found happiness. I had never met anyone who seemed so wise, so at peace with himself, so confident of his purpose in life. I was riddled with questions; he always had answers. I was anxious and driven; he was serene and relaxed in every situation. Despite his wealth and power, he was a completely humble man who cared little about his own material comforts and used his resources to serve God and help others.

During my years in Spartanburg, Mr. Littlejohn often reached out to me and cared for me in ways I had never known before. He became as much a father to me as my own father had been. Every time I was with Mr. Littlejohn, he said, "I love you, Pat." If any other man had said that to me, I would have thought it strange and awkward. When Mr. Littlejohn said those words, they seemed perfectly natural and fatherly.

I couldn't understand why Mr. Littlejohn took such a deep interest in my welfare. I remembered the Sunday School stories I had heard about Jesus when I was a boy, and Mr. Littlejohn reminded me again and again of Jesus.

I loved him like a father, and I worried about him when I learned that he was having heart problems and would eventually need a bypass operation. One day, I came into his office, and his secretary told me, "Mr. Littlejohn was having chest pains, so they took him to the hospital in Atlanta. They left just a few minutes ago."

With my heart in my throat, I got into my car and raced out onto the highway. I was afraid I would never see him again.

Ignoring the speed laws, I finally caught up with the car. I honked and motioned for them to pull over. Mr. Littlejohn's driver pulled the car onto the shoulder. I ran to the car and found Mr. and Mrs. Littlejohn in the back seat. I flung open the door, threw my arms around my boss and wept. As he had done so many times before, Mr. Littlejohn told me he loved me. He embraced me and said everything was going to be all right.

I let them continue on to Atlanta, and I got back in my car and returned to Spartanburg. As it turned out, Mr. Littlejohn was hospitalized for a short time, then he returned home and eventually resumed his work.

Though Mr. Littlejohn was bothered by chest pains, I was the one with serious "heart trouble."

READY TO SURRENDER

One Thursday evening in February 1968, I went to a folk music concert. Throughout the concert, I had my eye on one of the singers in the group—a pretty, petite blonde with a gorgeous smile. After the concert, I went up to her and introduced myself. I managed to casually work it into the conversation that I was a big-shot exec in minor league baseball. Just as I was about to ask her for a date, she adroitly changed the subject—

And started talking to me about Jesus.

I tried to switch the subject again. "I really admire your talent," I said. "I was thinking we could—"

"Thank you," she said. "I've dedicated my talent to serving Jesus Christ and sharing His message with other people."

Daggonit! She had switched the subject right back to Jesus! I was trying to make a pitch for this girl, and she was deflecting it with ease! We kept talking, and I kept trying to find an opening to ask her for a date—but it wasn't to be. "I need to go," she said, "but let me give you something to read. I think it will help you a lot." She handed me a little booklet, and I stuck it in my pocket. A booklet! I didn't want something to read! I wanted a date with a pretty blonde folk singer!

As she walked away, I realized that it wasn't just her hair, her eyes or her smile that attracted me. She had a radiance, a joy, an indefinable air of inner peace. It occurred to me that she had the same inner joy that I saw in Mr. Littlejohn. I wanted that for myself, but I didn't know where to find it.

I went home to my apartment, sat down on my bed and felt something jabbing me. I reached into my pocket and found the little booklet that the young lady had given me. It was entitled *Have You Heard of the Four Spiritual Laws?* I opened it and read it through in just a couple of minutes. The basic message of the booklet was this:

1. God loves you and offers a wonderful plan for your life.
2. Human beings are separated from God by sin, so we are unable to know and understand His love and plan for our lives.
3. Jesus Christ is God's only cure for human sin. Through Him we can experience God's love and know His plan for our lives.
4. We must individually receive Jesus Christ as Savior and Lord in order to receive God's cure for sin.

I closed the booklet and thought, *Is that what those people have that I don't? Is Jesus that elusive "something" that's missing from my life?*

I had to know more. I had to talk to the girl from the folk singing group again.

I didn't have much to go on. I knew that her name was Sandy Johnson, but where was she staying? On a hunch, I called the motel across the street from the auditorium. Sure enough, she was registered there. The desk clerk rang her room. When she answered, I told her, "I'd really like to talk to you again. Could you meet me for breakfast?"

"Well," she said, "our bus leaves at 11:00 in the morning—"

"Perfect," I said, "we can meet for breakfast at 9:00."

I could hear the reluctance in her voice, but she agreed. I'm sure she thought I was just trying to get a date. That may have been my original motive, but not anymore. The message of that little booklet had grabbed me by the throat. My mind was churning with questions, and I knew that Sandy Johnson had the answers.

I didn't sleep well that night.

The next morning over breakfast, I poured out my heart to her. One by one, she answered my spiritual questions. An hour went by like a flash. All too soon, it was time for her bus to leave.

I went back to my office, and the message of that booklet haunted me throughout the day. I couldn't work. I couldn't concentrate. Finally, I decided to talk to Mr. Littlejohn. I got in my car, drove to his office and told him everything I'd been going through.

He listened attentively, then said, "Pat, my wife and I have been praying for you ever since you came to Spartanburg. We were sure that you could have a great impact for Jesus Christ—if you would make a decision to follow Him."

As soon as he said that, I knew I was ready—

But in the very next moment, I felt a tug of self-will, a feeling of resistance. It was as if some part of me was saying, *Don't surrender control! If you give in to Jesus Christ, everything will change. What about your goals? What about fame and fortune? What about pleasure and power? You want those things, don't you? If you surrender to Jesus Christ, you may never get them!*

For a moment, I teetered on the knife-edge of indecision—but then I felt my inner resistance collapse. I knew I couldn't keep running after things that left me feeling empty and defeated. It was time to surrender. I wanted the same inner satisfaction that Mr. Littlejohn had—and if I had to give up all the fortune, fame, power and pleasure in the world to get it, so be it!

Mr. Littlejohn put his arm around me and asked, "Would you like me to pray with you?" I nodded, and he led me through a prayer of commitment:

Heavenly Father,

Thank You for loving me and having a plan for my life. I confess that I've sinned many times, but Lord, I'm sorry for my sins, and I want to turn away from my sin and live for You. I invite Jesus into my life as Lord and Savior. Thank You for hearing my prayer. Please seal this decision and help me to live the rest of my life for You!

Thank You in Jesus' name, Amen.

After praying that prayer, I felt an enormous sense of release. Tears flooded up from somewhere deep inside my soul. I don't know how to describe what I felt except to say that I felt completely regenerated, like I was a totally new man.

My long struggle was over. Jesus had won. After the tears of relief stopped flowing down my face, I looked up at Mr. Littlejohn. "I'm in now!" I said, grinning broadly.

He laughed. "Yes, Pat," he said. "You're in."

My "heart trouble" was cured.

ETERNITY IN OUR HEARTS

Until that day, I had not understood what it meant to have a personal relationship with Jesus Christ. Many times, Mr. Littlejohn had tried to explain his Christian faith to me. He had talked about Jesus as his Lord, his Savior and his personal Friend. He was trying to share a profound truth with me, but everything he said went in one ear and out the other. I thought it was all religious mumbo-jumbo. Though I respected Mr. Littlejohn and his beliefs, I didn't have any use for "religion" in my own life.

When I encountered the pretty blonde folk singer, I thought it was interesting but irrelevant that she, too, was "religious." It wasn't until I read the little booklet she gave me that it began to dawn on me that faith is not the same thing as "religion." To be "religious" is to know *about* God. To have faith is to *know* God in a personal way.

I recently received a letter from Tony Evans, the founder of The Urban Alternative and pastor of the Oak Cliff Bible Fellowship Church in Dallas. He is also the chaplain of the NBA's Dallas Mavericks. He wrote:

Do you know how Jesus defined 'eternal life'? As He was praying for His disciples toward the end of His earthly life, Jesus said, 'This is eternal life, that they may know You, the only true

God, and Jesus Christ whom You have sent'. . . . Money, power, relationships, reputation, status, appearance, education—these are what millions of people chase all their lives, hoping to find fulfillment. But chasing after what the world says will fulfill us has gotten us nowhere. No matter how much we attain, we are always hungry for something more.

I read those words and I thought, "Wow! Tony's telling my story!" Because that's exactly the way I was living until my encounter with Jesus Christ.

Tucked away in the Old Testament book of Ecclesiastes, there is a little verse that packs a huge wallop of meaning. There, Solomon writes that God has "set eternity in the hearts of men; yet they cannot fathom what God has done from beginning to end" (Eccles. 3:11). Let those words roll around between your ears for a few moments. God has set *eternity itself* within your heart and within mine. We weren't meant to set our hearts on anything as small and temporary as fortune, fame, power and pleasure. Our hearts were created to contain eternity itself!

The German philosopher Immanuel Kant once put it this way: "The human heart refuses to believe in a universe without a purpose." Now, why is that? It's because God has set eternity in our heart. He has created us to intuitively understand that there is an eternal purpose to our existence—and He has created us to seek that purpose until we find it and fulfill it.

Because God has placed eternity in our heart, we hunger for lasting significance. We want our life to matter. No one wants to die and be forgotten. We want to know that it made a difference that we lived on this planet. We want to know that the difference we made will endure long after we have physically departed.

The problem is that most people spend their lives in a vain attempt to build an earthly legacy. That's why so many people seem driven by inner demons to build monuments to themselves. There is a hole in their heart as big as eternity itself—and they try to fill it by building a financial empire, or by achieving the false "immortality" of fame, or by attaining political or military power and thus securing a place in the history books, or by achieving a Playboy lifestyle of hedonistic pleasure, so that they will become the envy of the world.

None of those achievements satisfies, because none of them measure up to the eternity that God has set in our heart. Our true and deepest longing is for Him—not for money, fame, power and pleasure. Those who try to fill an eternity-sized hole with things that can't last are doomed to the same futile chase that consumed my life—until I found a Purpose as vast as eternity itself.

YOU HAVE BEEN CALLED

As author and pastor Frederick Buechner once observed, "*Purpose* is the place where your deep gladness meets the world's needs." It's true. Once I stopped chasing my own selfish ambitions, God opened up a whole new purpose for my life—a place where my deep gladness in knowing Jesus Christ intersected with the crying and desperate needs of the world around me.

It's because of the joy of knowing Christ that I accepted this mission of adopting kids from around the world and encouraging others to consider international adoption. It's because of the joy of knowing Christ that I have stood before audiences around the world and shared my faith with thousands of people. In my younger years, it never occurred to me that I might write books or host radio talk shows—but because of the joy of knowing Christ, I now do that as well. I never planned to have the kind of exciting, full-throttle life I now enjoy—but my deep gladness in knowing Jesus Christ has plunged me into one adventure after another.

Another word often used to describe our purpose in life is "calling." For example, I know that I have a calling to devote my adult life to a career in professional sports—and my sports career gives me a platform for my calling as an author and speaker. The interesting thing about that word "calling" is that it requires us to have faith in Someone greater than ourselves. After all, you can't have a "calling" unless you have been called—and that means there must be a Caller, someone who gives you your purpose for living.

And that Someone, that Caller, is God.

The day I prayed in Mr. Littlejohn's office and gave my life to Jesus Christ, I knew beyond the shadow of a doubt that I had been called. God Himself had guided my steps and arranged my circumstances. He made sure that, when I was seven years old, I'd be sitting in Shibe Park, eating my fill of hot dogs and discovering a passion for sports that would propel me throughout my life. God led my steps from Wake Forest University to the Spartanburg Phillies. He led me to a Christlike man named Mr. R. E. Littlejohn—and He arranged for me to meet a pretty, blonde folk singer who gave me a booklet about The Four Spiritual Laws.

So, when Mr. Littlejohn prayed with me in his office that day, my heart had been prepared. I was ready. I knew that God had called me— and I was willing to follow Him wherever He might lead me. I had found my purpose for living.

YOUR ONE AND ONLY IRREPLACEABLE LIFE

Over the years, I've talked to many people who have no sense of their own purpose. Some don't know who their birth parents were or where they came from. Some have said to me, "My life is a mistake. I wasn't supposed to be conceived, and when I was born, my parents gave me away. My entire childhood has been miserable. I don't have a reason for living. I shouldn't have been born."

If you have ever had such thoughts, then I have good news for you: Every human being ever born is made in God's image and created for a purpose. God doesn't make mistakes. The circumstances of your birth and childhood don't matter. You are here because God put you here, and the world needs you. This is your one and only irreplaceable life, and God has called you to carry out His eternal purpose for your life. God has gifted you and provided you with passions, talents and abilities that can make a lasting difference in the world.

There is an exciting life ahead of you, my friend. No matter how young or old you are, or where you might be in life, God has an amazing adventure planned for you. The moment you put your trust in Jesus, wonderful things happen.

First of all, your sins—past, present and future—are instantly forgiven. The Bible tells us, "God made you alive with Christ. He forgave us all our sins. . . . He took it away, nailing it to the cross" (Col. 2:13-14).

Second, you receive eternal life—both a new eternal quality of life in the here and now, and the promise of everlasting life after you die. Jesus said, "I tell you the truth, whoever hears my word and believes him who sent me has eternal life and will not be condemned; he has crossed over from death to life" (John 5:24).

Third, you become a child of God. The Bible tells us, "Yet to all who received him, to those who believed in his name, he gave the right to become children of God" (John 1:12).

Fourth, you become a new creation. As 2 Corinthians 5:17 states, "Therefore, if anyone is in Christ, he is a new creation; the old has gone, the new has come!"

And that's just the beginning of the incredible things we experience the moment we commit our lives to Jesus Christ. As we move deeper into our relationship with Him, we discover more and more wonders on a daily basis.

Are you feeling overburdened and exhausted? Do you wonder how you can keep going with all the pressures and stresses that are loaded on your back? Jesus says to you, "Come to me, all you who are weary and burdened, and I will give you rest. Take my yoke upon you and learn from me, for I am gentle and humble in heart, and you will find rest for your souls. For my yoke is easy and my burden is light" (Matt. 11:28-30).

Are you facing a challenge that seems insurmountable and impossible? Jesus says to you, "What is impossible with men is possible with God" (Luke 18:27).

Is your world out of control? Do you wonder if all the suffering of this life is worth it or not? Then you have the assurance of God's Word, "And we know that in all things God works for the good of those who love him, who have been called according to his purpose. For those God foreknew he also predestined to be conformed to the likeness of his Son, that he might be the firstborn among many brothers" (Rom. 8:28-29).

Are you struggling with shame and an inability to forgive yourself for some sin in your past? God says to you, "Therefore, there is now no condemnation for those who are in Christ Jesus" (Rom. 8:1).

Do you feel physically and emotionally impoverished? Have you reached the end of your resources? The promise of God's Word is, "And my God will meet all your needs according to his glorious riches in Christ Jesus" (Phil. 4:19).

Are you struggling with anxiety or fear? Then you have this assurance: "For God has not given us a spirit of fear, but of power and of love and of a sound mind" (2 Tim. 1:7, *NKJV*).

Are you feeling unloved and lonely? God Himself has promised us, "I will never leave you nor forsake you" (Heb. 13:5, *NKJV*).

A grandfather once offered a wager to his young granddaughter. "I'll give you a quarter," he said, "if you can tell me where God is." The child wisely replied, "I'll give you two quarters if you can tell me where God *isn't*." There is no place we can go that God is not there. He will not leave us. He will not forsake us. He is always with us, and His love and power are always available to us.

For our fear, Jesus offers peace. For our worry, Jesus offers assurance. For our sin, Jesus offers forgiveness. For our shame, Jesus offers release. For our brokenness, Jesus offers wholeness. For our emptiness, Jesus offers fulfillment. For our worthlessness, Jesus offers affirmation. He replaces hatred and prejudice with love and acceptance. He replaces bondage and addiction with deliverance and freedom. He replaces death with eternal life.

When we give our life to Christ, He gives us an identity that transcends every other dimension of our life. Being a follower of Christ means more to us than our career, our political affiliation or any other label that defines us. NFL coach Tony Dungy put it this way: "I coach football, but the good I can do to glorify God along the way is my real purpose." And businessman Philip Armour (1832-1901), founder of the Armour meatpacking company, said, "I am a witness for Jesus Christ, but I pack sausages to meet expenses."

I see my own life the same way. I happen to be a husband, a father of 19, a sports executive with the Orlando Magic, an author and a public speaker. But first, last and always, I am a follower of Jesus Christ.

HOW TO GROW YOUR FAITH

Stan Buck, senior pastor of Sonrise Church in Fort Wayne, tells the story of a girl who, on the way home from church, asked, "Mommy, the preacher said that God is bigger than we are. Is that true?"

"That's right," her mother replied.

"And he said God lives inside of us. Is that true?"

"Yes."

"Well, if God is bigger than us and He lives in us, wouldn't He show through?"

That's a profound insight, isn't it? If we truly have Almighty God, Creator of heaven and Earth, living inside us, then there's no way to keep Him from showing through. His life should shine through our lives like the sun shining through a picture window. In fact, that's what Jesus was telling us when He said, "Let your light shine before men, that they may see your good deeds and praise your Father in heaven" (Matt. 5:16).

The Christian life is a journey of daily growth and maturity in which we learn in an ever-increasing way what it means to be like Jesus Christ—and what it means to have His life shining through us. The way we grow in our faith in God is by devoting ourselves to a few simple yet crucial disciplines on a daily basis. Let's take a look at those disciplines:

1. Study the Word of God

Keith Tower came to Orlando as a 6' 11" forward-center from Notre Dame. He made the Magic roster in 1993, at the launching of the Shaq era in Orlando. He played a limited role with the team, but he was a good-character guy, a good influence to have on our team.

Rich DeVos and the DeVos family had bought the Orlando Magic in the fall of 1991, and Rich took great delight in giving the players a special and personal kind of gift at Christmastime. For Christmas of 1993, he gave each of the Magic players a beautiful Bible with the player's name embossed on the cover. Keith opened his gift and his immediate reaction was to take it home and put it on a shelf, where it sat for three years.

Keith recently told me that, when he first saw that Bible, he thought, *Man, what a lame gift!* At that time, there were a lot of new, high-tech gadgets on the market—cell phones, computers, devices for listening to music and so forth. Keith thought, *Why couldn't he give us that kind of stuff? Other teams give their players all kinds of really cool electronic stuff. What do we get? Bibles!*

In 1996, Keith joined the Milwaukee Bucks. Before heading to training camp, he looked around his home for something to take to occupy his time. There's a lot of downtime at training camp, and Keith didn't want to be bored. By this time, he had acquired a lot of the "cool electronic stuff" he wanted—and most of his gadgets were already broken or outdated.

Then Keith saw the Bible sitting on his shelf. He took it down, blew the dust off of it and tossed it in his suitcase. Then he headed for Milwaukee.

One night in his hotel room, he started reading his Bible—and he was immediately convicted about his need for Jesus Christ. That night, he asked Jesus to take over as the Lord of his life.

Now in his late thirties, and retired from the game, Keith has moved back to Orlando. He and former Magic teammate Andrew DeClercq have cofounded HighPoint Church in Orlando. They started the church several years ago with four members, and their flock now numbers 165. And it's all because of the amazing, life-changing power of that so-called "lame gift" he received one Christmas, the gift of God's own Word.

The apostle Paul said, "Faith comes from hearing the message, and the message is heard through the word of Christ" (Rom. 10:17). He also said, "All Scripture is God-breathed and is useful for teaching, rebuking, correcting and training in righteousness" (2 Tim. 3:16). In other words, if we want to grow in our faith and understand the mind of God, then we need to study the Word that God Himself literally breathed into existence for our instruction.

Dr. James Borror, pastor of the El Dorado Park Community Church in Long Beach, California, urges us to take God's Word seriously. When the Bible says that "*all* Scripture is God-breathed," it means just that: *all* Scripture. To make his point, he quotes 1 Chronicles 26:18, an Old Testament verse that is often used as an example of how Scripture can seem meaningless when taken out of context. That verse, in the *King James Version*, reads: "At Parbar westward, four at the causeway, and two at Parbar." Yes, that is the entire verse.

When people have tried to argue doctrine with him, Dr. Borror would say, "Just read 1 Chronicles 26:18 and everything will be clear to you." So they would read, "At Parbar westward, four at the causeway, and two at Parbar"—and they'd think, "Huh? What does *that* have to do with the price of beans in Babylon?"

But one day, it occurred to Dr. Borror that if all Scripture is God-breathed and profitable for instruction, then that verse must have depths of meaning waiting to be discovered. So, as he studied that verse in its context, Dr. Borror realized that it actually illustrated some important spiritual principles.

In its historical context, the passage deals with King David's plans for the Temple in Jerusalem. The Temple would be filled with utensils made of gold, silver and precious stones. Those valuables needed to be guarded and protected from thieves. Parbar was a section of the city of Jerusalem, and a gate divided the Temple from Parbar. That gate opened on a causeway (an elevated pathway) into Parbar. So this verse was just a small part of a series of orders that David gave regarding the Temple layout and the positioning of the guards around the Temple. At this one site, there would be four temple guards stationed at the causeway, and there would be two additional guards stationed in the sector called Parbar.

At this point, you may be saying, "So?"

Well, there are some important principles embedded in this odd-seeming verse.

First, this verse shows us that every believer has a job to do, a function to fulfill as a servant of God. Sometimes we're tempted to think that our job isn't very important. The Temple guards who simply stood at the causeway or in Parbar might have been tempted to feel that way. After all, what were they doing? Just standing around. Yet if they were not there, that gate would be unguarded and the precious utensils of the Temple could easily be stolen. Even though they were "just standing around," they performed a crucial function in service to God. And so do we.

Second, this verse shows that every servant is important. David didn't order, "Post a few guards at the causeway, and maybe another guard or two at Parbar." He gave strict instructions: four guards at the causeway and two at Parbar. David was a king and a military commander and he expected his orders to be obeyed to the letter. The lesson for your life and mine: There are no "minor servants." Every member of God's kingdom is crucial and indispensable to God's plan.

If you do not do the job God has given you, it won't get done.

Third, the greatest ability you can offer God is your dependability. You may think, *I don't have a great talent. I can't sing, I can't preach, I can't write a book, I can't do much of anything.* Let me ask you this: Can you show up? If God tells you to simply stand at the causeway or at Parbar, can you do that? It doesn't take any great ability. It just takes dependability. If you can do that, it's enough.

Now, what do you think? Do you agree that all Scripture is God-breathed and profitable—even a verse like, "At Parbar westward, four at the causeway, and two at Parbar"? And that's one of the "lean and stringy" verses of Scripture! Imagine what you could get out of some of the really juicy, succulent, melt-in-your-mouth passages of Scripture! Study God's Word, my friend, and see how you grow.

2. Pray

God answers prayer. As you pray and experience His answers, your faith will grow stronger—and you will begin to rely on His power more and more.

My friend Jerry B. Jenkins is a gifted writer and the coauthor of the *Left Behind* series of novels. Jerry was also my writing partner on a number of books. A number of years ago, he was invited to help Dr. Billy Graham write his memoirs, which were published under the title *Just As I Am.* Looking back on that experience, Jerry called it "the privilege of a lifetime." Jerry recalls being impressed by Dr. Graham's profound humility—yet that same humility proved to be a problem.

His job was to interview the famed evangelist, dig deeply into the story of his life and uncover the sources of his spiritual strength—but Dr. Graham, in his deep humility, was reluctant to talk about himself. Jerry would say, "Most Christians see you as the epitome of—" and Dr. Graham would interrupt him with a wave of his hand and say, "People shouldn't see me as the epitome of anything. Sometimes I feel as low as that floor when I think of how often I've failed the Lord." Jerry wondered how he was going to write about the sources of Dr. Graham's spiritual strength if the man would only talk about his spiritual weaknesses.

After trying dozens of questions without getting anywhere, Jerry finally asked, "What is the secret of your personal spiritual disciplines?"

"Oh, that's no secret," Dr. Graham replied. "God tells us plainly and simply in the Bible that we are to pray without ceasing and search the Scriptures."

Jerry considered those words, especially the phrase "pray without ceasing" (1 Thess. 5:17, *KJV*). This, he knew, was a New Testament admonition written by the apostle Paul. Well, Jerry had always assumed that Paul was speaking figuratively, not literally, when he said that Christians should "pray without ceasing." But Dr. Graham seemed to take Paul's counsel quite literally.

"You pray without ceasing?" Jerry asked.

"I do," Dr. Graham replied. He went on to say that he had prayed nearly every waking moment since committing his life to Jesus Christ when he was a teenager. "In fact," he added, "I'm praying right now that this conversation and this book project will bring glory to God."[1]

Prayer isn't brain surgery. It's not rocket science. Prayer is simply the act of conversing with God, no more, no less. My friend, if you can chat with a friend over coffee or talk on a cell phone, you can pray. And because God is always with us, we can literally pray without ceasing. We can constantly be aware of God's presence, constantly include Him in our thoughts, constantly converse with Him wherever we are.

We don't have to express our prayers in lofty language, nor do our prayers need to only be about weighty problems or profound thoughts. We can ask God to bless a conversation we're having or an email we are sending. We can thank Him for the warmth of the sunshine and the music of songbirds when we step outside our door. We can ask Him to bring peace to a troubled part of the world—or to help us with our financial troubles.

Include God in the stream of your thoughts. Include Him in your conversations with friends. Feel free in the middle of a chat over coffee, an outing at a restaurant or a carpool ride to work, to stop and involve God in the activities of your day.

What should you pray for? Whatever you need or want at that moment. Wisdom and direction are always good things to ask for. The Old Testament tells us, "Trust in the LORD with all your heart and lean not on your own understanding; in all your ways acknowledge him, and he will make your paths straight" (Prov. 3:5-6). And the New Testament tells us, "If any of you lacks wisdom, he should ask God, who gives generously to all without finding fault, and it will be given to him" (Jas. 1:5).

Billy Graham recalls that, during a visit to New York City, he watched workers ease the great ocean liner *United States* into its berth in New York harbor. He saw the deckhands aboard the ship throw ropes down to the dockworkers on the pier. Once those ropes were secured to the pier, motorized winches reeled in the cable, closing the space between the ship and the pier. "Of course," Dr. Graham concluded, "the pier wasn't pulled out to the ship. The ship was moved snugly up to the pier. In the same way, prayer is the rope that pulls God and human beings together. But prayer doesn't pull God down to us. It pulls us up to Him."

I said earlier that God answers prayer. Does that mean He always gives us exactly what we ask for? No. Does it mean that the answer always comes in a way that we expect or immediately recognize? No. Why not? Because, just as a little child tends to ask her parents for sugary treats instead of healthy foods, the things we pray for are not always the things that are the best for us. As Anne Lamott once wisely observed, "I've seen prayers answered. But often, in my experience, if you get what you pray for, you've really shortchanged yourself." God, our loving Father, always gives us good gifts. If He does not give us what we ask for, we can trust that He will give us something better.

In December 2007, Jenna Bush, the daughter of President George W. Bush and his wife, Laura, was a guest on *The Ellen DeGeneres Show*, a syndicated TV talk show. Jenna was there to talk about her book *Ana's Story: A Journey of Hope*, which deals with her experiences working with UNICEF charities in Latin America. After interviewing the young author about her book, DeGeneres asked, "Can you call your dad on the phone anytime you want to?"

"Sure," Jenna Bush replied.

"Here's a phone," DeGeneres said. "Could you call him right now?"

So Jenna Bush dialed the private number. First Lady Laura Bush answered. "Hello?"

"Hi, Mom. It's Jenna. What's up?"

"Oh, hi, honey. I'm just sitting here with Daddy."

"Could I speak to him?"

Seconds later, the leader of the Free World was on the line. "Hello?"

"Daddy," the first daughter said, "it's Jenna. I'm on *The Ellen De-Generes Show*."

"Well, that's great!" said the president. "How's my little girl doing?"

Jenna asked if he was mad that she called him on national TV without warning him in advance.

"No, not at all!" he said jovially. "I'm glad to talk to you. I'm glad to talk to Ellen. . . . Ellen, I want to say Merry Christmas to your audience, and I want to tell my little girl I love her."[2]

Neither you nor I could have picked up the phone and placed a call to the president's private line. There isn't one head of state of any nation on Earth who could have placed that call. But Jenna Bush could pick up the phone, punch a few buttons and be instantly connected with the most powerful leader on the planet. Why? Because she was the child of the president.

You and I are children of the King of the Universe. We have instant access to Him through prayer. All of God's power and all of His love are available to us at the speed of thought. Use that power. Tap into that love. Pray without ceasing.

3. Face Adversity in Reliance upon God

Another way we grow in our faith is by facing adversity and overcoming painful circumstances through the power of God. The more difficult the trials we endure, the stronger our faith grows.

While writing his book *Disappointment with God*, Philip Yancey interviewed many people who were undergoing difficult trials. He interviewed one man he called Douglas. This man, who had devoted much of his life to urban ministry and helping the poor, had experienced a series of tragedies. In fact, Yancey said he was "the one person I know whose life most resembles Job's."

First, the man's wife was diagnosed with cancer. Despite extensive medical treatments, her health was going downhill. As if that weren't enough suffering for one family, Douglas and his 12-year-old daughter were injured in a head-on collision. Douglas's head injury rendered him prone to chronic double-vision and blinding headaches. After the accident, he could no longer read, not even from a large-print Bible.

When Philip Yancey interviewed Douglas, he said, "Tell me about your disappointment with God."

"To tell you the truth, Philip," Douglas replied, "I don't feel disappointed with God."

This answer startled Yancey. He had simply assumed that, after a string of tragedies, Douglas certainly must have felt that God had let him down.

"I have learned," Douglas explained, "first through my wife's illness and then especially through the accident, not to confuse God with life. I'm no stoic. I am as upset about what happened to me as anyone could be. I feel free to curse the unfairness of life and to vent all my grief and anger. But I believe God feels the same way about the accident as I do—grieved and angry. I don't blame Him for what happened. . . . We tend to think, 'Life should be fair because God is fair.' But God is not life. And if I confuse God with the physical reality of life—by expecting constant good health, for example—then I set myself up for a crashing disappointment."[3]

Adversity has a way of transforming our faith, and faith has a way of transforming our view of adversity. Sometimes when people go through tragedy, their faith is shattered. But many believers experience what Douglas discovered: There are lessons to be learned through a tragedy, and we should never waste those lessons. Even though life is unfair, Douglas chose to maintain his faith in the love and fairness of God.

When we live by faith, we learn that God can use all of the painful and tragic circumstances that we suffer to bring about growth and maturity in our life. Tough times often call us to reexamine our life and our priorities. Adversity often reminds us of God's love for us. As Rick Warren once observed, "We find out that God is all we need when God is all we've got." As the Old Testament tells us, "The righteous cry out, and the LORD hears them; he delivers them from all their troubles" (Ps. 34:17).

The Christian faith is not just about "pie in the sky when we die by and by." It's about a gradual transformation from the people we *were* to the people God wants us to be—and God uses all of our life experiences, including our pain, to achieve that transformation.

Near the end of the Old Testament story of Job, there is a scene that is rich in meaning for our lives. In the story, Job has undergone the loss of his wealth and property. His children have been killed. He has lost his health and is stricken by an outbreak of painful boils all over his body. His wife scorns him, and his best friends wrongly accuse him of bringing this suffering on himself. Throughout his painful trial, Job never lets go of God, and God never lets go of Job.

After Job emerges from his trial of suffering, he stands before God and says, "My ears had heard of you but now my eyes have seen you" (Job 42:5). In other words, "Before I went through this trial, I had heard about You, God. I thought I knew all about You. I had theological head knowledge. But now that I have gone through tragedy, pain and affliction with You, I feel I know You intimately and truly. Before I had only *heard* of you, but now I have *seen* you with my own eyes!" That is how facing adversity through faith in God serves to deepen our faith.

C. S. Lewis once said, "I don't want my image of God. I want God." That's what I want—and I'm sure you want that as well. We don't want to just know *about* God or have an *image* of God. *We want God Himself.* We want the reality of God and we want a relationship with God.

We often find that reality in a place called Adversity. Another word for Adversity is Adventure. Charles Swindoll expressed the Adventure of Faith in these words:

> If you really want to break the boredom syndrome, commit yourself to Jesus Christ. Life will start comin' at you! You will become effective, empowered from heaven, and the battle will rage. You never find people on the front lines going to sleep. They're in the fray. The war is exploding. It's terribly eventful when your life counts for Christ. Psalm 34 says, "Many are the afflictions of the righteous, but the Lord delivers him out of them all."
>
> I can promise you one thing: If your walk with Christ is consistent, all hell will break loose. But all heaven will come to your rescue! And you'll be right in the middle of cosmic, high-stakes warfare. . . . If you are willing to sign on as one of the Lord's commandos behind enemy lines, life will never be the same. . . . In fact, it's the only way to live![4]

The late pastor and author Ray Stedman told the story of Niccolò Paganini (1782–1840), probably the most brilliant violinist who ever lived. Paganini amazed audiences by performing entire sonatas on a single violin string. In a piece he composed, "Variations for the Fourth String," he pioneered a harmonic technique that enabled him to reach a note three octaves higher than the string could normally produce. No other violinist could produce that note.

As a showman, Paganini was unrivaled. To demonstrate his skill, he secretly attached a penknife to his right wrist and began performing a sonata on all four strings. At a dramatic moment, he drew the blade across the E string—*snap*! The crowd gasped, but Paganini played on. Moments later, the A string snapped, then the D string. Yet Paganini continued performing, brilliantly and effortlessly, on the one remaining string—and the sonata retained all the rich intricacy it had when played on all four strings.

God, the Master Artist, the Great Virtuoso, is performing His masterpiece through our lives. "His brilliance is displayed most dramatically," Ray Stedman concludes, "when he has the least to work with—when the strings of our lives have been broken, when there is nothing left for Him to play on but a single string."[5] When we have been reduced to a single strand, stretched taut by adversity, God can bring forth the most beautiful music from our life.

WHAT FADES—AND WHAT REMAINS

In April 2008, I flew from Orlando to Boston to run in the Boston Marathon for the twelfth time. I arrived on Saturday, and the weather was beautiful. So I put on my workout clothes and went jogging up to the Boston Common for a final tune-up before the marathon on Monday. Boston Common is the oldest city park in America, and dates back to 1634, so the Common and its surroundings are rich in history.

I jogged past the famed Park Street Church, with its brick walls and towering white steeple. Its pulpit has been home to some of the most influential evangelical preachers in America, including Harold Ockenga and Gleason Archer. There, on Independence Day 1829, William Lloyd Garrison delivered a blistering sermon attacking slavery. Two years later to the day, the song "America" by Samuel Francis Smith made its debut in the Park Street Church.

Adjacent to the church is the Granary Burying Ground, founded in 1660, the final resting place of such patriots as Paul Revere, Samuel Adams and John Hancock. Ben Franklin's parents are buried there (Ben himself lies in Philadelphia), and so is Crispus Attucks, an African-American killed at the Boston Massacre, the first martyr of the American Revolution. As I walked through that cemetery and studied those gravestones, I knew I was on holy ground.

Standing before the huge marker of John Hancock's grave, I heard the bells pealing from the church steeple, playing the hymn "Fairest Lord Jesus." The strains of that song floated across the cemetery, across Boston Common, across the busy streets and neighborhoods and shops and offices of central Boston. And as I listened to that hymn, I started to cry. I wasn't sure exactly why I felt so emotional. Perhaps it's because "Fairest Lord Jesus" was my mother's favorite hymn. Or perhaps it was because I stood among the monuments and grave markers of the brave heroes who risked their lives for independence.

As I listened to that hymn, with tears rolling unabashedly down my cheeks, I looked across that orchard of headstones. Some were so old and weather-beaten that I could hardly make out the names and dates— but "Fairest Lord Jesus" was alive and well. There were no weathered, timeworn stones to mark Jesus' gravesite. He's alive in time and space, and He's alive in my life and in the lives of millions of other believers.

Two hundred years from now, your name and mine will have faded from the earth, and it may well be that no one will be able to make out our names on our gravestones. But "Fairest Lord Jesus" will still live on.

My friend, don't waste your life chasing after money, fame, power or pleasure. The meaning of your life can only be found by answering God's call upon your life, by joining your finite life to His infinite and eternal life, and by immersing yourself in prayer and His Word.

Connect your heart to His, and He will lead you safely through this life and into the life that never ends.

WHAT ARE YOU DYING FOR?

Jameer Nelson is the starting point guard for the Orlando Magic. He was mentored, coached and raised in Chester, Pennsylvania, by his father, Floyd "Pete" Nelson, a welder and dock worker who built and maintained tugboats at a shop on the Delaware River. On August 30, 2007, Pete Nelson was reported missing from the job site. The police and rescue crews were called in, but Pete wasn't to be found. Jameer went home to Chester to help in the search for his 57-year-old father.

The NBA star couldn't stop thinking of all kinds of scenarios to explain his dad's disappearance—all of them bad. Had his dad been kidnapped? Would there be a ransom note demanding money from Jameer? Or had Pete suffered heatstroke or a heart attack and fallen into the water? The hardest part was not knowing.

On September 1, Jameer was at the Delaware River, taking part in the search, when Pete's body was found downriver, across from my hometown of Wilmington, Delaware. The fisherman who discovered the body notified the authorities, and Pete's body was pulled from the water two days after his disappearance.

Pete Nelson was a tough guy, a retired Marine who survived being wounded in Vietnam. He taught all of his boys, including Jameer, the importance of being strong in tough times. Jameer and his brothers called him "Pops."

Ask Jameer how he remembers his dad, and he'll tell you about Pete Nelson's ridiculous tall tales and his mouth-watering barbecue. Jameer will also tell you about the time when, at age nine or ten, he brought home a failing grade from school. His mom grounded him—and that meant no basketball.

So Jameer's dad took him aside and lectured him about the importance of bringing up those grades—and then he sneaked Jameer out to his basketball practices and games. Jameer's mom didn't find out that she'd been hoodwinked until more than a decade later, after her son was drafted into the NBA.

After Jameer achieved stardom in the NBA, he tried to talk his dad into retiring. "You don't have to work so hard anymore, Pops," he'd say. "Why don't you let me make things easier for you?" But Pete Nelson had always enjoyed working with his hands, and he wasn't ready to give it up.

Pete Nelson was reported missing around lunchtime. To this day, the cause of his death remains a mystery. No one knows how a tough Marine, a man who could handle himself in any situation, could have ended up being pulled from the Delaware River. It makes no sense. Jameer has given up trying to understand it, concluding, "All I can say is that it was his time to go."

BETTER, STRONGER, WISER

The funeral was held on September 7, at St. Luke's Community Christian Church in Chester. The Magic chartered the team plane, and we invited all of Jameer's teammates and the Magic staff to go to Chester for the funeral. I went on the plane with the team. Although we arrived at ten o' clock, an hour before the service, a huge throng of people already packed the pews. Pete Nelson was a much-beloved man in the area. He had coached youth sports and mentored many young people, and he had a huge cadre of fans and friends.

I had never attended a funeral quite like this one. First, every person in the church filed up to the front row to offer personal condolences to the Nelson family. That took about an hour. Then came the music, the Scripture readings and the eulogies. Jameer's Orlando Magic teammate, Dwight Howard, got up and told the congregation, "As Jameer's teammates, we've come to show that we're a team, we're a family. Jameer may have lost his earthly father, but nothing can take away his heavenly Father." The congregation was clearly moved by Dwight's words.

The officiating minister, Bishop Anthony Hanna, Sr., was Pete Nelson's son-in-law, married to Jameer's sister. He stood and said in a powerful, stirring voice, "You have heard for years that you are not to question God, that it's wrong to question God. Let me tell you, that's a fallacy. You can question God all you want. He can handle it.

"The question we are all asking is, 'Why did Pete Nelson have to die?' I'll tell you why Pete Nelson had to die. If he hadn't died, you wouldn't be in church today, would you? He died to make you better, to make you stronger, to make you wiser. Some of you need to be living better. Some of you are weak, and you need to be stronger. Some of you are making bad decisions, so you need to be wiser.

"I have to tell you something: There's only way one way for you to be better, stronger and wiser—only one way! And that's through Jesus Christ. He's the only one who can make you better, stronger and wiser."

Then Bishop Hanna led the congregation in a prayer of salvation. Finally, while everyone's head was bowed, Bishop Hanna said, "If you have prayed that prayer just now, I want you to put your hand up. I want to know if you made that decision today. I see that hand, I see that hand. Nine of you have prayed that prayer with me. Now, I have some good news for everyone here today! I can tell you exactly why Pete Nelson died. If he hadn't died, the nine of you wouldn't be in God's kingdom today — including Pete's son, Jameer. This is Jameer's day of salvation."

It was true. Jameer Nelson turned his life over to the Lord that day.

Soon after the funeral, Jameer told reporters, "My dad is still with me. He'll always be with me." So Jameer now has *two* fathers—an earthly father and a heavenly Father. And both of his fathers are with him in a very real way.

I think Pete Nelson knew what he was living for—and what he was dying for. He lived a life that truly mattered. And when his life was over, he left a powerful, life-changing legacy that will never die.

GOD SO LOVED . . .

While this book was being written, I learned of the death of a man I've known for quite a few years. He lived into his early nineties and was fortunate to have a good, sharp mind and relatively few health problems right up to the end. In fact, the day he died, he had gone to his computer and placed a bet on a major sporting event. Then he curled up on the living room sofa to take a nap—and he never woke up.

Later, when his son came home for the funeral, he told his mother, "You know, Dad enjoyed placing bets over the Internet. I'm going to check his computer."

So the son turned on the computer and found the bet his late father had placed shortly before he died—and he discovered that his dad had won about $600. The son collected the winnings, then took the cash to the parish priest. "Here," he said to the surprised clergyman. "Take these winnings for the church. I want to make sure Dad gets into heaven. This should take care of it."

Well, according to the Bible, you don't need money to get into heaven. Admission is free—or to be more accurate, admission to heaven is so expensive you and I can't possibly afford it. But Someone else has already paid the price so that we don't have to.

You're undoubtedly familiar with a verse in the New Testament, John 3:16. In the classic *King James Version*, it reads, "For God so loved the world, that He gave His only begotten Son, that whosoever believeth in Him should not perish, but have everlasting life." Those words have been called "the heart of the Bible" because the essential message of all Scripture is condensed into those few words. Someone has broken that verse down, line by line and phrase by phrase, to reveal its rich meaning:

GOD . . . . .the greatest Lover
SO LOVED . . . . .the greatest degree
THE WORLD . . . . .the greatest number
THAT HE GAVE . . . . .the greatest act
HIS ONLY BEGOTTEN SON . . . . .the greatest Gift
THAT WHOSOEVER . . . . .the greatest invitation
BELIEVETH . . . . .the greatest simplicity
IN HIM . . . . .the greatest Person
SHOULD NOT PERISH . . . . .the greatest deliverance
BUT . . . . .the greatest difference
HAVE . . . . .the greatest certainty
EVERLASTING LIFE . . . . .the greatest possession

How did God demonstrate this great love to all the world, and to each of us individually? By means of the cross. He loved the world so much that He sent His Son to Earth to die upon the cross, a sacrifice for your sin and mine, so that if we believe in Him, we don't have to perish in eternity, but we receive the gift of everlasting life.

There is nothing in this world as baffling and paradoxical as the cross of Jesus Christ. The cross is a thing of incomprehensible horror and suffering—and it's a beautiful symbol of God's amazing love for us. On the cross, the God who created the universe was tortured to death. Those who heard His last words on the cross, "It is finished," thought it was an admission of failure and despair—yet we now know it was a shout of triumph: His death on the cross meant, "Mission accomplished!"

The cross stretched Jesus' arms out wide to encompass the entire human race. Nailed to the cross, Jesus was suspended between the earth and sky, connecting humanity and God. The cross was an instrument of shame, yet it was there that Jesus was glorified. It symbolized defeat, yet it was there that He achieved victory. The cross killed Him, yet through His death we live.

The towering, bloodstained cross forces us to make a choice. If we run to the cross for refuge, it becomes a thing of indescribable beauty, a symbol of God's eternal love. If we turn away from the cross, it remains nothing but a grisly killing machine. But the cross does not permit us to remain neutral. Accept it or reject it—there is no third alternative.

Do you understand the pain that God the Father suffered in handing His Son over to die for you? Years ago, a preacher named Dwight L. Moody reached into his own feelings as a father, and he described what the cross must have meant to God:

> After I became a father and woke up to the realization of what it cost God to have his Son die, I began to see that God was to be loved just as His Son was. Why, it took more love for God to give His Son to die than it would to die Himself. You would have a thousand times sooner died yourself in your son's place than have him taken away. If the executioner was about to take your son to the gallows, you would say, "Let me die in his stead. Let my son be spared." Oh, think of the love God must have

had for this world that He gave His only begotten Son to die for it. And that is what I want you to understand: "The Father himself loves you because you have loved me." If a man has loved Christ, God will set His love upon him.[1]

God so loved the world that He gave His only Son. Do you see why Christians see this ugly, bloodstained instrument of torture as beautiful? The cross was the most cruel invention ever devised by man—yet God transformed it into a beautiful expression of His eternal love.

In 1998, media mogul Ted Turner, founder of CNN, established the United Nations Foundation with a pledge of $1 billion. A CNN reporter asked him what prompted him to make such a donation. Was he hoping for some reward from God?

"I'm not looking for any big rewards," Turner replied. "I am not a religious person. I believe this life is all we have. I'm not doing what I'm doing to be rewarded in heaven or punished in hell. I do it because I feel it's the right thing to do. Almost every religion talks about a savior coming. When you look in the mirror in the morning, when you're putting on your lipstick or shaving, you're looking at the savior. Nobody else is going to save you but yourself."[2]

Ted Turner's desire to use a portion of his wealth to do some good in the world is admirable. But his view of life and eternity is tragically shortsighted.

Compare Ted Turner's views with those of my late friend Dr. Bill Bright. Reflecting on his decision to commit his life to Jesus Christ, Bill once said, "I continually think back to a decision that Vonette and I made in the spring of 1951, to become slaves of Jesus. This means a total, absolute, irrevocable surrender to the person of Christ. We wrote and signed over the title deeds of our lives to Him and, 24 hours later, God gave Vonette and me the vision for the ministry we now call Campus Crusade for Christ. I am convinced that the vision was a result of that signed contract."

I thank God that Bill and Vonette Bright made that decision and became slaves of Jesus Christ. It was Campus Crusade for Christ that published the little booklet that changed my life, the booklet called *Have You Heard of the Four Spiritual Laws?* If they had not signed that contract with

God and had a vision for Campus Crusade, where would I be now? Would I have ever had the life-changing experience of committing my life to Christ? I don't know. I don't even like to think about it!

HOW DO WE KNOW IT'S TRUE?

In *Bill Gates Speaks: Insight from the World's Greatest Entrepreneur*, Janet Lowe tells us that the founder of Microsoft was raised in a church-going family. When Bill Gates was a boy, his pastor, Reverend Dale Turner of the University Congregational Church in Seattle, urged the congregation to memorize the entire Sermon on the Mount. As motivation, he offered a prize of dinner atop Seattle's famed Space Needle to anyone who could recite Jesus' famous sermon, which spans three chapters in the book of Matthew.

Eleven-year-old Bill Gates accepted the challenge. During a family road trip, he memorized the passage. When he returned home, he was the only member of the congregation who could recite the Lord's sermon flawlessly. Reverend Turner recalled that the boy (who would one day become the world's richest man and hold that distinction for 13 consecutive years) not only knew the passage word for word but had a strong grasp of its meaning.

In recent years, Bill Gates has told interviewers that there is no room for faith in his life. In a November 1995 interview on PBS, David Frost asked Bill Gates, "Do you believe in the Sermon on the Mount?" Gates replied, "I don't. I'm not somebody who goes to church on a regular basis. The specific elements of Christianity are not something I'm a huge believer in." In a *Time* magazine cover story (January 13, 1996), Gates told interviewer Walter Isaacson, "Just in terms of allocation of time resources, religion is not very efficient. There is a lot more I could be doing on a Sunday morning."

When Isaacson asked Gates if he believed in the existence of the immortal human soul, the billionaire entrepreneur's face became expressionless. He folded his arms and began rocking back and forth—an unconscious mannerism that Gates displays at moments of agitation. Tonelessly, the software king replied, "I don't have any evidence of that. I don't have any evidence of that."[3]

I can't help feeling sorry for one of the richest men in the world. It's not hard for me to believe in human immortality, eternal life and the miracle of the resurrection. I am convinced that on a certain Sunday morning, at a particular geographic location just outside the city of Jerusalem, a miraculous resurrection took place. A man who had been tortured to death on a cross and laid to rest in a tomb became alive again. He walked out of that tomb and was seen by many witnesses. As John Updike wrote in his "Seven Stanzas at Easter":

Make no mistake: if He rose at all
it was as His body . . .
Let us not mock God with metaphor.[4]

Here is just a brief overview of the evidence for my belief.

1. *The reliability of the Gospel accounts.* The four Gospels—Matthew, Mark, Luke and John—were written within two to five decades of the events that they describe. Matthew, Mark and Luke were written around A.D. 50–65; John was written somewhere between A.D. 80–95. Critics have suggested that John's Gospel was a later forgery. They claimed that the author misreported details and invented locations that did not actually exist.

Recent archaeological discoveries have shown that the author of John was correct about such once-doubted sites as Jacob's Well (where Jesus met the Samaritan woman) and the Pool of Bethesda (where Jesus performed a miracle of healing). The discovery of the Rylands Fragment, a papyrus fragment of John's Gospel, proved that it was written much earlier than the critics claimed. Whenever the historical accuracy of the four Gospels has been questioned, the best evidence has always confirmed them as reliable.

2. *The empty tomb.* When I visited Israel a number of years ago, I saw the places where Jesus walked. I looked up from the Jerusalem bus terminal and saw the hill where He was crucified, and it looked exactly as the Bible describes it. I visited the cave that many historians think was the tomb of Jesus. The story of the resurrection is found not only in the Bible, but in secular accounts. The Jewish historian Flavius Josephus wrote in his *Antiquities* (Book 18, Chapter 3):

At this time there was a wise man who was called Jesus. And his conduct was good, and [he] was known to be virtuous. And many people from among the Jews and the other nations became his disciples. Pilate condemned him to be crucified and to die. And those who had become his disciples did not abandon their discipleship. They reported that he had appeared to them three days after his crucifixion and that he was alive; accordingly, he was perhaps the Messiah, concerning whom the prophets have recounted wonders.[5]

The Christian faith began in Jerusalem, in the very city where Jesus was crucified and buried. His tomb was donated by a prominent citizen of Jerusalem, Joseph of Arimathea, a member of the ruling Sanhedrin. Any citizen of first-century Jerusalem could take a short stroll outside the city gates and visit the tomb. Many people undoubtedly did so and they found the tomb to be empty, a powerful and convincing proof of the resurrection.

Christianity could never have spread so quickly in Jerusalem and the region beyond if the very basis of Christianity could have been easily falsified. Yet Christianity gained literally thousands of adherents within weeks of the resurrection event. Obviously, many people examined the proof of the empty tomb and were convinced.

3. *Transformed lives.* During the first century of its existence, the Christian faith spread throughout Palestine, then north into modern-day Turkey, Greece, Italy, Spain and Britain. It spread south throughout Egypt, Ethiopia and across North Africa. It spread east through Persia and even as far as India. What is truly amazing is not merely how rapidly Christianity spread, but the fact that it spread in the face of extreme persecution and violence.

Tacitus, the Roman historian, wrote in his *Annals* (Book XV) that Emperor Nero blamed the great fire of Rome (A.D. 64) on the Christian sect and proceeded to arrest them, torture them and kill them by the thousands. The historian wrote:

Nero fastened the guilt and inflicted the most exquisite tortures on a class hated for their abominations, called Christians by the populace. Christus [Jesus Christ], from whom the name had its origin, suffered the extreme penalty [crucifixion] during the reign of Tiberius at the hands of one of our procurators, Pontius Pilatus, and a most mischievous superstition [Christianity and the story of the resurrection], thus checked for the moment, again broke out not only in Judaea, the first source of the evil, but even in Rome.[6]

Tacitus also records that Nero slaughtered many Christians by having them torn apart in the arena by wild animals. He ordered others crucified. And he had some bound and smeared with tar. When the tar was ignited, those brave Christians became human torches to illuminate the emperor's garden.

In spite of these horrors, the Christian faith spread quickly. The message was preached far and wide by the disciples of Jesus—the very same people who, after the crucifixion, hid behind locked doors, afraid that they were next in line to be killed. How did those disillusioned disciples become bold, fearless missionaries of the faith? In the face of persecution, they refused to be silenced. They went all across the Roman Empire, preaching with joy and conviction that their Master was raised from the dead. In fact, they claimed to have seen Him alive with their own eyes.

There is no way to explain the rapid spread of early Christianity apart from the reality of Jesus' resurrection. History records that the disciples all suffered torture and died martyrs' deaths, except John (he was exiled to the isle of Patmos). All claimed to be eyewitnesses of the resurrection—and they clearly believed their own claim. After all, who would suffer torture and execution for the sake of a lie?

RESURRECTION POWER TODAY

Two thousand years have come and gone, and one of the most powerful evidences for the resurrection is still the evidence of transformed lives—people today whose lives have been changed in dramatic, unexplainable ways. Take, for example, the two men I told you about at the beginning of this book—Major League Baseball's Josh Hamilton and the NBA's legendary "Pistol Pete" Maravich.

They both had it all: fortune, fame, power and all the pleasure their millions could buy. Yet they discovered that once they had everything they wanted, they no longer wanted what they had. So they flushed it all away with alcohol and drugs. Both Josh and Pete lived reckless, self-destructive lives—and both survived multiple suicide attempts.

You might ask, "What changed those two men?" That would be the wrong question. Don't ask *what* changed them. Ask *who* changed them. The answer: Jesus Christ.

"There were so many people praying for me," Josh Hamilton reflects today, "my aunt and uncle at their church, [people in] other churches, people I didn't even know. When I meet people for the first time, they say, 'We've been praying for you for years.' That's the reason I feel like I was allowed to live through all that—because all those prayers were going up for me."

When Josh was in the depths of his self-destructive, cocaine-binging lifestyle, he would hang out at the tattoo parlor, sometimes sitting for eight hours at a stretch while the tattoo artist injected ink into his flesh. Soon, his skin was graffiti-tagged with blue flames, tribal symbols and the faces of demons. "I have tattoos of demons with no eyes," he says. "And I didn't realize it at the time, but no eyes means 'no soul.' That's what I was at the time: a man with no soul."

One of the last images he had etched into his skin was a depiction of Jesus, located on the back of his leg. "I don't even know why I got that one," he now reflects. "I didn't realize it at the time, but I think it was like spiritual warfare—the devil versus Christ." Though he had no sense of Christ's presence in his life at the time, Josh now views his Jesus tattoo as a symbol of his transformation. Pointing to the image of Christ on his leg, he says, "It's like He's standing behind me, plugged into me. I'm not one of those guys who talks about God just because it sounds good. It's because He changed my life."

Josh isn't saying he no longer craves alcohol and cocaine. He does—every day. The evil one is relentless, and Josh's mind and body are a battlefield for the duel between Satan and Jesus. The Christian life demands a daily discipline of prayer, Bible study and accountable relationships with other Christians. Our enemy never gives us any rest; the battle goes on and on—but it's a good battle, and one worth fighting.

The fact that Josh was not destroyed by alcohol and drugs is proof that an amazing power is at work in his life—the power of the Resurrection. You can't argue with the evidence of a transformed life. No one escapes the grip of crack cocaine unless something truly radical has taken place. Ask Josh Hamilton why he is alive today, and he'll tell you: Jesus Christ.

The same was true of Pete Maravich. One night in November 1982, Pete felt bitter and lost. He wanted to die. In total despair, he called out to Jesus, "If You don't save me, nothing will save me. Come take over my life."

And the living Christ took over his life, drained all the poisonous rage and bitterness out of his soul, and replaced it with humility, peace and love for other people. I can personally testify to the change in Pete's life, because I knew him both before and after—and after Pete encountered Jesus, he was simply not the same person.

The most profound change I saw in Pete's life was that he became a complete zealot for the Lord. He wanted everyone he met to know Jesus as he did. Pete had received the best news anyone could ever hear—and he wanted to shout it to the world. I was with him at several public events when Pete told his story, and I never saw a more vibrant and compelling Christian witness in my life.

He only lived for five years after his life-changing encounter with Jesus Christ. But Pete Maravich packed more joy, enthusiasm and service to Christ into those five short years than most Christians display in a lifetime. Pete knew exactly what he was living—and dying—for.[7]

If you want evidence for the resurrection of Jesus Christ, just look at the lives of those who have been radically transformed by the life of Christ shining through them. Because Jesus was victorious over death, so are we—and that brings us to one of the most important questions to be answered in this book: What happens to us after we die?

LIFE AFTER LIFE

David Lloyd-George (1863-1945) was a Welsh-British statesman who served as prime minister during the second half of World War I. "When I was a boy," he once recalled, "the thought of heaven used to frighten me more than the thought of hell. I pictured heaven as a place where there would be perpetual Sundays with perpetual services, from which there would be no escape, as the Almighty, assisted by cohorts of angels, would always be on the lookout for those who did not attend. It was a horrible nightmare. The conventional heaven, with its angels perpetually singing, nearly drove me mad in my youth."[8]

Through the years, I've been surprised to notice how many people, both believers and nonbelievers, have cartoonish and stereotyped images of heaven. Another prime example is Ted Turner, who once called Christianity "a religion for losers." He explained, "I don't think I'd like to go to heaven. I just can't see myself sittin' on a cloud and playin' a harp day in and day out."[9]

Ted Turner's mental image of heaven being an ethereal realm of fluffy clouds, populated by harp-plucking saints, seems to be based on clichéd imagery borrowed from Bugs Bunny cartoons and cornball movies like *Heaven Can Wait* and *The Horn Blows at Midnight*. Such conceptions of heaven certainly don't come from the Scriptures. Unfortunately, most people—including most Christians—have very little idea what the Bible actually says about heaven. As John Eldredge wrote in *The Journey of Desire*:

> Nearly every Christian I have spoken with has some idea that eternity is an unending church service. After all, the Bible says that the Saints "worship God in heaven," and without giving it much more thought we have settled on an image of the never-ending sing-along in the sky, one great hymn after another, forever and ever, amen.
>
> And our heart sinks. *Forever and ever? That's it? That's the good news?* And then we sigh and feel guilty that we are not more "spiritual." We lose heart, and we turn once more to the present to find what life we can. . . . And since we're not all that sure about what comes after, we search hard now.[10]

The tragic irony of our misconceptions about heaven is that the reality of heaven is what every human heart truly desires. The biblical heaven is a place of exquisite beauty, boundless pleasure and endless joy—a place where we will be reunited with the ones we love. God Himself planted those desires within us so that we would want to be with Him for eternity. We were made for heaven.

One of the most important and inspiring books ever written is *Heaven* by Randy Alcorn. In his book, Alcorn describes our innate longing for the wonders of heaven:

> We are homesick for Eden. We are nostalgic for what is implanted in our hearts. It's built into us, perhaps even at a genetic level. We long for what the first man and woman once enjoyed—a perfect and beautiful Earth with free and untainted relationships with God, with each other, animals, and our environment. Every attempt at human progress has been an attempt to overcome what was lost in the Fall.[11]

The Scriptures do not portray heaven as a vague and insubstantial realm of gauzy, ethereal nothingness, populated by insubstantial spirits. In the Bible, heaven is always portrayed as a concrete reality—substantial, tangible and definite. It's described as a place of gardens and cities, where people with real, substantial bodies live in real, substantial buildings. Heaven is not an analogy or a metaphor. It's not a state of mind. It is, as Randy Alcorn says, a "physical, tangible *place*."[12] He adds, "Many religions, including Buddhism and Hinduism, characterized the afterlife as vague and intangible. Christianity specifically refutes this notion."[13]

If the Bible is clear and definite about the nature of heaven, why are so many Christians unclear and indefinite about it? Randy Alcorn explains that our conception of heaven, even in the Christian community, has been infected by the views of the Greek philosopher Plato (c. 427–c. 347 B.C.). Plato taught that the material world is merely a reflection of a higher idealized truth. According to Plato, the things of heaven are immaterial and ideal, while the things of Earth are material and corrupt. The human soul, Plato believed, is immaterial and belongs to a higher plane of existence; the human body is earthly and material and subject to corruption.

Platonism (Plato's teachings) heavily influenced a Hellenistic Jewish philosopher, Philo of Alexandria (20 B.C.–A.D. 50), whose writings in turn had a major influence on two leading Alexandrian scholars of the early church, Origen (A.D. 185–254) and Clement of Alexandria (c. A.D. 150–216). Both Origen and Clement tried to merge Greek philosophical traditions with Christian truth—and the result was that the truth of heaven as a literal and substantial realm of reality was replaced by a spiritualized and metaphorical view of heaven as a place where souls live in a disembodied state. These tragic misconceptions about heaven are still with us today.

We need to regain a clear and biblical view of heaven. We need to understand, as evangelist R. A. Torrey once declared, "We are not to be disembodied spirits in the world to come, but redeemed spirits, *in redeemed bodies*, in a redeemed society, in a redeemed universe."[14] Let's take a look at what heaven will truly be like, and what our lives will be like as citizens of heaven.

First, we will have resurrected, physical bodies. When Jesus was resurrected, He was not a ghost or spirit. He walked out of the tomb, and His feet left footprints on the grass.

When Jesus appeared to the disciples after His resurrection, they thought He was a ghost. But Jesus said to them, "Look at my hands and my feet. It is I myself! Touch me and see; a ghost does not have flesh and bones, as you see I have" (Luke 24:39). The Bible goes on to tell us that Jesus "will transform our lowly bodies so that they will be like his glorious body" (Phil. 3:21) and "when he appears, we shall be like him" (1 John 3:2).

This is especially good news for those of us who are suffering the effects of illness, injury or advanced age. Christian artist and author Joni Eareckson Tada has been a quadriplegic since breaking her neck at age 17, in a 1967 diving accident in Chesapeake Bay. In her book *Heaven: Your Real Home*, she wrote:

> I, with shriveled, bent fingers, atrophied muscles, gnarled knees, and no feeling from the shoulders down, will one day have a new body, light, bright, and clothed in righteousness—powerful and dazzling. No other religion, no other philosophy promises new bodies, parts, and minds. Only in the Gospel of Christ do hurting people find such incredible hope.[15]

This has always been the hope of believers, even in Old Testament times. Job, the suffering saint, said, "And after my body has decayed, yet in my body I will see God! I will see him for myself. Yes, I will see him with my own eyes. I am overwhelmed at the thought!" (Job 19:26-27, *NLT*).

Second, we will live on a new Earth, and the capital of the new Earth will be a city designed and built by God. In the book of Revelation, heaven is pictured as a real place of beauty and wonders, with mountains, forests, rivers and magnificent cities. Unlike the present Earth, there will be no pollution, no natural disasters, no sin and no death. Throughout the Scriptures, in both the Old and New Testaments, we find promises of a new heaven and a new Earth.

"Behold," God told the prophet Isaiah, "I will create new heavens and a new earth. The former things will not be remembered, nor will they come to mind" (Isa. 65:17). Peter said, "We are looking forward to a new heaven and a new earth, the home of righteousness" (2 Pet. 3:13). And John said, "Then I saw a new heaven and a new earth, for the first heaven and the first earth had passed away" (Rev. 21:1).

Heaven is pictured as a city—the perfect dwelling place for humanity, a place of shining light and beautiful architecture, a place of culture and community, a "city with foundations, whose architect and builder is God" (Heb. 11:10). The Bible even reveals the exact dimensions of heaven (see Rev. 21:15-17). In this city of wonders, we will be given exciting work to do—work that may well take us far beyond the city, out to the distant corners of the universe. God's headquarters ("the throne of God") will be in the city, but you and I as His servants will have all of infinity and all of eternity in which to joyfully serve Him (see Rev. 22:3).

By the way, I hope you enjoy juicy, sweet fruit, because the Bible tells that the tree of life in the middle of heaven will bear "twelve crops of fruit, yielding its fruit every month" (rev. 22:2). Health nut that I am, I'm glad to know there will be plenty of good, healthy fruit to eat.

Third, when we leave this world, we instantly enter the next world. Jesus was crucified on the middle cross between two thieves. One of the thieves believed in Jesus, and Jesus told him, "Today you will be with me in paradise" (Luke 23:43). That word "paradise," in the original language, refers to an enclosed park or garden, like the great walled palace gardens of the ancient kings. Jesus did not speak in a metaphor or an allegory.

He promised the believing man that he would, on that very day, join Jesus in an actual physical place of intense beauty, joy and pleasure.

This paradise that Jesus spoke of is mentioned elsewhere in Scripture. In the book of Revelation, for example, Jesus said, "To him who overcomes, I will give the right to eat from the tree of life, which is in the paradise of God" (Rev. 2:7). When do we experience this paradise in the presence of Jesus? The moment that we pass from this life to the next (see Phil. 1:23; 2 Cor. 5:8). As my friend Dr. Bill Bright once observed, "While your family tends to your funeral, you are beholding the face of Christ."

God sometimes allows His people to catch a glimpse of heaven while they are still here on Earth. In the book of Acts, Stephen, the first Christian martyr, was about to be stoned to death. The account tells us that as the angry mob surrounded him, Stephen "looked up to heaven and saw the glory of God, and Jesus standing at the right hand of God. 'Look,' he said, 'I see heaven open and the Son of Man standing at the right hand of God'" (Acts 7:55-56). At that, the mob proceeded to execute Stephen.

Evangelist Dwight L. Moody (1837–1899), founder of the Moody Bible Institute, had a similar experience before his death. Moody preached his final sermon in Kansas City, Kansas, on November 16, 1899. His friends who heard him preach were alarmed to see that he had gained considerable weight in just a few weeks. What they didn't know was that his body was retaining water due to undiagnosed congestive heart failure. Moody knew he was dying, and he told friends, "Soon you will read in the newspaper that I am dead. Don't believe it for a moment. I will be more alive than ever before."

On December 22, he lay on his deathbed, surrounded by family and friends. He opened his eyes wide, and his face shone with joy. He seemed to be looking at something that no one else in the room could see. "Earth recedes!" he said. "Heaven opens before me!" Moments later, he left this world and graduated to eternity.

When I think of those awe-inspiring last words of Dwight L. Moody, I'm reminded of Coach Ray McCall of Lamesa, Texas, the high school coach I told you about in chapter 1. The words he wrote to me in an email still challenge me: "What are you dying for, Mr. Williams?"

Dwight L. Moody knew what he was *living* for—and *dying* for. And as he died, heaven itself opened up for him.

CHRONOS AND KAIROS

Eternity is beyond our comprehension, yet amazingly, God has placed eternity within our grasp. John Newton wrote in the great old hymn "Amazing Grace":

> When we've been there ten thousand years,
> Bright shining as the sun,
> We've no less days to sing God's praise
> Than when we first begun.

The apostle Paul tells us, "Since, then, you have been raised with Christ, set your hearts on things above, where Christ is seated at the right hand of God" (Col. 3:1). The more we think about heaven and eagerly await our future home, the more motivated and excited we will be about the things that matter most.

Money can't get its hooks into those who are intent on a heavenly goal. Fame has no attraction. Power loses its allure. Earthly pleasures pale in comparison to the pleasures that await us in eternity. In *Mere Christianity*, C. S. Lewis put it this way: "I was made for another world. . . . I must keep alive in myself the desire for my true country, which I shall not find till after death; I must never let it get snowed under or turned aside; I must make it the main object of life to press on to that other country and to help others to do the same."[16]

Yes! Let's press on together to that other country—and let's help others to get there as well. On the other side of the door called Death, all of eternity awaits us. But on this side of the door, time is short.

So let's talk for a moment about time.

Did you know there are two kinds of time? The ancient Greeks had a specific name for each kind of time. One kind of time is called *chronos*. The other is called *kairos*. *Chronos* is sequential time—the time of the clock or sundial, the time that passes second by second, hour by hour, year by year. *Kairos* time is the moment of significance, the moment of opportunity—a frozen instant of time when something takes place that will matter for all eternity.

Like sands falling through an hourglass, our supply of *chronos* moments is finite and we eventually run out of it. But *kairos* time has no quantity that we can measure. *Kairos* is a *quality* of time that will endure long after our mortal lives have ended.

Those who spend their lives chasing the false values of money, fame, power and pleasure are living in *chronos* time. They will have a span of their mortal lifetime to enjoy those things, and when their time is up, they will have nothing. But those who live for character, influence, parenthood and faith are accumulating *kairos* moments that will last throughout eternity.

The instant you committed your life to Jesus Christ is a *kairos* moment that will remain with you throughout eternity. The moment you demonstrate a character quality, such as courage under fire or compassion toward a stranger or unconditional love toward an enemy, you have transformed a bit of *chronos* into *kairos*. When you use your influence to change one life or to change your world, when you make a positive difference in the life of a child, you create a lasting *kairos* legacy. When we choose to live our lives in a series of meaningful moments, then even after our *chronos* has all been spent, our *kairos* remains.

As someone once said, "Life is not measured by the number of breaths we take, but by the moments that take our breath away."

Heaven does not operate on Greenwich Mean Time or Eastern Standard Time or Daylight Savings Time. The only time that matters in eternity is *kairos*. It is the time that existed before God said, "Let there be light!" *Kairos* is God's time. It's the time that matters most.

In his book *Led by the Carpenter*, D. James Kennedy told the true story of a man named John Carmody. This man stood looking out a second-story window in his home, remembering the events of a few days earlier . . .

John Carmody had arrived home from the office, his briefcase filled with reports. He sat at his desk and took out the reports—then he felt a tug at his sleeve. He looked down. There was his five-year-old daughter, Margie, beaming up at him. "Look, Daddy!" she said, holding up a picture book.

"That's nice, Margie," Carmody said. "But Daddy's very busy. Run along now."

Margie insisted, "Would you read me a story, Daddy? Please?"

"Not now, honey. Ask your mother, okay?"

"Mommy's busy in the kitchen. Read me just one little story—please?"

"I'm sorry, sweetie. I have to study these reports. Run along."

Margie pouted. "Okay, Daddy," she said, placing the picture book on the corner of her father's desk. "But when you get through with your work, would you just read one little story to yourself? But read it loud, so I can hear it."

John Carmody sighed. "Okay—but later, okay? Run along and play now."

"Okay, Daddy." Margie went out of the room, leaving the picture book behind.

That was the event John Carmody remembered as he stared out the window. Strange that such a seemingly minor incident now loomed so large.

He looked down at the book in his hands. Margie's picture book.

John Carmody never got to read the book to Margie. She had gone out to the front yard to play, just as he had told her to do. While she was playing, a drunk driver careened into the front yard. Margie died instantly.

A voice called from downstairs. "John?" said his wife. "It's time."

It's time, he thought. *Time to go to the funeral home and say good-bye to Margie. I always thought there was plenty of time. Whatever happened to the time?*

"Just a moment," he said hoarsely.

He sat down and opened the book, remembering: *Daddy, when you get through with your work, would you just read one little story to yourself? But read it loud, so I can hear it.*

"Once upon a time," he read aloud, "there was a little girl who was oh so fair—" He hoped Margie could hear it too.[17]

Time is short. Children need *kairos* moments with you too. Make every moment count.

LIVING GRACE AND DYING GRACE

I want to go to heaven, but I don't want to die. That's normal. We were made to live, to enjoy life and to cling to life as long as we can. The survival instinct is hardwired into us.

In a 2005 commencement address at Stanford University, Apple co-founder Steve Jobs told the story of his brush with death. The previous year, he underwent a procedure that showed that he had a tumor on his pancreas. "I didn't even know what a pancreas was," he said. "The doctors told me this was almost certainly a type of cancer that is incurable, and that I should expect to live no longer than three to six months."

Throughout the day, Jobs thought about all the things this diagnosis meant to him: getting his business and personal affairs in order, saying goodbye to family and friends, grieving the loss of his one and only life.

That same evening, the doctors performed a biopsy on the tumor. Jobs was sedated during the procedure, so he was not aware of what the doctors were doing. His wife, however, was present, and she was startled when she saw the doctors place the biopsied cells under a microscope—then weep openly! And they were weeping for joy!

When Steve Jobs awoke from the sedation, his wife and the doctors told him that he had a very rare form of pancreatic cancer. Unlike the more common and incurable form, which the doctors thought he had, this rare form is curable with surgery. Steve Jobs had escaped a medical death sentence. He had the surgery and is doing well today.

"This was the closest I've been to facing death," he said, "and I hope it's the closest I get for a few more decades. . . . No one wants to die. Even people who want to go to heaven don't want to die to get there. And yet death is the destination we all share."

Most people avoid even *thinking* about death, but Steve Jobs says that he finds the thought of death helps him to focus his priorities. "Remembering that I'll be dead soon," he said, "is the most important tool I've ever encountered to help me make the big choices in life. Because almost everything—all external expectations, all pride, all fear of embarrassment or failure—these things just fall away in the face of death, leaving only what is truly important."[18]

One good thing about our mortality: It forces us to focus on our priorities. Charles Swindoll put it this way: "The prospect of death has a way of quickly putting things into perspective. When viewed through the lens of eternity, material wealth suddenly becomes infinitesimally small compared to the things that transcend death, things like relationships and the abundant life Jesus promised. The issue is not whether you have a lot of cash or material possessions, but do they have you?"[19]

But just as our survival instinct is hardwired into us, so is the longing for heaven. We are, as the Scriptures say, "longing for a better country—a heavenly one" (Heb. 11:16). So we have two competing and contradictory instincts within us: We want to go to heaven but we don't want to die. The good news, which liberates us from this internal contradiction, is the fact that Jesus has come and has conquered death. As the Bible tells us, He chose to share in our humanity and go through death in order to destroy the power of death "and free those who all their lives were held in slavery by their fear of death" (Heb. 2:15).

When we are free of the fear of death, we are free indeed! As Dr. Martin Luther King, Jr., once told a crowd at a civil rights rally in 1963, "No man is free if he fears death. But the minute you conquer the fear of death, at that moment you are free. . . . I submit to you that if a man hasn't discovered something that he will die for, he isn't fit to live!"[20]

There is only one statement of Jesus' that is recorded in all four Gospels (and in two Gospels, more than once). I believe that by repeating this statement throughout the Gospels, God was underscoring this truth to make sure we wouldn't miss it. Jesus said, "For whoever wants to save his life will lose it, but whoever loses his life for me and for the gospel will save it" (Mark 8:35; see also Matt. 10:39; 16:25; Luke 9:24; 17:33; John 12:25).

In other words, there are things in this world that are more important than life itself—things that are truly worth dying for. If all we care about is saving our own skin, we will lose everything that truly matters to us. We will end up having lived our entire life for nothing. But if we commit ourselves, body and soul, to Jesus Christ and His cause, then even if we lose our mortal life, we will save what is truly important: our character, our influence and our eternal life with Him.

While this book was being written, I lost my good friend Dr. Wendell Kempton.

Wendell was a Christian leader, a Bible teacher and a friend to many people, especially in the sports world. He was in great demand as a speaker for various professional sports teams and was a chapel speaker at three Super Bowls and a World Series. He mentored many athletes, coaches and sports executives, including Mike Schmidt, Bobby Jones, Julius Erving and Joe Gibbs.

I got to know Wendell when I was in Philadelphia as the general manager of the 76ers. He was a friend and Bible teacher for many athletes in Philly, and his Bible studies were an important source of growth and strength for a number of Christian players on our team.

I remember one conversation I had with Wendell when I lived in Philly in the late 1970s. We were talking about death and eternity, and I said to him, "Wendell, I don't want to die. I know that, as a Christian, I shouldn't feel that way, but I can't help it. Even though I look forward to heaven, I have absolutely no interest in dying!"

"Pat," he said, "there are three kinds of grace that God gives us in our life. First, there is saving grace, which is the grace He gives us at the moment we commit our life to Him and we are saved. Second, there is living grace—the drive, focus, intensity and enthusiasm for living that He gives us each day so that we can go about our work with zeal and energy. Third and finally, there is dying grace. When the time comes for you to leave this world, God will prepare you for it and the transition will be easy."

That conversation gave me a lot of comfort. I've often thought about those words.

On December 13, 2007, my friend Wendell Kempton began to make that transition from living grace to dying grace. That was the day his body first signaled to him that something was wrong.

At age 75, Wendell maintained one of the busiest travel and speaking schedules of anyone I knew. He had racked up over 300,000 miles in 2007 alone. He was traveling in the Midwest when he noticed a lump on his arm, a growth that shouldn't be there. At the same time, he began to experience flu-like symptoms. He was supposed to fly to Phoenix, but his illness forced him to cancel his trip and return to Lancaster, Pennsylvania. He went to the hospital emergency room where tests revealed that his internal organs were riddled with a previously unde-tected cancer.

At first the doctors thought he had months to live, but it soon be-came apparent that he had only weeks. After two weeks in the hospital, Wendell decided that he wanted to go home to die. So he returned to his home in Lititz, near Lancaster, where he received hospice care in the final days of his life. His entire family came to say good-bye—his 6 chil-dren, 20 grandchildren, and his sister.

His wife, Ruth, told me, "God was loving and kind to Wendell dur-ing the final days of his life. His whole family was with him. He talked to us and recognized us right up until the morning he went to be with the Lord."

While he still had strength, Wendell planned his own funeral. He was sitting up in bed, dictating plans to his son Tim, when his six-year-old granddaughter Audrey tiptoed into the bedroom. "What are you doing, Pop-Pop?" she asked.

"I'm planning a party!" Wendell said.

"Will there be balloons?" Audrey asked.

"Yes, indeed!" he replied, smiling.

Wendell wanted to make sure that everyone who came to the fu-neral would hear the good news of Jesus Christ. He told one of his as-sociates, "Call Pat Williams. He knows all the sports people in my life, and he'll take care of getting them to the funeral." When I got that word, I moved immediately and invited six of Wendell's friends from the sports world to come speak at the service.

His strength declined quickly, and he spent less than a week at home. By Saturday, January 5, it was clear that his fight was nearly over. His oldest son, Stan, stayed with him through the night. At about 3:40 A.M., on Sunday morning, January 6, Stan noticed that his dad had be-gun to tremble—a sign that death was near.

Stan remembered that when his dad would step into the pulpit at church, one of his favorite opening lines was, "Good morning, it's Res-urrection Day!" So Stan leaned toward the bed and whispered in Wendell's ear, "Dad, it's Resurrection Day. It's Sunday morning, your favorite day of the week. Dad, you've come to the end of the race. You're about to break the tape. You've done your job, and now you're going to your eternal reward. Get your best sermon ready, Dad. You're going into glory."

And with those words, Wendell's son ushered him from this life into eternal life. Wendell couldn't speak, but Stan was convinced that his father was aware and heard every word. And I'm convinced that everything Wendell once told me about "dying grace" is true.

Wendell's funeral was held in the early afternoon of Friday, January 11, 2008. I introduced the six men I had invited to come speak at the funeral. All of them—Bobby Jones, Mike Schmidt, Bob Boone, Garry Maddox, Terry Harmon and Doug Collins—had quickly juggled their schedules to be there. Doug had even spent the night on a red-eye flight to Lancaster after broadcasting an NBA game in Salt Lake City. Each of them told me they wouldn't have missed being there for the world. Speaking to a crowd of about 800 people, those men shared, some through tears, how Wendell introduced them to the Lord.

Wendell had planned his "going home party" well. It was a celebration of a life well lived and triumphantly concluded. And just as Wendell had promised his granddaughter, there were balloons at the reception. The entire event was a powerful reminder that these reassuring words of the apostle Paul are still true:

> When the perishable has been clothed with the imperishable, and the mortal with immortality, then the saying that is written will come true: "Death has been swallowed up in victory."
>   "Where, O death, is your victory?
>   Where, O death, is your sting?" (1 Cor. 15:54-55).

What are you living for? What are you dying for? My friend, don't waste your life on money, fame, power or pleasure. Those things fade and crumble to dust. Live to build your character. Live to influence your world. Live to make a positive difference in the lives of children. And when it's time to die, die at peace in the arms of Jesus.

Live a life that truly matters. Leave a legacy that never dies.

ENDNOTES

Chapter 1: What Are You Living For?

1. Ken Snyder, "Josh Hamilton: Silver Lining," *Sports Spectrum*, May-June 2008, pp. 26-29; Bob Nightengale, "Hamilton on the Comeback Trail," *USA Today*, June 7, 2006, electronically retrieved at http://www.usatoday.com/sports/baseball/al/devilrays/2006-06-06-hamilton-cover_x.htm; John Eligon, "Devil Rays Prospect Moves a Step Closer to Playing Again," *New York Times*, July 4, 2006, electronically retrieved at http://www.nytimes.com/2006/07/04/sports/04hamilton.html?r=1&n=Top/News/Sports/Baseball/Major%20League/Tampa%20Bay%20Rays&oref=slogin; "In His Own Words," Interview, Josh Hamilton and Tim Keown of ESPN, electronically retrieved at http://thewalkwithchrist.blogspot.com/2008/05/josh-hamilton.html.
2. Dennis Miller, guest appearance on *The O'Reilly Factor*, Fox News Channel, Wednesday, October 10, 2007.
3. Laura Ingraham and Robi Ludwig, Psy.D., *The O'Reilly Factor*, Friday, February 8, 2008.

Chapter 2: Chasing Fortune

1. Statistics and sources cited are from "Land of the Broke? Consumption and Debt in Overdrive," Moneyspot.org, retrieved at http://www.mdmproofing.com/iym/brokethink.shtml.
2. Greg Gittrich, "Saddam, Sons Likely Alive," *New York Daily News*, Saturday, March 22, 2003, retrieved at http://www.nydailynews.com/archives/news/2003/03/22/2003-03-22_saddam__sons_likely_alive.html.
3. Chuck Colson with James S. Bell, Jr., *Lies That Go Unchallenged in Popular Culture* (Carol Stream, IL: Tyndale House, 2005), p. 348.
4. Charles Spezzano, quoted by John C. Maxwell in *The 360 Degree Leader Workbook: Developing Your Influence from Anywhere in the Organization* (Nashville, TN: Thomas Nelson, 2006), p. 87.
5. Harvey Mackay, "How to Tell When You're Rich," InspirationalStories.com, retrieved at http://www.inspirationalstories.com/7/798.html.
6. Geoffrey Giuliano, *The Lost Lennon Interviews* (New York: Omnibus Press, 1999), p. 239.
7. Anthony Bromberg, "Remembering George Harrison," *UCLA Daily Bruin*, December 3, 2001, retrieved at http://www.dailybruin.ucla.edu/archives/id/17377/.
8. Rick Warren, *The Purpose-Driven Life* (Grand Rapids, MI: Zondervan, 2002), p. 29.
9. Ted Engstrom and Paul Cedar, *Compassionate Leadership* (Ventura, CA: Regal Books, 2006), pp. 45-46.
10. Associated Press, "The Pop Princess Is a Big Spender," *The Houston Chronicle*, November 3, 2007, p. A2.
11. Stephen King, Commencement Address, Vassar College, May 20, 2001, retrieved at http://commencement.vassar.edu/2001/010520.king.html.

Chapter 3: Chasing Fame

1. "Tom Brady: The Winner—Patriots Quarterback Discusses His Career and Other Aspects of His Life," *60 Minutes*, November 3, 2005, retrieved at http://www.cbsnews.com/stories/2005/11/03/60minutes/main1008148_page3.shtml.
2. Janet Lowe, *Ted Turner Speaks: Insights from the World's Greatest Maverick* (New York: John Wiley and Sons, 1999), pp. 28,39,48; Porter Bibb, *Ted Turner: It Ain't as Easy as It Looks: A Biography* (Boulder, CO: Johnson Books, 1993), p. 130; William A. Henry III, "Shaking Up the Networks," *Time*, August 9, 1982, retrieved at www.time.com/time/magazine/article/0,9171,925663,00.html; Unsigned article, "Celebrity Profiles: Ted Turner, Media Mogul," retrieved at http://www.skillcircle.com/resources/articles/3442.html; "The Rejects: Harvard's Biggest Mistakes," *02138 Magazine*, May-June 2007, retrieved at http://www.02138mag.com/magazine/article/1267-2.html.

3. Jon Krakauer, *Into Thin Air: A Personal Account of the Mt. Everest Disaster* (New York: Anchor, 1999), p. 3.

4. Unsigned article, "People, Places and Things in the News: Margot Kidder," *South Coast Today* (Massachusetts), retrieved at http://archive.southcoasttoday.com/daily/07-96/07-29-96/a04wn026.htm; Unsigned article, "Actress Margot Kidder Found Dazed, Frightened," CNN, April 25, 1996, retrieved at http://www.cnn.com/SHOWBIZ/9604/25/margot.kidder/index.html; "Margot Kidder Mental Wellness Page," Margot Kidder website, retrieved at http://www.margotkidder.com/activist.shtml.

5. Leslie Halliwell, quoted in *Halliwell's Filmgoer's Companion*, 1984, retrieved at http://www.bartleby.com/66/37/7337.html.

6. Henry Blackaby and Richard Blackaby, *Called to Be God's Leader: How God Prepares His Servants for Spiritual Leadership* (Nashville, TN: Thomas Nelson, 2004), p. 37.

7. Blackaby and Blackaby, *Called to Be God's Leader: How God Prepares His Servants for Spiritual Leadership*, pp. 36-37; Paul Johnson, *Napoleon* (New York: Viking-Penguin, 2004), pp. 75-77; "Napoleon," *Encyclopedia Britannica*, 15th Edition, Macropedia, Vol. 24 (Chicago: Encyclopedia Britannica, Inc., 1986), p. 742ff.

8. Mark Bowden, "Tales of the Tyrant," *Atlantic Monthly*, May 2002, retrieved at http://www.theatlantic.com/doc/200205/bowden.

9. George Harrison, quoted by Marc Shapiro in *Behind Sad Eyes: The Life of George Harrison* (New York: St. Martin's, 2003) pp. 4, 58.

10. George Harrison, quoted by Geoffrey Giuliano in *Dark Horse: The Life and Art of George Harrison* (New York: Dutton, 1990), p. 40.

11. Muhammad Ali with Hana Yasmeen Ali, *The Soul of a Butterfly: Reflections on Life's Journey* (New York: Simon & Schuster, 2004), p. 32.

12. Ibid., pp. 39-41.

13. Gary Smith, "Ali and His Entourage," *Sports Illustrated*, 16 April 1988, pp. 48-49.

14. "Prominent NBC Journalist Dies in Iraq: David Bloom Dead of Pulmonary Embolism at 39," CNN.com, April 6, 2004, retrieved at http://www.cnn.com/2003/US/04/06/sprj.irq.journalist.death/.

Chapter 4: Chasing Power

1. Cal Thomas, *Blinded by Might* (Grand Rapids, MI: Zondervan, 2000), p. 54.

2. Anne Edwards, *The Reagans: Portrait of a Marriage* (New York: St. Martin's, 2004), pp. 134-135.

3. Johanna McGeary, "Inside Saddam's World," *Time*, May 6, 2002, retrieved at http://archives.cnn.com/2002/ALLPOLITICS/05/06/time.saddam/.

4. Mark Bowden, "Tales of the Tyrant," *Atlantic Monthly*, May 2002, retrieved at http://www.theatlantic.com/doc/200205/bowden.

5. Calvin Miller, *Jesus Loves Me: Celebrating the Profound Truths of a Simple Hymn* (Nashville, TN: FaithWords, 2002), pp. 21-22.

6. Mary Soames, ed., *Winston and Clementine: The Personal Letters of the Churchills* (Boston: Houghton Mifflin, 2001), p. 454.

7. Winston Churchill, quoted in "Finest Hour," *Time* magazine, Monday, February 14, 1949, retrieved at http://www.time.com/time/magazine/article/0,9171,794604,00.html.

8. Peter W. Schramm, "Constancy," *On Principle*, vol. 10, no. 4, August 2002, retrieved at http://www.ashbrook.org/publicat/onprin/v10n4/schramm.html.

9. John P. Foley, editor, *The Jeffersonian Cyclopedia: A Comprehensive Collection of the Views of Thomas Jefferson* (New York: Funk & Wagnalls Co., 1900), p. 766.

10. Oprah Winfrey, quoted by Jack Canfield, Mark Victor Hansen, Lisa Nichols and Tom Joyner in *Chicken Soup for the African American Soul* (Deerfield Beach, FL: Health Communications, Inc., 2004), p. 243.

11. Oprah Winfrey, quoted by Jodi Wilgoren, "Words of Advice for Graduates on the Threshold of the Millennium," *The New York Times*, May 29, 2000, retrieved at http://query.nytimes.com/gst/fullpage.html?res=9C02E3DF163CF93AA15756C0A9669C8B63&sec=&spon=&pagewanted=3.

Chapter 5: Chasing Pleasure

1. "Online Couple Cheated with Each Other," *The Daily Telegraph*, September 18, 2007, retrieved at http://www.news.com.au/dailytelegraph/story/0,22049,22439156-5012895,00.html.

2. Meghan Daum, "Confidence a Wet T-Shirt?," *The Orlando Sentinel*, Saturday, March 22, 2008, p. A17 (reprinted from *The Los Angeles Times*).

3. Michael W. Eysenck, *Psychology: An International Perspective* (New York: Psychology Press, 2004), p. 57.

4. Oscar Wilde, *De Profundis*, transcribed from the 1913 Methuen & Co. edition, retrieved at http://www.gutenberg.org/files/921/921.txt.

5. Mary Jane Ryan, quoted by Lauren Daley in "Tame the Beast: How to Really Stick with Your New Year's Resolution," SouthCoastToday.com (Massachusetts), retrieved at http://www.south coasttoday.com/apps/pbcs.dll/article?AID=/20080106/LIFE/801060321/-1/LIFE.

6. George Orwell, "Pleasure Spots," a 1946 essay, retrieved at http://www.george-orwell.org/Pleasure_Spots/0.html.

7. Julie Sevrens Lyons, "Stanford-Caltech Study Links Wine Price to Drinker's Pleasure," *San Jose Mercury News*, January 15, 2008, retrieved at http://www.mercurynews.com/breakingnews/ci_7981068?nclick_check=1.

8. Blaise Pascal, *Pensées*, translated by A. J. Krailsheimer (London: Penguin, 1993), p. 45.

9. Alan Bullock and Stephen Trombley, *The Norton Dictionary of Modern Thought* (New York: W. W. Norton & Co., 1999), p. 369.

10. Grace Lee Whitney, *The Longest Trek: My Tour of the Galaxy* (Clovis, CA: Quill Driver Books, 1998), pp. 17-23.

Chapter 6: Pursue Good Character

1. Tony Dungy, quoted by Hal Habib in "On His Terms: Colts' Dungy Stays True to Principles," *Palm Beach Post*, January 23, 2007, retrieved at http://www.palmbeachpost.com/sports/content/sports/epaper/2007/01/23/a1c_dungy_0123.html.

2. Tony Dungy, quoted by Mike Bianchi in "Dungy-Belichick Pits Class vs. Crass," *The Orlando Sentinel*, November 4, 2004, retrieved at http://www.baltimoresun.com/sports/football/bal-sp.nflcolumn04nov04,0,5198394.story.

3. Richard Goldstein, "Ralph Beard, a Star Tarnished by Point Shaving, Is Dead at 79," *The New York Times*, December 3, 2007, retrieved at http://www.nytimes.com/2007/12/03/sports/ncaabasketball/03beard.html?_r=1&n=Top/Reference/Times%20Topics/Organizations/N/National%20Collegiate%20Athletic%20Assn&oref=slogin.

4. Tanya Caldwell, "Breaking Rules Necessary to Get Ahead, Teens Say," *The Orlando Sentinel*, December 6, 2007, page A1.

5. Jim Denney, *Answers to Satisfy the Soul: Clear, Straight Answers to 20 of Life's Most Important Questions* (Clovis, CA: Quill Driver Books, 2002), p. 5.

6. David Maraniss, "In Clinton, a Past That's Ever Prologue," *The Washington Post*, January 25, 1998, p. A01.

7. Fred Rogers, *The World According to Mister Rogers: Important Things To Remember* (New York: Hyperion, 2003), p. 53.

8. Ibid., p. 8.

Chapter 7: Pursue Influence

1. Anthony McCarron, " 'Roid Regret: Two-Time MVP Murphy," *The New York Daily News*, April 1, 2007, retrieved at http://www.nydailynews.com/sports/baseball/2007/04/01/2007-04-01_roid_regret.html; David Whitley, "Murphy Swings Away at Steroids in Our Pastime," *The Orlando Sentinel*, June 24, 2007, pp. C1,C9; Jeff Schultz, "Murphy Takes His Cuts at Clemens," *The Atlanta Journal-Constitution*, January 14, 2008, retrieved at http://www.ajc.com/sports/content/printedition/2008/01/14/schultz0114.html.

2. Kurt Warner, quoted by the *Sports Spectrum* website, retrieved at http://www.sportsspectrum.com/daily/archives/051121.html; and by Mike Ostrom, "Kurt Warner: Beyond the Hype," *Today's Pentecostal Evangel*, date unknown, retrieved at http://keybearers.org/Articles2001/4525_warner.cfm.

3. Glen Wesley, quoted by the *Sports Spectrum* website, retrieved at http://www.sportsspectrum. com/daily/archives/060206.html.
4. Kevin Shea, "Stanley Cup Journal No. 12," *Hockey Hall of Fame*, date unknown, retrieved at http://www.hhof.com/html/exSCJ06_12.shtml.
5. Mike Huckabee, *Character Makes a Difference: Where I'm From, Where I've Been, and What I Believe* (Nashville: B&H Publishing Group, 2007), pp. 174-175.
6. Philip Yancey, "A Quirky and Vibrant Mosaic," *Christianity Today*, June 2005, retrieved at http://www.christianitytoday.com/ct/2005/june/24.37.html?start=4.
7. Kenneth Blanchard and Norman Vincent Peale, *The Power of Ethical Management* (New York: William Morrow, 1988), p. 27.

Chapter 8: Pursue Parenthood

1. Mark Clements, "The Consequences of Fatherlessness," Fatherhood.com, retrieved at http:// www.fathers.com/content/index.php?option=com_content&task=view&id=391.
2. "Scouts' Honor," *Investor's Business Daily*, October 22, 2007, p. A18.
3. Peter Vecsey, "NBA report: Russell reflects on remarkable career," *The Japan Times Online*, June 27, 2007, retrieved at http://search.japantimes.co.jp/cgi-bin/sp20070627pv.html.
4. Dan Kindlon, Ph.D., and Michael Thompson, Ph.D., *Raising Cain: Protecting the Emotional Life of Boys* (New York: Ballantine, 2000), p. 103.
5. Joyce Landorf Heatherley, *Balcony People* (Georgetown, TX: Balcony Publishing, 2004), p. 9.
6. Kindlon and Thompson, *Raising Cain*, p. 104.
7. Ibid., p. 103.
8. Associated Press, "Girl Loses Hannah Montana Tickets for Lying," *USA Today*, December 29, 2007, retrieved at http://www.usatoday.com/news/offbeat/2007-12-29-fake-essay_N.htm; Associated Press, "Hannah Montana Essay Winner a Fake," *Comcast.net TV*, December 29, 2007, retrieved at http://www6.comcast.net/tv/articles/2007/12/29/Fake.Essay/.
9. Steven J. Lawson, *The Legacy*, quoted in the *Better Families* newsletter, May 2008, vol. 32, no. 5, published by The Relationship Resource Group, Inc., p. 1.

Chapter 9: Pursue Faith

1. Vernon McLellan, ed., *Billy Graham: A Tribute from Friends* (New York: Warner Books, 2002), pp. 111-114.
2. "Ellen Has Guest Jenna Bush Call Dad," UPI.com, December 5, 2007, retrieved at http:// www.upi.com/NewsTrack/Entertainment/2007/12/05/ellen_has_guest_jenna_bush_call_ dad/6271/.
3. Philip Yancey, *Disappointment with God* (Grand Rapids, MI: Zondervan, 1997), p. 183.
4. Charles R. Swindoll, *Moses, Great Lives Series*, Volume 4 (Nashville: Thomas Nelson, 1999), p. 299.
5. Ray Stedman, *Let God Be God* (Grand Rapids, MI: Discovery House Publishers, 2007), p. 225.

Chapter 10: What Are You Dying For?

1. Dwight L. Moody, *The Gospel Awakening: Sermons and Addresses* (Chicago: Fleming H. Revell, 1883), p. 287; for the sake of clarity, the form of the quotation from John 16:27 has been altered by the author from *KJV* to *NIV*.
2. Quoted by Jill Lieber, "He Wants to Save the World," *USA Today*, February 17, 2000, p. C1.
3. Janet Lowe, *Bill Gates Speaks: Insight from the World's Greatest Entrepreneur* (Hoboken, NJ:, Wiley & Sons, 1998), pp. 3-4,7; John Lofton, "Warren Buffett 'Agnostic,' Bill Gates Rejects Sermon on the Mount," *The American View*, May-September 2006, retrieved at http://www.theameri canview.com/index.php?id=649; Austin Cline, "Warren Buffett: Atheist Philanthropist?" *About.com*: Atheism/Agnosticism, July 7, 2006, retrieved at http://atheism.about.com/ b/a/ 257812.htm.
4. John Updike, *Telephone Poles and Other Poems* (New York: Knopf, 1963), pp. 72-73.
5. From the tenth-century Arabic translation into English by Shlomo Pines, *An Arabic Version of the Testimonium Flavianum and Its Implications* (Jerusalem: Israel Academy of Sciences and Humanities, 1971), p. 69.

6. Tacitus, *The Annals of Publius Cornelius Tacitus*, translated by Alfred John Church and William Jackson Brodribb, Modern Library edition of Church and Brodribb's text, published as *The Complete Works of Tacitus*, retrieved at classics.mit.edu/Tacitus/annals.11.xv.html.

7. Ken Snyder, "Josh Hamilton: Silver Lining," *Sports Spectrum*, May-June 2008, pp. 26-29; Dave Sheinin, "New Life at the Plate: Hamilton Looks to Resurrect a Once-Promising Career Derailed by Drugs," *The Washington Post*, Tuesday, February 13, 2007, p. E01; Associated Press, "With Faith, Hamilton Overcomes Addictions, Gets Another Chance," Monday, February 25, 2008, electronically retrieved at http://www.christianpost.com/article/20080225/31320_With_Faith%2C_Hamilton_Overcomes_Addictions%2C_Gets_Another_Chance.htm.

8. David Lloyd-George, quoted by Peter Rowland in *Lloyd George* (London: Barrie and Jenkins, 1975), p. 13.

9. Ted Turner, quoted by Janet Lowe in *Ted Turner Speaks* (New York: Wiley, 1999), p. 46.

10. John Eldredge, *The Journey of Desire: Searching for the Life We've Only Dreamed Of* (Nashville: Thomas Nelson, 2000), p. 111.

11. Randy Alcorn, *Heaven* (Wheaton, IL: Tyndale, 2004), p. 77.

12. Ibid., p. 15.

13. Ibid., p. 77.

14. R. A. Torrey, *Real Salvation and Whole-Hearted Service* (Chicago: Fleming H. Revell, 1905), p. 73, emphasis in the original.

15. Joni Eareckson Tada, *Heaven: Your Real Home* (Grand Rapids, MI: Zondervan, 2001), pp. 48-49.

16. C. S. Lewis, *Mere Christianity* (New York: HarperOne, 2001), p. 137.

17. D. James Kennedy, *Led by the Carpenter* (Nashville: Thomas Nelson, 1999), pp. 168-169.

18. Steve Jobs, "Commencement Address," Stanford University, June 12, 2005, published in the *Stanford Report*, June 14, 2005, retrieved at http://news-service.stanford.edu/news/2005/june15/jobs-061505.html.

19. Charles Swindoll, *Great Lives: Jesus, the Greatest Life of All* (Nashville: Thomas Nelson, 2008), p. 69.

20. Quoted by Johann Christof-Arnold, *Seeking Peace* (New York: Penguin/Plume, 2000), p. 193.

ACKNOWLEDGMENTS

———◉———

With deep appreciation I acknowledge the support and guidance of the following people who helped make this book possible:

Special thanks to Bob Vander Weide, Alex Martins, and Rich DeVos of the Orlando Magic.

Hats off to my associates Andrew Herdliska and Latria Leak, my proofreader Ken Hussar, and my ace typist Fran Thomas.

Thanks also to my writing partner, Jim Denney, for his superb contributions in shaping this manuscript.

I also want to express deep gratitude to Bill Greig III, Kim Bangs, Steven Lawson, and Mark Weising of Regal Publishing Group. Thank you for believing we had something important to say.

And finally, special thanks and appreciation go to my wife, Ruth, and to my wonderful and supportive family. They are truly the backbone of my life.

AUTHOR CONTACT

———◉———

You may contact Pat Williams at:

Pat Williams
c/o Orlando Magic
8701 Maitland Summit Boulevard
Orlando, FL 32810
phone: (407) 916-2404
pwilliams@orlandomagic.com

Visit Pat Williams's website at:

www.PatWilliamsMotivate.com

If you would like to set up a speaking engagement for Pat Williams,
please call or write his assistant, Andrew Herdliska, at the above address
or call him at 407-916-2401. Requests can also be faxed to 407-916-2986
or emailed to aherdliska@orlandomagic.com.
We would love to hear from you. Please send your comments about
this book to Pat Williams at the above address or in care of our publisher
at the address below. Thank you.

Pat Williams
c/o Regal Publishing Group
1957 Eastman Ave.
Ventura, California 93003

ALSO AVAILABLE FROM
PAT WILLIAMS

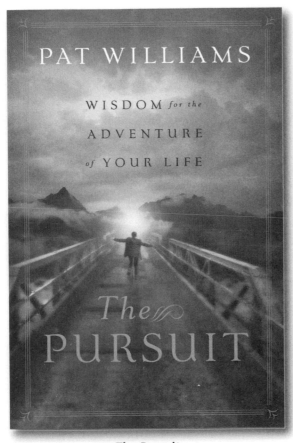

The Pursuit
Wisdom for the Adventure of Your Life
Pat Williams with Jim Denney
ISBN: 08307.45998
ISBN: 978.08307.45999

Everyone wants to pursue a life of meaning, a life that matters, a life of authentic success and lasting satisfaction. But what's the secret to living the life you've always dreamed of? In this personal, relevant and engaging book of wisdom, Pat Williams shares his six powerful and practical insights that aren't taught in school but are essential in the pursuit of a successful and rewarding life. Packed with page-turning stories, *The Pursuit* illustrates the life-changing concepts that Pat learned from his mentor, R.E. Littlejohn, the long-time co-owner of a minor league baseball club and Pat's former boss. These six principles are at the heart of this captivating quick-start manual for anyone who wants to hit the ground running and take on the world.